HYEONSEO LEE lived in North Korea u̲... she came to Seoul where she now lives ̲... Hankuk University of Foreign Studies. Leader at the Centre for Strategic and International Studies, a journalist at the Ministry for Unification and a selected member of the 'English for the Future' programme at the British Embassy in Seoul. She now campaigns internationally for North Korean human rights and refugee issues, speaking all over the world, including at the UN and the Oslo Freedom Forum. Her 2013 TED talk has had over 4 million views and was described by Oprah Winfrey as 'the most inspirational TED talk ever'.

DAVID JOHN is a writer and editor who has lived in Seoul and has spent time in North Korea. His first novel, *Flight from Berlin*, was published by HarperCollins in 2012.

Praise for Hyeonseo Lee:

'Stirring and brave . . . true, committed, unvarnished and honest. Lee has made her own life the keyhole to the present, inside and outside of North Korea' *Scotsman*

'Remarkable bravery fluently recounted' *Kirkus*

'Hyeonseo Lee brought the human consequences of global inaction on North Korea to the world's doorstep . . . Against all odds she escaped, survived, and had the courage to speak out'

Samantha Power, US representative to the United Nations

'I have spoken with countless numbers of defectors over the years. When I first met Hyeonseo Lee, the unflinching manner in which she told her story, although full of sadness and hurt, was inspirational. That is the story now written in this book . . . Every time she navigated treacherous terrain and overcame seemingly insurmountable obstacles, she had to change her name to protect her new identity. She became the

Girl with Seven Names . . . But one thing that she held on to was her humanity, ever stronger as she continuously sublimated her hardships into hope'

Jang Jin-sung, founder of New Focus International and author of *Dear Leader: Poet, Spy, Escapee – A Look Inside North Korea*

'This is a powerful story of an escapee from North Korea. In the hallowed meeting rooms of the United Nations in New York, ambassadors from North Korea recently sought to shout down stories like this. But these voices will not be silenced. Eventually freedom will be restored. History will vindicate Hyeonseo Lee and those like her for the risks they ran so that their bodies and their minds could be free. And so that we could know the truth'

The Honourable Michael Kirby, Chair of the UN Commission of Inquiry on Human Rights Abuses in North Korea, 2013–14

'Perhaps the richest part of the story is Hyeonseo Lee herself. She is a real, textured human with flaws, and her vulnerability in the writing makes for a thrilling story that not only provides suspense for readers, but also frustration, compassion and everything in between. Hyeonseo Lee's work is a rare, fascinating glimpse into the daily life of growing up in North Korea, and the consequences that accompany defectors. Freedom, as it turns out, is much more complicated than first imagined.' *Associated Press*

'A gripping memoir that proves once again that truth can be stranger than fiction.' *New York Post*

'Hyeonseo Lee brought the human consequences of global inaction on North Korea to the world's doorstep . . . Against all odds she escape, survived and had the courage to speak out.'

Samantha Power, U.S. permanent representative to the United Nations

THE GIRL WITH SEVEN NAMES

Escape From North Korea

Hyeonseo Lee

With David John

WILLIAM COLLINS

William Collins
An imprint of HarperCollins*Publishers*
1 London Bridge Street
London SE1 9GF
WilliamCollinsBooks.com

First published in Great Britain by William Collins in 2015

This William Collins paperback edition published 2016

18 19 20 LSCC 20 19

Copyright © Hyeonseo Lee 2015

Hyeonseo Lee asserts the moral right to
be identified as the author of this work

A catalogue record for this book
is available from the British Library

ISBN 978-0-00-755485-0

Maps by John Gilkes

Set in Janson Text by Palimpsest Book Production Limited,
Falkirk, Stirlingshire

Printed and bound in the United States of
America by LSC Communications

Find out more about HarperCollins and the environment at
www.harpercollins.co.uk/green

CONTENTS

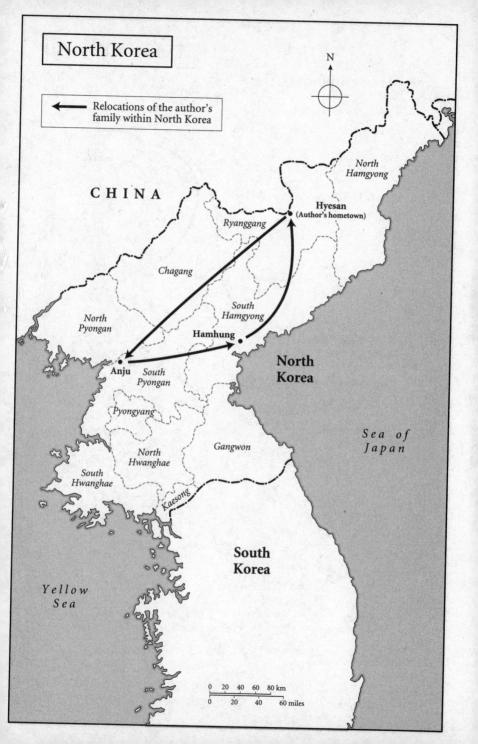

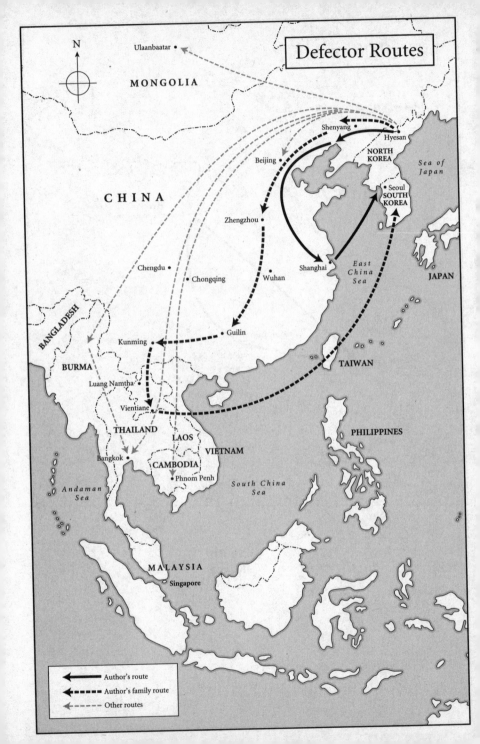

Defector Routes

N

MONGOLIA

Ulaanbaatar

CHINA

Shenyang
Hyesan
NORTH
KOREA

Beijing

Sea of
Japan

Zhengzhou

Seoul
SOUTH
KOREA

Chengdu

Chongqing

Wuhan

Shanghai

East
China
Sea

JAPAN

Guilin

Kunming

TAIWAN

BANGLADESH

BURMA

Luang Namtha

Vientiane

THAILAND

LAOS

VIETNAM

PHILIPPINES

Bangkok

CAMBODIA

Phnom Penh

South China
Sea

Andaman
Sea

MALAYSIA

Singapore

→ Author's route
→ Author's family route
→ Other routes

Author's Note

To protect relatives and friends still in North Korea, I have changed some names in this book and withheld other details. Otherwise, all the events described happened as I remembered or was told about them.

Introduction

13 February 2013

Long Beach, California

My name is Hyeonseo Lee.

It is not the name I was born with, nor one of the names forced on me, at different times, by circumstance. But it is the one I gave myself, once I'd reached freedom. Hyeon means sunshine. Seo means good fortune. I chose it so that I would live my life in light and warmth, and not return to the shadow.

I am standing in the wings of a large stage, listening to the hundreds of people in the auditorium. A woman has just blushed my face with a soft brush and a microphone is being attached to me. I worry that it will pick up the sound of my heart, which is thumping in my ears. Someone asks me if I'm ready.

'I'm ready,' I say, though I do not feel it.

The next thing I know I'm hearing an amplified announcement. A voice is saying my name. I am being introduced.

A noise like the sea rises in the auditorium. Many hands are clapping. My nerves begin to flutter wildly.

I'm stepping onto the stage.

I feel terrified suddenly. My legs have turned to paper. The spotlights are faraway suns, dazzling me. I can't make out any faces in the audience.

Somehow I motion my body toward the centre of the stage. I inhale slowly to steady my breathing, and swallow hard.

This is the first time I will tell my story in English, a language still new to me. The journey to this moment has been a long one.

The audience is silent.

I begin to speak.

I hear my voice trembling. I'm telling them about the girl who grew up believing her nation to be the greatest on earth, and who witnessed her first public execution at the age of seven. I'm telling them about the night she fled across a frozen river, and how she realized, too late, that she could never go home to her family. I describe the consequences of that night and the terrible events that followed, years later.

Twice I feel tears coming. I pause for an instant, and blink them back.

Among those of us who were born in North Korea and who have escaped it, the story I am telling is not an uncommon one. But I can feel the impact it is having on the people in the audience at this conference. They are shocked. They are probably asking themselves why a country such as mine still exists in the world.

Perhaps it would be even harder for them to understand that I still love my country and miss it very much. I miss its snowy mountains in winter, the smell of kerosene and burning coal. I miss my childhood there, the safety of my father's embrace, and sleeping on the heated floor. I should be comfortable with my new life, but I'm still the girl from Hyesan who longs to eat noodles with her family at their favourite restaurant. I miss my bicycle and the view across the river into China.

Leaving North Korea is not like leaving any other country. It is more like leaving another universe. I will never truly be free of its gravity, no matter how far I journey. Even for those who have suffered unimaginably there and have escaped hell, life in the free world can be so challenging that many struggle to come to terms with it and find happiness. A small number of them even give up, and return to live in that dark place, as I was tempted to do, many times.

My reality, however, is that I cannot go back. I may dream about freedom in North Korea, but nearly seventy years after its creation, it remains as closed and as cruel as ever. By the time it might ever be safe for me to return, I will probably be a stranger in my own land.

As I read back through this book, I see that it is a story of my awakening, a long and difficult coming of age. I have come to accept that as a North Korean defector I am an outsider in the world. An exile. Try as I may to fit into South Korean society, I do not feel that I will ever fully be accepted as a South Korean. More important, I don't think I myself will fully accept this as my identity. I went there too late, aged twenty-eight. The simple solution to my problem of identity is to say I am Korean, but there is no such nation. The single Korea does not exist.

I would like to shed my North Korean identity, erase the mark it has made on me. But I can't. I'm not sure why this is so, but I suspect it is because I had a happy childhood. As children we have a need, as our awareness of the larger world develops, to feel part of something bigger than family, to belong to a nation. The next step is to identify with humanity, as a global citizen. But in me this development got stuck. I grew up knowing almost nothing of the outside world except as it was perceived through the lens of the regime. And when I left, I discovered only gradually that my country is a byword, everywhere, for evil. But I did not know this years ago, when my identity was forming. I thought life in North Korea was normal. Its customs and rulers became strange only with time and distance.

Thus I must say that North Korea is my country. I love it. But I want it to become good. My country is my family and the many good people I knew there. So how could I not be a patriot?

This is my story. I hope that it will allow a glimpse of the world I escaped. I hope it will encourage others like myself, who are struggling to cope with new lives their imaginations never prepared them for. I hope that the world will begin, finally, to listen to them, and to act.

Prologue

I was awoken by my mother's cry. Min-ho, my kid brother, was still asleep on the floor next to me. The next thing I knew our father came crashing into the room, yelling 'Wake up!' He yanked us up by our arms and herded us, pushed us, out of the room. My mother was behind him, shrieking. It was evening and almost dark. The sky was clear. Min-ho was dazed from sleep. Outside on the street we turned and saw oily black smoke pouring from our kitchen window and dark flames licking the outside wall.

To my astonishment, my father was running back into the house.

A strange roar, a wind rushing inward, swept past us. We heard a *whumpf*. The tiles on one side of the roof collapsed, and a fireball like a bright orange chrysanthemum rose into the sky, illuminating the street. One side of the house was ablaze. Thick, tar-black smoke was belching from the other windows.

Where was my father?

Our neighbours were suddenly all around us. Someone was throwing a bucket of water – as if that would quench this blaze. We heard the groan and splitting of wood and then the rest of the roof went up in flames.

I wasn't crying. I wasn't even breathing. My father wasn't coming out of the house.

It must only have been seconds but it seemed like minutes. He emerged, running toward us, coughing his lungs up. He was blackened by smoke, his face glistening. Under each arm he was holding two flat, rectangular objects.

He wasn't thinking of our possessions, or our savings. He'd rescued the portraits. I was thirteen, old enough to understand what was at stake.

Later my mother explained what had happened. Some soldiers had given my father a large can of aviation fuel as a bribe. The can was in the kitchen, which was where we had an iron stove that burned *yontan* – the circular charcoal cakes used for heating everywhere in North Korea. She was in the act of decanting the fuel into another container when it slipped from her hands and splashed onto the coals. The combustion was explosive. The neighbours must have wondered what on earth she'd been cooking.

A wall of intense heat was advancing from the blaze. Min-ho began to wail. I was holding our mother's hand. My father put the portraits down with great care, then hugged the three of us – a public display of affection that was rare between my parents.

Huddled together, watching the remains of our home collapse in a rippling glow, the neighbours might have felt sorry for us. My father looked a sight – his face was filthy and his new civilian suit ruined. And my mother, who was house-proud and always made an effort to dress nicely, was seeing her best bowls and clothes go up in smoke.

Yet what struck me most was that neither of my parents seemed that upset. Our home was just a low, two-room house with state-issue furniture, common in North Korea. It's hard to imagine now how anyone would have missed it. But my parents' reaction made a strong impression on me. The four of us were together and safe – that was all that mattered to them.

This is when I understood that we can do without almost anything – our home, even our country. But we will never do without other people, and we will never do without family.

The whole street had seen my father save the portraits, an act of heroism that would win a citizen an official commendation. As it turned out, matters had gone too far for that. We did not know it, but he was already under surveillance.

PART ONE

The Greatest Nation on Earth

Chapter 1

A train through the mountains

One morning in the late summer of 1977, a young woman said goodbye to her sisters on the platform of Hyesan Station and boarded the train for Pyongyang. She had received official permission to visit her brother there. She was so excited she'd slept little the night before. The Capital of the Revolution was, to her mind, a mythic and futuristic place. A trip there was a rare treat.

The air was still cool and smelled of fresh lumber from the nearby mill; the humidity was not yet too high. Her ticket was for a window seat. The train set off, creaking slowly southward along the old Hyesan Line through steep pine-clad mountains and over shaded gorges. Now and then a white-water river could be glimpsed far below. But as the journey progressed she found herself being distracted from the scenery.

The carriage was full of young military officers returning to the capital in high spirits. She thought them annoying at first, but soon caught herself smiling at their banter, along with the other passengers. The officers invited everyone in the carriage to join them in playing games – word games and dice games – to pass the time. When the young woman lost a round, she was told that her forfeit was to sing a song.

The carriage fell quiet. She looked down at the floor, gathered her courage, and stood up, keeping herself steady by holding on to the luggage rack. She was twenty-two years old. Her shiny black hair was pinned back for the journey. She wore a white cotton frock printed with small red flowers. The song she sang was from a popular North Korean movie of that year called *The Story of a General*. She sang it well, with sweet, high notes. When she finished, everyone in the carriage broke into a round of applause.

She sat back down. A grandmother was sitting on the outside seat and her granddaughter sat between them. Suddenly a young officer in a grey-blue uniform was standing over them. He introduced himself with great courtesy to the grandmother. Then he picked up the little girl, took the seat next to the young woman, and sat the little girl on his lap.

'Tell me your name,' was the first thing he said.

This was how my mother met my father.

He sounded very sure of himself. And he spoke with a Pyongyang lilt that made my mother feel uncouth and coarse with her northern Hyesan accent. But he soon put her at her ease. He was from Hyesan himself, he said, but had spent many years in Pyongyang and was ashamed to admit to her that he had lost his accent. She kept her eyes lowered but would steal quick glances at him. He wasn't handsome in the conventional way – he had thick eyebrows and strong, prominent cheekbones – but she was rather taken with his martial bearing and his self-assurance.

He said he thought her frock was pretty and she gave a shy smile. She liked to dress well because she thought this made up for plain and ordinary looks. In fact she was prettier than she knew. The long journey passed quickly. As they talked she noticed him repeatedly look at her with an earnestness she had not experienced before from a man. It made her face feel hot and flushed.

He asked her how old she was. Then he said, very formally: 'Would it be acceptable to you if I were to write you a letter?'

She said that it would, and gave him her address.

Later my mother was to recall little of the visit to her brother in Pyongyang. Her mind was filled with images of the officer on the train, and the dappled light in the carriage, of sun shining through mountain pines.

No letter came. As the weeks went by my mother tried to put him out of her mind. He had a girlfriend in Pyongyang, she thought. After three months she'd got over the disappointment and had given up thinking about him.

On an evening six months later, the family was at home in Hyesan. It was well below freezing but the skies had been clear for weeks, making a beautiful autumn and winter. They were finishing dinner when they heard the clip of steel-capped boots approaching the house, and a firm knock on the door. A look of alarm passed around the table. They were not expecting anyone so late. One of my mother's sisters went to open the door. She called back to my mother.

'A visitor. For you.'

The power in the city had gone off. My mother went to the door holding a candle. My father was standing on the doorstep, in a military greatcoat, with his cap tucked under his arm. He was shivering. He bowed to her, and apologized, saying that he had been away on military exercises and had not been permitted to write. His smile was tender and even a little nervous. Behind him the stars reached down to the mountains.

She invited him into the warmth. They began courting from that evening.

The next twelve months were dreamlike for my mother. She had never been in love before. My father was still based near Pyongyang, so they wrote letters to each other every week and arranged meetings. My mother visited his military base, and he took the train to see her in Hyesan, where her family got to know him. For her, the weeks between their encounters were filled with the sweetest planning and daydreaming.

She told me once that everything during that time acquired a kind of lustre and magic. People around her seemed to share her optimism, and she may not have been imagining it. The world was at the height of the Cold War, but North Korea was enjoying its best years. Bumper harvests several years in a row meant that food was plentiful. The country's industries were modern by the standards of the communist world. South Korea, our mortal enemy, was in political chaos, and the hated Yankees had just lost a bruising war against communist forces in Vietnam. The capitalist world seemed to be in decline. There was a confidence throughout the country that history was on our side.

When spring came and the snow on the mountains began to recede my father made a trip to Hyesan to ask my mother to marry him. She accepted with tears. Her happiness was complete. And to cap it all, both his family and hers had good *songbun*, which made their position in society secure.

Songbun is a caste system that operates in North Korea. A family is classified as loyal, wavering or hostile, depending on what the father's family was doing at the time just before, during and after the founding of the state in 1948. If your grandfather was descended from workers and peasants, and fought on the right side in the Korean War, your family would be classified as loyal. If, however, your ancestors included landlords, or officials who worked for the Japanese during the colonial occupation, or anyone who had fled to South Korea during the Korean War, your family would be categorized as hostile. Within the three broad categories there are fifty-one gradations of status, ranging from the ruling Kim family at the top, to political prisoners with no hope of release at the bottom. The irony was that the new communist state had created a social hierarchy more elaborate and stratified than anything seen in the time of the feudal emperors. People in the hostile class, which made up about 40 per cent of the population, learned not to dream. They got assigned to farms and mines and manual labour. People in the wavering class might become minor officials, teachers, or hold military ranks removed from the centres of power. Only the loyal class got to live in Pyongyang, had the opportunity to join the Workers' Party, and had freedom to choose a career. No one was ever told their precise ranking in the *songbun* system, and yet I think most people knew by intuition, in the same way that in a flock of fifty-one sheep every individual will know precisely which sheep ranks above it and below it in the pecking order. The insidious beauty of it was that it was very easy to sink, but almost impossible to rise in the system, even through marriage, except by some special indulgence of the Great Leader himself. The elite, about 10 or 15 per cent of the population, had to be careful never to make mistakes.

At the time my parents met, a family's *songbun* was of great importance. It determined a person's life, and the lives of their children.

My mother's family possessed exceptionally good *songbun*. My grandfather was distinguished for his deeds during the Second World War, becoming a hero for infiltrating the Japanese imperial police when Korea was a Japanese colony, passing intelligence to the local communist partisans in the mountains, and freeing some of them from police cells.

After the war he was decorated and widely admired in his community. He kept an old photograph of himself wearing the Japanese police uniform and had written a manuscript telling his story, but after he died my grandmother burned it all in case the story should one day be misunderstood and bring disaster upon the family.

My grandmother had become an ardent communist when she was a college student. She had studied in Japan in the 1940s, and had returned to Korea as part of a small intellectual elite, bringing with her educated ways and refinements that were rare among Koreans at that time, when most people did not even finish elementary school. She joined the Party when she was just nineteen. My grandfather, after marrying her, moved to her hometown of Hyesan, instead of taking her to his own province, as was the custom. He became a local government official. In the autumn of 1950, when American troops entered the city in the first year of the Korean War, he fled to the deep mountains to avoid capture. The Americans were conducting house-to-house searches for members of the Party. My grandmother, who at the time was carrying a baby on her back, one of eight she was to have, hid their Party membership cards between bricks inside the chimneystack.

'If they'd found the cards, the Americans would have shot us,' she told me.

Her safekeeping of the cards ensured the family's high *songbun*. Those who destroyed their cards as the Americans approached were later to fall under suspicion. Some were purged violently and sent to the gulag. For the rest of her life, my grandmother wore her Party card on a string around her neck, concealed beneath her clothing.

After their twelve months of courtship my parents should have been married. But that was not how events turned out.

The problem was my mother's mother. My grandmother refused to give permission for the marriage. She was unimpressed with my father's prospects and his career in the air force. She thought my mother could do better, and marry a man who could provide her with a more comfortable life. For all her education in Japan and her progressive communist credentials, my grandmother belonged to a generation that saw love as a secondary matter when it came to a suitable match. Financial security came first. With luck, the couple could fall in love after the marriage.

She saw it as her duty to find my mother the best candidate. In this, my mother could not go against her will. It was unthinkable to defy one's parent.

My mother's blissful year began to turn into a nightmare.

Through connections my grandmother had met a glamorous woman who had a career as an actress in Pyongyang's booming film industry. The woman's brother was an official at the National Trading Company in the capital, and it was arranged for my mother to be introduced to him. My mother could not believe what was happening to her. She had no interest in this official, pleasant though he was. She was in love with my father. Before she knew it a marriage was being arranged for her.

My mother suffered an emotional breakdown, and for weeks her eyes were sore from crying and lack of sleep. Her pain took her to the edge of despair. She was made to break off relations with my father. When she wrote to tell him the news, he said little in return. She knew she had broken his heart.

My mother married the official from Pyongyang on a bright cold day in spring 1979. It was a traditional wedding. She wore an elaborately embroidered red silk *chima jeogori*, the national Korean dress – a long skirt wrapped high on the body, and a short jacket over it. Her groom wore a formal, Western-style suit. Afterwards, wedding photographs were taken, as was customary, at the feet of the great bronze statue of Kim Il-sung on Mansu Hill. This was to demonstrate that however much a couple might love each other their love for the Fatherly Leader was greater. No one smiled.

I was conceived during the honeymoon, and born in Hyesan in January 1980. My birth name was Kim Ji-hae.

It would seem that my mother's future, and mine, was sealed.

Love, however, was setting a course of its own, cutting through my grandmother's best-laid plans, like water finding its way to the sea.

My mother was born and brought up in Hyesan, the capital of Ryanggang Province in the northeast of the country – a mountainous region of spruce, larch and pine. There is little arable land there, and life can be rugged. In Korean folklore, the character of Hyesan people is tenacious and stubborn. They are survivors. A proverb has it that if you drop them in the middle of the ocean, they will find their way to land. Like all such sayings they are simplifications, and yet I recognized these traits strongly in my mother. In time, Min-ho and I would display similar characteristics – especially the stubbornness.

My mother could not live with the official, my biological father, and left him just after I was born. In the Korean way of measuring age, a child is one year old at the beginning of its first year and not, as in most countries, at the end of the first year. I was age one.

A divorce came soon after. Now it was my grandmother's turn to suffer sleepless nights. A divorced daughter was shameful enough, but a divorced daughter with a baby on her back would make her chances of making a successful match with someone else almost impossible. My grandmother insisted that I be given up for adoption.

One of my mother's brothers succeeded in finding a young highborn couple in Pyongyang who were seeking to adopt. The couple made the long journey to Hyesan to meet me and to take me back with them. They brought with them a box of toys and good-quality clothes.

There followed a terrible scene at the house. My mother tearfully refused to give me up. She would not let my grandmother wrest me out of her arms. I began to wail loudly. The couple from Pyongyang watched aghast as my grandmother vented her fury at my mother, then began to panic and implore her. Soon the couple became angry themselves and accused my family of misleading them.

Not long after this, my mother travelled to the military base of my father the officer. In an emotional reunion he accepted her straight away. Without even hesitating he also accepted me as his daughter.

They were so much in love that my grandmother conceded defeat, and she changed her mind about my father from then on. He had an air of authority that struck everyone who met him, yet he was gentle and kind. He never touched alcohol, or lost his temper. The strength of my parents' feelings for each other, however, was a worry to my grandmother. She warned them that if a couple loved each other too much it would condense all the affection that should last a lifetime into too short a period, and one of them would die young.

My mother and father were finally to marry. But now they had a new problem – this time, his parents. They would strongly have disapproved of the match if they'd known that my mother already had a child by another man, so my parents attempted to keep my existence a secret. In a city like Hyesan, however, where so many people knew each other, such a secret was not easily kept. Word got out, and just a few days before my parents' wedding my grandparents learned the truth about my existence. They withdrew their permission for my father to marry my mother. My father implored them with passion. He could not bear it if his marriage to my mother were thwarted a second time.

With great reluctance, therefore, my grandparents gave their consent, but on one condition: that my name be changed altogether to symbolize my joining a new family. In North Korea, as elsewhere, it was common for a child's surname to change if a mother remarried, but it was highly unusual for the first name to change, too. My mother was given no choice in the matter. And so, I was four years old when my identity was changed the second time, just after my parents married. My new name was Park Min-young.

The wedding was a quiet affair in Hyesan. This time there was no elaborate *chima jeogori*. My mother wore a smart dress suit. My father wore his uniform. His parents made little effort to hide their disapproving faces from my mother's family.

I was too young to be aware of these tensions. Nor was I aware of the truth of my own parentage. I would not discover the secret until several years later, when I was at elementary school. There is a part of me that still wishes I had never found out. In time, the discovery would have heartbreaking consequences for me, and for the kind and loving man I'd known until then as my father.

Chapter 2

The city at the edge of the world

For the first four years of my life, I grew up among a large extended family of uncles and aunts in Ryanggang Province. Despite the nomadic life that was to come after my parents married, moving with my father's career to various cities and military bases around the country, these early years formed the deep emotional attachment to Hyesan that has remained with me all my life.

Ryanggang Province is the highest part of Korea. The mountains in summer are spectacular. Winters are snowy and extremely cold. During the colonial period (1910–45), the Japanese brought the railroad and the lumber mills. On some days the air everywhere smelled of fresh-cut pine. The province is home both to the sacred revolutionary sites surrounding Mount Paektu, North Korea's highest peak, and, conversely, to the hardscrabble penal region of Baekam County, where families that have fallen foul of the regime are sent into internal exile.

When I was growing up Hyesan was an exciting place to be. Not because it was lively – nowhere in the country was noted for its theatre scene, restaurants or fashionable subcultures. The city's appeal lay in its proximity to the narrow Yalu River, Korea's ancient border with China. In a closed country like North Korea, Hyesan seemed like a city at the edge of the world. To the citizens who lived there it was a portal through which all manner of marvellous foreign-made goods – legal, illegal and highly illegal – entered the country. This made it a thriving hub of trade and smuggling, which brought many benefits and advantages to the locals, not least of which were opportunities to form lucrative partnerships with Chinese merchants on the other side of the river, and make hard currency. At times it could seem like a semi-lawless place where the government's iron rule was not so strong. This was because almost everyone, from the municipal Party chief to the lowliest border guard, wanted a share of the riches. Occasionally, however, there were crackdowns ordered by Pyongyang, and they could be brutal.

People from Hyesan were therefore more business-minded and often better off than people elsewhere in North Korea. The grown-ups would tell me that we were fortunate to live there. It was the best place in the whole country after Pyongyang, they said.

My earliest memory is from Hyesan, and it was very nearly my last.

Strangely, I remember the dress I was wearing. It was pretty and pale blue. I had wandered alone down the grassy bank behind our house and was sitting on a wooden sleeper, gathering stones into my lap. The dress and my hands became filthy. Suddenly there was a noise so loud it split the air and echoed off the mountains. I turned and saw a vast, blackened mass the size of a building coming around a curve in the track between the pine trees. It was heading straight at me. I didn't know what it was.

I have a series of confused images – blazing headlights, screeching metal, a sharp, burning smell. Voices shouting. The horns blasting again.

The black mass was in front of me, over me. I was underneath it. The noise and burning smell were tremendous.

The train driver later told my mother that he'd spotted me on the curve, about a hundred yards up the track, too short a distance to brake and avoid hitting me. His heart nearly stopped, he said. I crawled out from under the fourth carriage. For some reason, I was laughing. There were now many people on the bank. My mother was among them.

She picked me up by my arms and yelled: 'How many times have I said it, Min-young? Never – go – down – there!' Then she clutched me to her waist and began weeping uncontrollably. A woman in the crowd came over and told her that this was a good omen. To survive such a disaster so young meant that I would have a long life. For all her common sense, my mother was a superstitious person. Over the years she would repeat this woman's saying. It became a kind of deliverance myth, and I would remember it in moments of danger.

***

My mother was one of eight siblings – four sisters and four brothers – all of whom possessed the characteristic Hyesan stubbornness. They were to have curiously diverse careers. At one extreme was Uncle Money. He was an executive at a successful trading company in Pyongyang and could obtain luxurious Western goods. We were very proud of him. At the opposite end was Uncle Poor, who had sunk in the *songbun* system after marrying a girl from a collective farm. He was a talented artist and could have been one of the elite few permitted to paint the Leaders, but instead lived out his days painting the long red propaganda placards that stood in fields, exhorting tired farmworkers to 'unleash the transformative phase of economic growth!' and so on. The other brothers were Uncle Cinema, who ran the local movie theatre, and Uncle Opium, a drug dealer. Uncle Opium was quite an influential figure in Hyesan. His high *songbun* protected him from investigation and the local police welcomed his bribes. He would sit me on his knee and tell me fabulous folktales of the mountains, of animals and mythical beasts. When I remember these stories now, I realize he was probably high.

Family was everything to my mother. Our social life took place within the family and she formed few friends outside. In that way she was like my father. They were both private people. I would never see them hold hands or catch them cuddling in the kitchen. Few North Koreans are romantically demonstrative in that way. And yet their feelings for each other were always clear. Sometimes, at the dinner table, my mother would say to my father: 'I'm so happy I met you.' And my father would lean towards me and whisper, loud enough for my mother to hear: 'You know, if they brought ten truckloads of women for me and asked me to choose someone else, I would reject them all and choose your mother.'

Throughout their marriage they remained smitten. My mother would giggle and say: 'Your father has the most beautiful ears!'

When my father was away on military business, my mother would take me to stay with my grandmother or with one of my aunts. The eldest sister was Aunt Old, a melancholy and solitary woman, whose tragic marriage I was not to learn about until years later. The youngest was a generous woman known as Aunt Tall. The most beautiful and talented of my mother's sisters was Aunt Pretty. As a girl, she'd had hopes of becoming an ice-figure skater, but after a slip in which she'd chipped a tooth, my grandmother put paid to her dreams. Aunt Pretty had a real head for business – a talent my mother also possessed – and made a lot of money sending Chinese goods for sale in Pyongyang and Hamhung. She was tough, too, and once underwent an appendectomy by candlelight when the hospital had neither power nor enough anaesthetic.

'I could hear them cutting me,' she said.

I was horrified. 'Didn't it hurt?'

'Well, yes, but what can you do?'

My mother was a born entrepreneur. This aspect of her was unusual for a woman of high *songbun*. Many such women during the 1980s and early 1990s would have regarded making money from trade as immoral and beneath their dignity. But my mother was from Hyesan, and had a nose for a deal. Over the years ahead she would run many small, profitable ventures that would keep the family alive through the worst imaginable times. 'Trade' and 'market' were still dirty words when I was growing up, but within a few years attitudes would change radically, when it became a matter of survival.

She was strict with me, and I was brought up well. She had high standards for everything. She taught me it was rude to bump into older people, talk too loudly, eat too quickly, and eat with my mouth open. I learned that it was vulgar to sit with my legs apart. I learned to sit on the floor with my legs folded and tucked underneath, Japanese-style, and my posture bolt upright. She taught me to say goodbye to her and my father in the mornings with a full, ninety-degree bow.

When one of my girl friends dropped by once and saw me do this, she said: 'What d'you do that for?'

The question surprised me. 'You don't do it?'

My friend became weak with laughter. I was teased after that with extravagant, mock-formal bows.

In the house my mother hated untidiness and could be obsessively orderly. In public she always looked her best – she never wore old clothes and had an eye for the fashion trends, although she was seldom satisfied with her appearance. In a society where round-faced women with large eyes and almond-shaped lips are considered beautiful, she bemoaned her narrow eyes and angular face, usually in a way that made fun of herself: 'When I was pregnant I was worried you'd look like me.' I acquired my liking for fashion from her.

***

I was expecting to start kindergarten in Hyesan, but it was not to be. One evening in December my father returned home from work grinning broadly. It was snowing hard outside and his cap and uniform were powdered white. He clapped his hands together, asked for some hot tea, and told us he had received a promotion. He was being transferred. We were moving to Anju, a city near North Korea's west coast.

Chapter 3

The eyes on the wall

At the beginning of 1984, the three of us arrived in Anju. I was five years old. My mother's heart sank when she saw the place. The region's main industry is coal mining, and the Chongchon River, which runs through the city centre to the Yellow Sea, was black with silt and coal slag. We were informed that it smelled badly in summer and was prone to flooding the city in the rainy season. As with other cities in North Korea, much of Anju was rebuilt after the Korean War. All share a similarly drab, colourless look. Concrete blocks of flats lined the main roads in the centre. There were a few Soviet-style state buildings and a public park with the obligatory bronze statue of Kim Il-sung. Squat, tiled-roof houses made up the rest of the city. Hyesan, it has to be said, was not much different, but the mountain backdrop and our colourful family life there made it a magical place to us.

My mother had severe regrets about leaving Hyesan, knowing that she would not be able to visit her mother and siblings easily or often, but at the same time she knew that we were leading a privileged life. Most North Korean families never got to go anywhere. They stayed in the same place all their lives and needed a travel permit even to leave their local county. My father's job gave him access to goods most other people didn't have. We ate fish or meat with most meals. I did not know then that many North Koreans ate fish or meat so seldom that they could often remember the dates on which they did so – usually the birthdays of the Leaders, when extra rations were distributed.

We did not like our new house, which was on my father's military base. It had a wall-mounted radio with a speaker. It could not be turned off, and had no volume control, and would occasionally blast instructions and air-raid drill announcements from the *banjang* – the head of our neighbourhood people's unit. The *banjang* was usually a woman in her fifties whose job it was to deliver warnings from the government, check that no one was staying overnight without a permit, and to keep an eye on the families in her block. The day we moved in she presented us with the two portraits for our home. These were identical to the portraits in our house in Hyesan, and we hung them on the wall before we'd even eaten our first meal there.

Our entire family life, eating, socializing and sleeping, took place beneath the portraits. I was growing up under their gaze. Looking after them was the first rule of every family. In fact they represented a second family, wiser and more benign even than our own parents. They depicted our Great Leader Kim Il-sung, who founded our country, and his beloved son Kim Jong-il, the Dear Leader, who would one day succeed him. Their distant, airbrushed faces took pride of place in our home, and in all homes. They hung like icons in every building I ever entered.

From an early age I helped my mother clean them. We used a special cloth provided by the government, which could not be used for cleaning anything else. Even as a toddler I knew that the portraits were not like other household items. Once, when I pointed a finger at them, my mother scolded me loudly. 'Never do that.' Pointing, I learned, was extremely rude. If we needed to gesture towards them, we did so with the palm of the hand facing upward, with respect. 'Like this,' she said, showing me.

They had to be the highest objects in the room and perfectly aligned. No other pictures or clutter were permitted on the same wall. Public buildings, and the homes of high-ranking cadres of the Party, were obliged to display a third portrait – of Kim Jong-suk, a heroine of the anti-Japanese resistance who died young. She was the first wife of Kim Il-sung and the sainted mother of Kim Jong-il. I thought she was very beautiful. This holy trinity we called the Three Generals of Mount Paektu.

About once a month officials wearing white gloves entered every house in the block to inspect the portraits. If they reported a household for failing to clean them – we once saw them shine a flashlight at an angle to see if they could discern a single mote of dust on the glass – the family would be punished.

Every time we took them down for cleaning we handled them with extreme caution, as if they were priceless treasures from Koryo tombs, or pieces of enriched uranium. Damage to them due to humidity, which could make spots of mould appear on the paper in summer, was acceptable. Damage from any other cause could get a homeowner into serious trouble. Each year, stories of portrait-saving heroics would be featured in the media. My parents would hear a radio report commending a grandfather who'd waded through treacherous flood water holding the portraits above his head (he'd saved them, but sacrificed his own life in the attempt), or see a photograph in the *Rodong Sinmun*, the national daily, of a couple sitting precariously on the tiled roof of their hut after a catastrophic mudslide, clutching the sacred portraits. The newspaper exhorted all citizens to emulate the example of these real-life heroes.

This intrusion of the state into our home did not seem oppressive or unnatural to me. It was unthinkable that anyone would complain about the portraits. On the biggest dates in the calendar – the birthdays of Kim Il-sung and Kim Jong-il – the three of us would line up in front of them and make a solemn bow.

That small family ceremony was the only time politics entered our house. When my father came home from work, and the table was laid with rice, soup, kimchi and pickles, which we ate with every meal, my mother waited for me to say: 'Thank you, Respected Father Leader Kim Il-sung, for our food' before we picked up our chopsticks. But over dinner my parents chatted only of personal matters, or family. There was usually plenty of innocuous family news from Hyesan to talk about.

Serious topics were never discussed. I learned to avoid them in the way children acquire a sense for the dangers of the road. This was for my own protection, and we were no different from other families in that respect. Since there was no aspect of life, public or private, that fell outside the authority of the Party, almost every topic of conversation was potentially political, and potentially dangerous. My parents would not risk an incautious remark that might be repeated innocently by me, or misunderstood.

Growing up, I sensed this danger. I knew it was out there, but at the same time it was normal, like air pollution, or the potential for fire to burn. I didn't worry about it, and neither did Min-ho, when he came along. We seldom even mentioned the Leaders whose eyes shone upon us from the wall. Saying Kim Il-sung's name, for example, and forgetting to affix one of his titles – Great Leader, Respected Father Leader, Comrade, President or Marshal – could result in serious punishment if anyone reported the offence.

I played and quarrelled with other children, just like children anywhere else in the world. My parents did the worrying for me. My mother, in particular, seemed to have a talent for warding off trouble. Part of this came from the self-confidence of being a woman of high *songbun*. But she also possessed a natural tact in dealing with people, which would save us from disaster several times. She was good at managing the *banjang*, and would go out of her way to befriend her at the weekly block meetings, and give her small gifts. Most of the *banjang* women we knew were tough, reasonable types my mother could relate to. But she was always careful about what was on view in our house so as not to draw the state's attention or cause envy.

If my mother couldn't solve a problem with reason and good will, she'd try to solve it with money.

The week after we arrived in Anju she was stopped in a city-centre street by five volunteers wearing red armbands. These vigilantes would prowl the city looking for violators of North Korea's myriad social laws – anyone in jeans, men whose hair was a touch too long, women wearing a necklace or a foreign perfume – all of which were unsocialist and symbolic of moral degeneracy and capitalist decadence. The volunteers could be aggressive and arrogant in their zeal. Their nastiest trick was to catch people during the morning rush hour who had left home forgetting to wear their pin of the Great Leader's face, a small round badge worn by all adult North Koreans over their hearts. Those caught could find themselves with a delicate problem. No one could say they had 'simply forgotten' the Great Leader.

My mother's crime that morning was that she happened to be wearing trousers in public, not a skirt. This was prohibited, since the leadership had decreed that trousers were unbecoming of the Korean woman. The volunteers surrounded her and demanded to know why she was wearing them. To avoid a scene, she paid the fine, then slipped them a bribe so that the offence would not be entered in her ID passbook.

My mother bribed people confidently. There was nothing unusual in this, as long as you weren't caught. In North Korea, bribery is often the only way of making anything happen, or of circumventing a harsh law, or a piece of nonsense ideology.

Gradually we got used to life on the military base. Military life, I found, was not so different from civilian life. Everyone knew each other, and there was little security. My father joked that the whole country was a military base. None of us made friends easily at that time.

Like my father, my mother avoided being sociable. She knew how to keep her distance from people. This reserve served her well in a country where the more people you knew the more likely you were to be criticized or denounced. If I brought a friend home to the house, she would be hospitable rather than welcoming. But this was not really the person she was. One of the tragedies of North Korea is that everyone wears a mask, which they let slip at their peril. The mask my mother presented to people outside the family was of a hardened, no-nonsense woman of high *songbun*. In truth, it hid a sense of fun and a deep compassion for others. She would risk everything for those she loved. She regularly helped out siblings who were not so well off, especially Uncle Poor and his family on the collective farm, with food, clothes and money – so much so that I am ashamed to say that I resented it and complained. And for all her practicality she had a spiritual nature. She felt strongly in touch with her ancestors and would honour them with food and offerings at their grave-sides at the lunar New Year and at *Chuseok*, the autumn harvest festival. At such times she would speak in a hushed voice and tell me: 'Careful what you say.' The ancestors were listening.

My closest friend at this time was my tiny pet dog – it was one of the cute little breeds that people in other countries put frocks on. I wouldn't have been allowed to do that, because putting clothes on dogs was a well-known example of capitalist degeneracy. The Yankee jackals care more about dogs than people. This is what the teachers in my kindergarten told me. They even dress them up in clothes. That's because they are like dogs themselves.

I was six when I entered kindergarten in Anju. And although I was far too young to notice it, this marked a subtle change in my relation-ship with my parents. In a sense, I no longer belonged to them. I belonged to the state.

Chapter 4

The lady in black

The school year started in September, with a long vacation in the winter, not the summer, due to the difficulty of keeping the schools warm in North Korea's harsh winters. My kindergarten had a large wood-burning stove in the middle of the classroom and walls painted with colourful scenes of children performing gymnastics, children in uniform, and of a North Korean soldier simultaneously impaling a Yankee, a Japanese and a South Korean soldier with his rifle bayonet.

Ideological indoctrination began on the first day.

The teachers read us stories of child heroes who'd fought the Japanese during the period of colonial rule in Korea, and legends from the boyhood of Kim Il-sung – of how he'd suffered for the people's happiness even as an infant, giving away his own food and shoes to children less fortunate.

Whenever the Leaders were mentioned, the teachers adopted low, tremulous voices, as if they were intoning the names of living gods. The walls displayed photographs of Kim Il-sung as a young guerrilla; Kim Il-sung surrounded by smiling orphans; Kim Il-sung in his white marshal's uniform, as the father of our nation. He was tall and striking, and his brave wife, Kim Jong-suk, who had fought alongside him, seemed like a lady from a folktale. It was not difficult to adore them.

The story of the nativity of their son, the Dear Leader Kim Jong-il, brought me out in goose bumps. His birth was foretold by miraculous signs in the heavens – a double rainbow over Mount Paektu, swallows singing songs of praise with human voices, and the appearance of a bright new star in the sky. We listened to this and a shudder of awe passed through our small bodies. My scalp tingled. This was pure magic. The teachers encouraged us to draw and paint the snow-covered wooden cabin of his birth, with the sacred mountain behind it, and the new star in the sky. His birthday, on 16 February, was the Day of the Bright Star. The kindergarten also had a little model of the cabin, with painted-on snow, beneath a glass case.

This was a very happy time for me. We were the children of Kim Il-sung, and that made us children of the greatest nation on earth. We sang songs about the village of his birth, Mangyongdae, performing a little dance and putting our hands in the air on the word 'Mangyongdae'. His birthday, on 15 April, was the Day of the Sun, and our country was the Land of the Eternal Sun.

These birthdays were national holidays and all children were given treats and candies. From our youngest years we associated the Great Leader and Dear Leader with gifts and excitement in the way that children in the West think of Santa Claus.

I was too young not to believe every word. I believed absolutely that this heroic family had saved our homeland. Kim Il-sung created everything in our country. Nothing existed before him. He was our father's father and our mother's father. He was an invincible warrior who had defeated two great imperial powers in one lifetime – something that had never happened before in five thousand years of our history. He fought 100,000 battles against the Japanese in ten years – and that was before he'd even defeated the Yankees. He could travel for days without resting. He could appear simultaneously in the east and in the west. In his presence flowers bloomed and snow melted.

Even the toys we played with were used for our ideological education. If I built a train out of building blocks, the teacher would tell me that I could drive it to South Korea to save the starving children there. My mission was to bring them home to the bosom of Respected Father Leader.

Many of the songs we sang in class were about unifying Korea. This was a matter close to my heart because, we were told, South Korean children were dressed in rags. They scavenged for food on garbage heaps and suffered the sadistic cruelty of American soldiers, who used them for target practice, ran them over in jeeps, or made them polish boots. Our teacher showed us cartoon drawings of children begging barefoot in winter. I felt desperately sorry for them. I really wished I could rescue them.

The teachers were nice to us, in accordance with the Great Leader's oft-repeated view that children are the future and should be treated like royalty. There was no corporal punishment in schools. We sang a song called 'We Are Happy' and meant every word of it. We felt loved, confident and grateful.

My parents never dared criticize our schooling in front of me, or later, in front of Min-ho. That would have been dangerous. But neither did they comment on it, or reinforce what we learned. In fact they never mentioned it. My mother did, however, teach me to praise the Great Leader and the nation for anything good that came our way. This came from her acute sense of caution. Not to do so would have reflected on her, and might have been noticed by an informer. And there were informers everywhere – on the military base where we lived, in the city streets, in my kindergarten. They reported to the provincial bureau of the Ministry of State Security, the *Bowibu*. This was the secret police. The translation doesn't convey the power the word *Bowibu* has to send a chill through a North Korean. Its very mention, as the poet Jang Jin-sung put it, was enough to silence a crying child.

The *Bowibu* didn't watch from street corners or parked cars, or eavesdrop on conversations through walls. They didn't need to. The citizenry did all that for them. Neighbours could be relied upon to inform on neighbours; children to spy on children; workers to watch co-workers; and the head of the neighbourhood people's unit, the *banjang*, maintained an organized system of surveillance on every family in her unit. If the authorities asked her to place a particular family under closer watch, she would make the family's neighbours complicit. Informers often received extra food rations for their work. The *Bowibu* weren't interested in the real crimes that affected people, such as theft, which was rife, or corruption, but only in political disloyalty, the faintest hint of which, real or imagined, was enough to make an entire family – grandparents, parents and children – disappear. Their house would be roped off; they'd be taken away in a truck at night, and not seen again.

I never noticed my parents' silence on the subjects we were taught. This would only take on significance for me years later. Neither did I ever question their loyalty or doubt that they believed the selfless and superhuman feats of Kim Il-sung in saving our nation.

During a summer vacation from kindergarten, my mother took me on a visit to our family in Hyesan. That trip is memorable because I heard another myth that was to shape my childish idea of the world. It was told to me by Uncle Opium, the drug dealer, at the house of my grandmother.

Opium wasn't hard to come by in North Korea. Farmers had been cultivating poppies since the 1970s, with state laboratories refining the raw produce into high-quality heroin – one of the few products the country made to an international standard. It was sold abroad to raise foreign currency. North Koreans, however, were forbidden to use it or trade with it. But in such a bribe-dependent economy, plenty of it found its way into the general population. My uncle was selling it illegally in Hyesan and over the river in China, where there was a strong demand. My grandmother used it regularly. Many people did – painkillers and pharmaceutical medicines were often hard to come by.

Uncle Opium had enormous shining eyes, much larger than any of my mother's other siblings. It was years before the penny dropped and I realized why his eyes looked like this. He told me a lady came down from the sky every time it rained.

'She is dressed in black,' he said mysteriously, sucking on a cigarette of rough tobacco and blowing a ring of yellow smoke. 'If you grab hold of her skirts she'll take you up there with her.'

Back in Anju I waited days for it to rain. When finally I heard thunder I ran out of the house and looked up at the clouds. The raindrops splashed on my face. If the Respected Father Leader Kim Il-sung could appear in the east and in the west at the same time, it seemed quite reasonable to me that there would be a lady in black who flew among the clouds. I began to picture her realm up there in the sky. The thought of this lady scared the wits out of me, but I was too curious not to look for her. I held on to the steps in case she came down as fast as the rain and snatched me.

My mother quickly ruined the magic.

'What are you doing?' she yelled from the front door. 'Get in here.'

'I'm waiting for the lady in black.'

'What?'

Then her expression changed, as if she were remembering something. She clearly had some recollection of this story from Uncle Opium, and then realized I'd completely fallen for it. Suddenly she was laughing so hard she was bent over with her arms wrapped around herself. Then she hugged me and I could feel her body shaking. She was still laughing hours later when my father came home and she was cooking the rice for dinner, dabbing her eyes with her sleeve.

Now I was confused.

Some magical stories I was supposed to believe in with all my heart and could never doubt. Others I believed in at a cost to my dignity. I had really wanted to believe in the lady in black.

The world inside the kindergarten was clear. The teachers had simple answers for everything good and everything bad. Outside the kindergarten, the world was more confusing. Uncle Opium could probably have explained it to me, if I'd ever been able to have a normal conversation with him.

At his house once I saw a solid gold bar on the table, and next to it a gluey lump that looked like tar. I asked him what it was and he told me it was opium.

'Stick the end of your pencil in and take a bit,' he said.

'What do I do with it?'

He gave a breathy, hissing laugh. 'Eat it, of course.'

I had a cold at the time and wasn't feeling too good. The symptoms disappeared within minutes.

Anju may have been grimy and bleak but the hills surrounding it were beautiful. I enjoyed three idyllic childhood summers there, picnicking in fields of wild flowers. In certain months of the year the air would be buzzing with dragonflies. They hovered and flashed in iridescent blues and greens. We would chase them, running through the long grass. All the kids did this. At the weekend, my father would join in. Some kids bit off the heads and ate them, saying they tasted nutty.

On one outing we laid out our picnic mat in a copse of tall pine trees. My mother started hitting the trees with a long branch and suddenly it was raining pine cones. I ran around gathering them in a sack. We had never laughed so much together.

That scene is vivid in my mind as a moment of pure happiness just before a painful personal tragedy for me. We arrived home to find that my little dog had been killed. One of the trucks at the military base had run her over. I cried so much. My father told me there would not be another pet dog. They were too hard to obtain.

But it wasn't that event that overshadowed my memories of Anju. There was far worse to come.

Chapter 5

The man beneath the bridge

On a hot afternoon when I was seven years old, my mother sent me on some errand into town. It was unpleasantly humid. A fetid smell came off the river. There were flies everywhere. I was heading home along the riverbank when I saw the crowd ahead of me. A dense mass of people had gathered on the road beneath the railroad bridge. I had an odd intuition that this was something bad, but I could not resist going to look. I slipped my way into the crowd to see what was going on. The people near the front were looking upward. I followed their gaze, and saw a man hanging by his neck.

His face was covered with a dirty cloth sack and his hands were tied behind his back. He was wearing the indigo uniform of a factory worker. He wasn't moving but his body swayed slightly on a rope tied from the iron railing of the bridge. Several soldiers were standing about, stony-faced, with rifles on their backs. The people watching were still and quiet, as if this were some sort of ceremony. The rope creaked. I caught a reek of male sweat. The scene confused me because people were watching but no one was moving and no one was helping the man.

The most random detail stuck in my mind. I remember how the man standing next to me lit a cigarette and held it down by his side so that the smoke gathered foggily in his fingers. There was no breeze. Suddenly it seemed like there was no air to breathe.

I had to get out of there. I almost fought my way out.

When I told my mother what I'd seen she went as pale as a fish. She turned her back to me and pretended to busy herself with something. Then she muttered: 'Don't ever watch those things.'

Over the next few days there was a spate of hangings across the city, and my mother became unnerved. One of the victims was someone she knew – a woman named Baek Kyeong-sul. She was accused of seducing a state bank official in order to steal money, and was sentenced at a people's trial. My mother was there. These were not actually trials at all – the charges were simply read out and the victim executed on the spot. If the accused were to pass out from terror beforehand, the authorities were meant to adjourn to another day, so the victim was kept from knowing what was happening until the last moment.

It was near the start of the rainy season and the skies over Anju had been rumbling with thunder all morning, which further set my mother's nerves on edge. She was pregnant with Min-ho, and not feeling herself.

The woman emerged from the back of a police van and found herself facing eight judges seated behind a table set up in a public square, which was surrounded by a cordon of police and a large silent crowd. Her hands were bound behind her back and her face so blackened and puffy from beatings that my mother hardly recognized her. She was disorientated and stared about with an animal terror in her eyes.

In a hail of static, the charges were read out through a loudspeaker.

The woman fell to her knees and began to whimper, saying she was deeply sorry and ashamed for what she had done. My mother knew that the woman had a son who was a police officer; the woman must have believed that her son's connections would save her.

'The sentence is death by hanging.'

The woman's head jerked upward in shock. She looked around at the crowd as if appealing to them. Behind the police vans was a tall wooden pole with a noose hanging from it that had been kept hidden from her view. Police grabbed her at once and frogmarched her to the pole. She struggled and kicked out and wailed, but the noose was over her head in an instant. The rope was yanked taut, lifting her up into the air. She writhed and twitched for a few seconds before going limp.

When my mother returned home, the rain was coming down in lead rods. She had an odd, vacant stare in her eyes. She said she hadn't realized until then that it was as easy to kill a person as to kill an animal. The corpse had been thrown roughly onto the back of a truck. She'd asked one of the court officials where it was to be buried, and was told it would be taken to a garbage pit and covered in ash.

That was the detail that unhinged my mother.

Without an ancestral grave for her descendants to honour, the woman's spirit would find no rest. It would haunt the living.

That summer my father's work had been taking him to military bases all over the country. Without his reassuring presence, my mother was having problems sleeping after the hangings. At breakfast she'd be hollow-eyed, saying she'd seen the ghosts of the victims in nightmares. She couldn't concentrate on the simplest task. She was badly spooked and wanted to get out of Anju. I'm not sure whether it was after pressure from her, or simply an extraordinary coincidence, but she was immensely relieved when my father announced that we were relocating – to North Korea's second-largest city, Hamhung.

We left Anju, but did not go immediately to Hamhung. My parents wanted the new baby to be born in our home city, Hyesan, so that his birth documentation would be registered there, the same as the rest of the family's. So it was in Hyesan that my little brother was born. North Korean families have a tradition of naming children with the same first syllable, so although I was Min-young, my brother became Min-ho. I was seven years old, and feeling peevish at all the cooing and adoring the new arrival was receiving, and the stream of family visitors – Aunt Old, Aunt Pretty, Aunt Tall, Uncle Opium and Uncle Cinema – coming to see him, with congratulations and armfuls of gifts, but my mother was radiant, and overjoyed to be surrounded by family members and old neighbours once again.

There was one family matter, however, that she was not looking forward to. My father's parents wanted to meet their new grandson. At this time I still had not learned the truth about my parentage. I thought my father's parents were my blood grandparents, but for reasons obscure to me we had never got around to meeting them.

Their house had cold wooden floors. I didn't like being there. Neither, I sensed, did my mother. My grandfather was a forbidding presence who did not invite conversation. At dinner, he sat on the floor away from us, at a separate table. My grandmother served him first. It was a mark of respect, but it seemed to put a distance between everyone. My father, who normally exuded calm and confidence, was decidedly tense and talking too much to fill the silences. There was none of the chatter that surrounded us when we visited my mother's mother and my uncles and aunts.

I sensed the moment I arrived at their house that these grandparents liked Min-ho much more than me. The only time their faces lit up was when they held him, or when he gurgled and cried. With him they were affectionate. With my mother and me they were cool and civil. I told myself it was because Min-ho was a boy and these formal, old-fashioned people preferred grandsons to granddaughters. He was my parents' only son, which gave him a position of supreme importance in the family. Over the coming years, each time we visited, they would have gifts for Min-ho, but not for me. I realize now that my mother must have known that this was how it would be. It was why she went out of her way to be generous and bighearted toward me, to give me pocket money and sweets when I asked for them, and nice clothes. It was also the reason she presented me, on my ninth birthday, with the most marvellous gift I ever received in North Korea.

Chapter 6

The red shoes

I was very excited about the move to Hamhung, on the east coast. At that time Hamhung was a major industrial hub, famous as a centre for the production of Vinylon – a synthetic fibre, used in uniforms, that was invented in North Korea. It was an achievement we were so proud of that patriotic songs were sung about it. It held dye badly, shrank easily, was stiff and uncomfortable to wear, but it was marvellously flame-resistant. The city also boasted many restaurants and a grand new theatre – the largest in North Korea.

I couldn't stop pointing at the numbers of vehicles everywhere; there were far more than in Anju, and more bicycles, too. The streets were broad, grand boulevards with trolley buses that trailed sparks from the overhead cables, and the buildings weren't so shabby. The air was badly polluted, however. On some mornings the sky had a sulphurous yellow tint and stank of chemicals from the vast Hungnam ammonium fertilizer complex, which the Great Leader himself had visited several times and delivered on-the-spot guidance. His words were everywhere, on red-painted placards throughout the city, carved on stone plaques, and in letters six feet high on the side of Mount Tonghung. His image was omnipresent, in murals of coloured glass, in statues of marble and bronze, in portraits on the sides of buildings, which depicted him as soldier or scientist; as stern ideologue or jovial friend of children.

Despite my father's high rank in the air force the accommodation was barely adequate. This time our home was on another military base in a six-storey concrete apartment block with no elevator. We had three rooms and cold running water. It was decorated with yellowed wallpaper, which my mother immediately had changed for a better-quality washable type. She had the bathroom walls tiled blue. In winter the pipes froze; in summer mould would turn the outside walls black.

I was very lucky, however, although I still did not fully understand quite how lucky. My father's rank not only gave him access to goods many people didn't have, but he received a lot of food and household items as gifts and bribes,

In theory the government provided for everyone's needs – food, fuel, housing and clothing – through the Public Distribution System. The quality and the amount you received depended on the importance of your work. Twice a month your workplace provided you with ration coupons to exchange for the goods. Until a few years previously, the Party had still seriously been thinking of abolishing money. When the system actually worked, money was only needed as pocket money, or for the beauty parlour. But most of the time, the communist central planning system was so inefficient that it frequently broke down, rations dwindled or disappeared through theft, and people relied more and more on bribery or on unofficial markets for their essentials – for which cash, and often hard foreign currency, not the Korean won, was required.

We ate out quite often at restaurants that served *naengmyeon*, for which Hamhung is famous. These are noodles served in an ice-cold beef broth with a tangy sauce, although there are many variations. My mother would eat *naengmyeon* with her eyes closed in pure pleasure. She loved it to the point of addiction.

On Sundays, I played with neighbourhood girl friends outside on the concrete forecourt of our apartment block. We would skip or play a type of hopscotch called *sabanchigi*.

For the other six days of the week I was either at school or busy with school-related activities. It wasn't just the children's time that got filled up. Everyone – factory workers, cadres, soldiers, dock workers, farmers, teachers, housewives, pensioners, and my parents included – was kept constantly busy with some kind of after-hours organizational meeting or mind-numbing activity, such as ideological 'study groups' or 'discussions', which often involved memorizing the speeches of the Great Leader and the Dear Leader, or attending lectures that could last for hours after work, on everything from the revolutionary history of the early Party and new techniques for pig rearing, to hydroelectric power and the poetry of Kim Jong-il. This was part of the communist way – to ensure that no one could ever deviate into a selfish, individualistic or private life – but it was also a system of surveillance. Perpetual communal participation meant that the hours in each day when we were not being watched, by someone, were few.

I had begun elementary school in Anju, but now I had to join a new one in Hamhung, which filled me with apprehension. My mother had real trouble getting me to enter the building on my first day. The children seemed rough, and had a different accent; there was no 'village' feel as there had been at the school in Anju. Banners in the school corridors made our priorities clear: 'Let us study for our country!' and 'Always be on the alert for Marshal Kim Il-sung!'

But I was outgoing, and curious about my new classmates. I soon made some good friends among the girls. That came from the confidence a loving family gave me.

It was at school in Hamhung that I received my initiation into 'life purification time', or self-criticism sessions. These have been a basic feature of life in North Korea since they were introduced by Kim Jong-il in 1974, and are the occasions almost everyone dreads. They start in elementary school and continue throughout a person's life. Ours were held every Friday, and involved my entire class of forty students. Our teacher presided. Everyone took turns to stand up, accuse someone, and confess something. No one was excused for shyness. No one was allowed to be blameless.

It must have been humiliating and painful for the adults, standing up to criticize a colleague for some work-related or personal failing in front of the whole workforce. But there was only so much for which young children could be held guilty. The atmosphere in class was deadly serious. The teacher would not tolerate the mildest levity, even though the accusations were often ludicrous. The formula was to open the session with a commandment from Kim Il-sung or Kim Jong-il and then stand up and accuse the child who had violated it. When the accusations started to fly and fingers started to point, this was the only time, ironically, that we called each other 'comrade'.

These sessions could create an atmosphere of great fear and bitterness, even among children. But often, through a humanity we all possess, adults and children alike would find ways of taking the poison out of them. If I couldn't face accusing someone I'd sometimes accuse myself, which was permitted. Or a friend and I would strike a deal where she would criticize me one week, and I would criticize her the following week with some prearranged made-up charge. And so my friend would stand and say: 'Our Respected Father Leader said that children must focus on their studies with dedication in their hearts and a clear mind.' Then she'd point at me. 'In the last week I have noticed that Comrade Park is not listening in class.' I would hang my head and try to look chastened. The next week would be my turn. That way we stayed friends. My mother would make a similar pact with colleagues at her workplace; so did Min-ho when he got to elementary school. The sessions taught me a survival lesson. I had to be discreet, be cautious about what I said and did, and be very wary of others. Already I was acquiring the mask that the adults wore from long practice.

Often, students would find themselves criticized unexpectedly. When this happened, they took revenge. In rare cases, it could be lethal. On one occasion, in my final year of secondary school, a boy in my class pointed at another boy and said: 'When I went to your house, I saw that you had many things you didn't have before. Where did you get the money to pay for them?' The teacher reported the criticism to the headmaster, who reported it to the *Bowibu*. They investigated and found that the family had a son who had escaped the country and was sending them money from South Korea. Three generations of the family were arrested as traitors.

Like the ever-present danger of informers, I took the self-criticism sessions to be part of normal life. But I also had the sense there was nothing positive about them; they were entirely negative.

The biggest milestone of my youth came at the age of nine, in Hamhung. With all other children my age, I entered the Young Pioneer Corps, North Korea's communist youth movement. Ceremonies were held at schools all over the country on the same day, with parents and teachers assembling at large public places for the occasion. This is considered one of the proudest days in a North Korean's life.

Joining the Pioneers is compulsory between the ages of nine and fourteen, but not everyone is accepted at the same time. First, there is a formidable test of memorizing: I had to show that I'd learned the Young Pioneer's rights and duties by heart. From now on, I followed the orders of the Great Leader and the Dear Leader, no matter where, no matter what. I must think and act in accordance with their teachings. I must reject and denounce anyone who directed me to do anything against their will. I was good at memorizing, and passed the test easily. And as I'd done well in the most important subjects on the school curriculum – the revolutionary history of Kim Il-sung and Kim Jong-il – I was selected for the first induction ceremony of the year, on Kim Jong-il's birthday, 16 February, in 1989.

A few days before the ceremony my mother bought me a pair of new shoes especially for the occasion. They were foreign-made and from a dollar store – a special shop for people who had access to foreign currency and wanted to spend it. I was so excited about these shoes that, in order to calm me down, she let me take a peek at them. They were patent-leather Mary Janes, fastened with a buckle, and were a luscious deep red – nothing like the cheap state-issue shoes we all wore, and which only came in black. My mother wouldn't let me take them out of the box until the night before the ceremony.

At the ceremony we were to receive a red cotton scarf and a small silver Pioneer badge to pin on our blouses. To me the scarf was the mark of a grown-up and meant that I was no longer a kid. But this excitement was displaced unexpectedly by my anticipation of the red shoes. The wait was agonizing. The night before the ceremony I slept with them next to me on the bed – I woke a few times to check they were still there.

When the morning came at last I was ecstatic. The event was held in my school hall. The walls were adorned for the occasion with paintings and collages that the children had made – of the secret guerrilla base in the forests of Mount Paektu where the Dear Leader was born, and of the new star that had appeared in the heavens on the night of his birth. Amplified speeches boomed from the headmaster and the teachers on the stage, whose centrepiece was an enormous bouquet of kimjongilia, a fleshy red begonia that is the flower of Kim Jong-il. Everyone then stood to sing the 'Song of General Kim Jong-il', and finally the Pioneers stepped up to the stage to receive, with great solemnity, their scarves and badges. The parents in the audience applauded each one.

I walked up to receive mine, bursting with pride for my red shoes. It surprises me now to think that there were no repercussions. All present in the school hall must have noticed them. It did not strike me until years later what an unusual gift they were. Most kids at the ceremony – several hundred of them – were wearing the state-issue black shoes. My mother was a cautious woman, but, consciously or not, she was encouraging a distinct individualism in me.

We took many group photos and family photos. It was a proud day for my parents. My father wore his air force uniform. My mother was carrying Min-ho, aged two.

Classmates not selected for that day's ceremony had to wait until the next ceremony on Kim Il-sung's birthday, 15 April.

One girl I was friendly with had not been accepted for the February induction and was often absent from class. For some reason our teacher decided that she and some of the girl's friends should visit the girl's home to see if she was all right. It was in a run-down area of the city where hoodlums hung about. The housing was very squalid. Our visit was a terrible mistake. Her house was bare, and smelled of sewage. She had obviously hoped to hide her poverty from us, but there we were, crowded into one of her two small rooms, staring at our feet while our teacher, flushed with embarrassment, suggested to her mother that our friend should try to attend school every day.

The experience was deeply confusing for me. I knew there were degrees of privilege, but we were also equal citizens in the best country in the world. The Leaders were dedicating their lives to providing for all of us. Weren't they?

Schooling in North Korea is free, though in reality parents are perpetually being given quotas for donations of goods, which the school sells to pay for facilities. My friend had not been attending because her parents could not afford these donations. None of us was cynical enough to realize that our schooling was not really free at all. The donations were a patriotic duty – rabbit-fur for the gloves and hats of the soldiers who kept us safe; scrap iron for their guns, copper for their bullets; mushrooms and berries as foreign currency-earning exports. Sometimes a child would be criticized by the teacher in front of the class for not bringing in the quota.

In early 1990, when I was ten years old, my father announced that we were moving again, this time back to Hyesan. My mother had had enough of the pollution and grind of life in Hamhung, and missed her family and the clean air. She did not think an industrial city was a good place to bring up Min-ho. Once again, we looked forward to the move. My parents talked incessantly of Hyesan and of the people there.

We were going home.

Min-ho, my mother, and I all waved goodbye to my father, and to Hamhung, from the train window. My father would follow in a day or two. That journey home would not have stuck in my mind but for a drama we experienced on the way that made a lasting impression on my mother and me.

On the way north we had to change trains at a town called Kil-ju on the east coast. Train stations in North Korea have a rigorous inspection of travellers' documents, with passengers often having to pass through cordons of police and ticket inspectors. No one can board a train without a travel permit stamped in their ID passbook, together with a train ticket, which is valid for four days only. The documentation is then checked all over again at the destination station. A woman ticket inspector examined my mother's ticket and told her brusquely that it had expired. She was the type of official most North Koreans are familiar with – a mini Great Leader when in uniform. She took my mother's ID passbook and ticket and told her to wait.

My mother's face fell into her hands. Now we had a problem. She would have to get permission from Hamhung again before we could buy new tickets. That would take time and she had two children in tow, and luggage. We were stranded. Min-ho was crying loudly. My mother took him off her back and held him and together we slumped onto a bench inside the station. I held her hand. We must have looked a desolate bunch, because a middle-aged man in the grey cap and uniform of the Korean State Railway came up to us and smiled. He asked what the matter was. My mother explained, and he went to the ticket inspector's office. The woman was not there, but he brought back my mother's ticket and ID passbook, and gave them to her.

In a low voice he said: 'When the train stops, jump on. But if she comes looking for you, hide.'

My mother was so grateful that she asked for his address so that she could send him something.

He held up his palms. 'No time for that.'

The train was creaking into the station, bringing with it a reek of latrines and soldered steel. It screeched to a stop and the doors began flying open.

We boarded. The carriage was crowded. My mother quickly explained our predicament to the passengers and asked if we could crouch down behind them. Sure enough, a minute later we heard the voice of the ticket inspector, asking people on the platform about us. Next thing we knew she had entered the carriage.

'Have you seen a woman with a baby and a little girl?' She was shouting. 'Did she get on the train?'

'Yes.' Two of the passengers in front of us said this in unison. 'They went that way.'

The woman got off, still looking left and right for us. We heard her asking more people on the platform. We were holding our breath. Why wasn't the train moving? A minute seemed to pass. Finally we heard the shrill note of a whistle. The train shunted forward, couplings banging together. My mother looked at me and finally exhaled. She'd been terrified Min-ho would start bawling again.

Kindness toward strangers is rare in North Korea. There is risk in helping others. The irony was that by forcing us to be good citizens, the state made accusers and informers of us all. The episode was so unusual that my mother was to recall it many times, saying how thankful she was to that man, and to the passengers. A few years later, when the country entered its darkest period, we would remember him. Kind people who put others before themselves would be the first to die. It was the ruthless and the selfish who would survive.

Chapter 7

Boomtown

Our new home in Hyesan was another house allocated to us by the military. Our neighbours were other military officials and their families. The accommodation was good by North Korean standards. It had two rooms and a squat toilet. The heating in the floor was piping hot, making the glue beneath the *reja* – a kind of linoleum – give off a smell like mushrooms, but the building was poorly insulated. In winter we'd have warm backsides and freezing noses. We had to boil water when we wanted a hot bath.

My mother did her usual makeover, replacing the wallpaper and the furniture. She didn't mind. She was thrilled to be back in Hyesan and reconnected with our family social circles. We felt settled.

Hyesan had been booming in the years we'd been away. The illicit trade coming over the border from China seemed greater than ever and my mother wanted to get in on some deals. She had found a job with a local government bureau, but her salary, as with all state jobs, was negligible. She wanted to make serious money, like Aunt Pretty, Uncle Money and Uncle Opium.

It seemed that everything was available in Hyesan – from high-value liquor and expensive foreign perfume to Western-brand clothing and Japanese electronics – at a price. Smugglers brought goods from the county of Changbai, on the Chinese side, across the narrow, shallow river for collection by a Korean contact, or across the Changbai–Hyesan International Bridge (known to locals as the Friendship Bridge). Illegal trade across the bridge required bribing the North Korean customs officials; smuggling across the river required bribing the border guards. When the river froze solid in winter smugglers crept over the ice; the rest of the year they waded across at night, or in broad daylight, if the guards at key points had been bribed and were in on the deal.

We could see the prosperity. This would not have been at all obvious to outsiders, since North Koreans are poor and do not wish to draw the state's attention. Anyone looking across from China would have seen a city in deep blackout at night, with a few kerosene lamps flickering in windows, and a colourless, drab place by day, with people cycling joylessly to work. But the signs were all around us. The special hotel for foreigners, where our parents sometimes took Min-ho and me for an overnight stay as a treat (the manager was a friend of my mother's), was always full with Chinese business people. In the morning we'd join them for breakfast but never talk to them, in case any informers or *Bowibu* agents were listening. The city's dollar store, opposite Hyesan Station, had plenty of customers spending hard currency on goods not obtainable anywhere else, and certainly not through the state's Public Distribution System. Going there was like being admitted into a magical cavern. I couldn't believe how brightly the goods were packaged – foreign-made cookies and chocolates in wrappers of silver and purple that made them irresistibly tempting, and fruit juices – orange, apple, grape – in clear bottles marked with Western letters, that came from some faraway land of plenty. Outside the store, a few illegal moneychangers hung about like flies. My mother walked straight past them and would have nothing to do with them, saying they swindled people by wrapping newsprint into a bundle and putting a few genuine notes on top, knowing that anyone illegally trying to change money couldn't complain. The state beauty parlour was always fully booked, with women having their hair permed (not dyed, which was prohibited), and the state restaurants were doing a roaring trade. Most significantly, business was brisk and busy at the open-air local markets.

Markets occupy an ambiguous place in North Korean society. The government tried several times to ban them altogether, or narrowly restrict their opening times, since Kim Jong-il, who was now effectively running the country for his father, declared that they were breeding grounds for every type of unsocialist practice. (He was right about that.) But he couldn't abolish them while the Public Distribution System kept breaking down or failing to provide people with sufficient essentials. Occasionally, during some crackdown ordered by Pyongyang, the markets would be closed without notice, only to sprout up again within days, like sturdy and fertile weeds. The rules for market traders changed as often as the wind. For many years it was illegal to sell rice because rice was sacred and a gift of the Great Leader. But when I went to the markets, quite regularly with my mother, rice was for sale, along with meat, vegetables, kitchenware, and also Chinese fashions, cosmetics and – concealed beneath mats at enormous personal risk to vendor and buyer alike – cassette tapes of foreign pop music. Goods from Japan were considered the best quality. Next were South Korean products (with the archenemy's labels and trademarks carefully removed), and lastly Chinese.

My mother wasted no time. Soon she had made contacts among the Chinese traders just across the river in Changbai and was arranging for goods to be sent over, which she would sell on, and make a nice profit. Her chief trading partners were a Mr Ahn and a Mr Chang, both Korean-Chinese, who had houses on the Chinese side of the riverbank.

It was in connection with my mother's thriving business activities that she took me to a fortune-teller in the second year after we arrived back in Hyesan.

We woke extremely early, while it was still dark. My father and Min-ho were asleep. It was spring, and vivid green shoots were starting to sprout along the empty dirt streets. We hurried to the station to catch the first commuter train for Daeoh-cheon, the village where the fortune-teller woman lived.

My mother knew a number of these mystics and spent a lot of money on them. I was irritable about being woken so early, but she told me that the channel to the spirits is clearest at dawn. 'She'll be more accurate.'

My mother also wanted to beat the queue. Sometimes she'd arrive to find the fortune-teller out. A neighbour would say she'd been driven away in a Mercedes-Benz with tinted windows, for a discreet session with a high-ranking Party cadre. North Korea is an atheist state. Anyone caught in possession of a Bible faces execution or a life in the gulag. Kim worship is the only permitted outlet for spiritual fervour. Shamans and fortune-tellers, too, are outlawed, but high cadres of the regime consult them. We'd heard that even Kim Jong-il himself sought their advice.

The fortune-teller's house was very old. Single-storey, and wood-framed with walls of mud and a thatched roof. I hadn't known that such houses still existed. It was at a tilt and smelled damp. The lady was elderly, with thick, dishevelled hair. She was raising a granddaughter on her own.

'I have a question about trade,' my mother said in a whisper. 'My Chinese partner has goods. I wish to know when to receive them.'

In other words, she wanted to know the best day to smuggle and not get into trouble. Sometimes, if the date was already fixed, my mother would pay for a ceremony to ward off bad luck.

The lady spilled a fistful of rice on the tabletop and used her finger-nails to separate individual grains into portions. She examined this little pile intensely, then she started to speak in a rapid patter. I couldn't tell if she was addressing us, or the spirits. She spoke of the day on which it was most propitious to receive the goods.

'When you leave the house that morning, you must step out with your left foot first. Then spread some salt around and pray to the mountain spirit for good fortune.'

My mother nodded. She was satisfied.

'This is my daughter,' she said, and told her the time and date of my birth. The fortune-teller looked straight at me in a way that unnerved me. Then she closed her eyes theatrically.

'Your daughter is clever,' she said. 'She has a future connected with music. She will eat foreign rice.'

As we walked back to the station the sun was coming up and the air was beautifully clear and crisp. The crags at the tops of the mountains were etched sharply against the sky but a white mist lingered in the foothills among the pines. My mother walked slowly down the dirt track, holding my hand. She was thinking about the prediction. She interpreted 'foreign rice' to mean that I would live overseas. Then she sighed, realizing she'd probably wasted her money. No ordinary North Koreans were allowed to travel abroad, let alone emigrate. That's how it was with fortune-tellers. They told you things and you chose what you believed. But despite my scepticism about predicting dates for smuggling, I was more accepting of what the woman had said about me. I too thought my future was in music. I had been learning the accordion from a private tutor and was good at it. Accordion playing is popular in North Korea, a legacy from the end of the Second World War when our half of the peninsula was filled with Russian troops of the Soviet Red Army, although the Party never acknowledged any foreign influence on our culture. I thought the old woman's prophecy meant that I would have a career as a professional accordionist and marry someone from another province. Maybe I would live in Pyongyang. That would be a dream come true. Only privileged people lived there. I fantasized about this for weeks until an event occurred that obliterated my daydreams and cast a shadow over my whole childhood.

Chapter 8

The secret photograph

A few months after the visit to the fortune-teller, during the summer school vacation, my mother had taken Min-ho somewhere and had left me at my grandmother's house for the day. She was a fascinating woman, intelligent, and always full of stories. Her silver hair was pinned back in the old Korean style, with a needle through the bun. On this particular visit, however, she told me a story that devastated me.

To this day I'm not sure why she did it. She wasn't being mischievous. And I don't think her mind was weakening, making her forgetful of what should stay secret. The only explanation I can think of is that she thought I should know the truth while I was young, because I'd find it easier to come to terms with as a girl than if I discovered it later, as a grown woman. If that's what she was thinking, she made a terrible misjudgement.

It was a warm Saturday morning and the door and windows were open. Outside in the yard, jays were chirping and drinking water from a bowl. We were sitting at her table when she began looking at me with an odd intensity. She said softly: 'You know, your father isn't your real father.'

I didn't take in what she'd said.

She reached across and squeezed my hand. 'Your name is Kim. Not Park.'

There was a long pause. I didn't see where this was going, but I might have smiled uncertainly. This could be one of her jokes. Like my mother, she had quite a sense of humour.

Seeing my confusion, she said: 'It's the truth.'

She stood and went over to the glass cabinet where she kept her best bowls and plates. It had a small drawer in the bottom. She bent down stiffly. At the back of her neck I could see the string on which she kept her Party card. She retrieved a cardboard envelope, and handed it to me. It smelled damp.

'Open it.'

I put my hand inside and pulled out a black and white photograph. It showed a wedding party. I recognized my mother at once. She was the bride in the centre, wearing a beautiful *chima jeogori*. But the scene didn't make sense. The groom next to her was not my father. He was tall and handsome with slicked-back hair, and dressed in a Western-style suit. Behind them was a vast bronze statue of Kim Il-sung, arm outstretched, as if giving traffic directions.

My grandmother pointed to the groom in the suit. 'That's your father. And this lady . . .' She pointed to a beautiful woman to the man's right. '. . . is his sister – your aunt. She's a film actress in Pyongyang. You strongly resemble her.' She sighed. 'Your real father was a nice man, and he loved you a lot.'

The room seemed to go dim. Whatever tethered me to reality had just been cut. I was floating in unreality, and deeply confused.

She explained that my mother had loved my father so much that she could not live with the man she'd married, my biological father. She'd divorced him.

My father is not my father? My eyes started brimming with tears. *How could she say that?*

I said nothing. She seemed to read the next question forming in my mind. I couldn't open my mouth to ask it. I think if I'd opened my mouth I would have fallen apart.

'Min-ho is your half-brother,' she said, nodding.

I stared at her, but she ploughed on.

'A couple of years ago, when your mother visited your Uncle Money in Pyongyang, she bumped into your real father in the street . . .'

A chill went through me. I did not like her calling this person my father.

'. . . She had a photo of you in her purse and showed it to him. He didn't say anything. He just looked at it for a long time, then he slipped it into his pocket before she could stop him, and walked away. So he has your picture.' My grandmother's eyes drifted to the window and the mountains. 'After that, I wrote to his sister the actress to ask what had happened to him. She told me he had remarried soon after the divorce and had twin girls, one of whom he named Ji-hae, after you.'

Ji-hae, my birth name.

A shadow passed over my grandmother's face. 'He shouldn't have done that.'

There is a superstition in North Korea that if someone remarries and gives a child of the second marriage the same name as a child from the previous marriage, the second to receive the name will die.

'When the girl was young, she fell sick and died.'

I left my grandmother's house in a daze. I felt hollowed out, tearful and numb at the same time. She'd said nothing about keeping this a secret, but I knew I would never mention it to my mother or my father or anyone. I was too young to know that talking about it is exactly what I should have done. Instead I buried it inside me, and it started to gnaw at my heart. I was still utterly confused. The only thing I kind of understood was that it explained the coolness of my father's parents toward me, and their generosity toward Min-ho. He had their blood. I didn't.

When I got home Min-ho was sitting on the floor drawing a picture with coloured crayons. What he'd drawn stunned me, and I felt tears again. And something like anger. It was crude and charming and showed stick figures of me, him, my mother and my father, all holding hands together beneath a shining sun. Inside the sun was a face of a man wearing glasses – Kim Il-sung.

Min-ho was now five years old. He was growing up into a good-natured boy, who liked to help our mother. He had a very cute smile. But now I felt as if a glass wall had gone up between us. He was a half-brother.

Our relationship changed from then on. I became an older sister who provoked him and started fights with him that he could never win. I feel so sorry about that now. My mother would say: 'What's wrong with you? Why can't you be more like Min-ho?'

It would be years before I could process maturely the information my grandmother had given me, and reach out to him.

At dinner that evening I said nothing. My mother chatted about some business venture of Aunt Pretty's; Min-ho was told not to hold his chopsticks in the air; my father was calm as usual, as if nothing had changed. Eventually he said: 'What's up with you? You're as quiet as a little mouse.'

I stared at my bowl. I could not look at him.

In North Korea family is everything. Bloodlines are everything. *Songbun* is everything. *He's not my father.*

I began to push him away and withdraw from him, thinking I had lost my love for him. The pain I was feeling was making me think this.

I began to avoid him.

Chapter 9

To be a good communist

I joined the other children assembling on the street. No one was ever late. We straightened our red scarves, and got into formation. The class leader, who was also our marching-group leader, held up the red banner, and we fell in step behind him, swinging our arms and singing at the tops of our voices.

Who is the partisan whose deeds are unsurpassed?
Who is the patriot whose deeds shall ever last?

In September 1992 I had started secondary school in Hyesan, and marched there each morning at eight. We knew all the songs so well that we'd fall into harmony spontaneously.

So dear to our hearts is our glorious General's name,
Our beloved Kim Il-sung of undying fame!

By now the red scarf I'd longed to wear had become an irritation to me. From my mother I was acquiring a distinct care for how I looked. I didn't want the drab North Korean clothes. I wanted to look different. I'd also grown more conscious of my body after an incident earlier that year, in the spring.

My mother had come to my school to have lunch with me. We were sitting in the sun just outside the school building, eating rice balls on the riverbank, when a boy shouted from my classroom window on the second floor, so loud they would have heard him in China: 'Hey, Min-young, your mother's ugly. Not like you.' There was laughter from other boys behind him. I was only twelve but my face was scarlet with fury. I'd never thought my mother was not pretty. I felt far more humiliated than she did. She actually laughed and told me to calm down. Then she pinched my cheek and said: 'Boys are noticing you.'

We had classes in Korean, maths, music, art, and 'communist ethics' – a curious blend of North Korean nationalism and Confucian traditions that I don't think had much to do with communism as it is understood in the West. I also began to learn Russian, Chinese characters, geography, chemistry and physics. My father was especially strict with me about learning Chinese calligraphy, which he said was important. Many words in Korean and Japanese derive from ancient Chinese, and although the languages have diverged over time, the people of these nations often find they can communicate through calligraphy. I did not see much point to this, when I had clothes and boys to think about. I did not know that a time would come when I would thank my father in prayers for making me study Chinese. It was a gift of great good fortune from him. One day it would help save my life.

Again, the most important lessons, the most deeply studied subjects, centred on the lives and thoughts of our Leaders Great and Dear. Much of the curriculum was taken up by the cult of Kim. The Kim 'activities' of elementary school became serious study in secondary school. The school had a 'study room' devoted to Kim Il-sung, Kim Jong-il, and Kim Jong-il's mother, Kim Jong-suk. It was the most immaculate room in the school, made of the best building materials, and had been paid for with compulsory donations from parents. It was sealed shut so that dust did not settle on the photographs. We took our shoes off outside the door, and could only enter if we were wearing new white socks.

History lessons were superficial. The past was not set in stone, and was occasionally rewritten. My parents had learned at school that Admiral Yi Sun-shin, a naval commander whose tactics had defeated a massive Japanese invasion in the sixteenth century, was one of the great heroes of Korean history. By my day, his heroism had been downgraded. Admiral Yi had tried his best, we were told, but society was still backward at that time, and no figure in Korean history truly stood out until Kim Il-sung emerged as the greatest military commander in the history of humankind.

Lessons were taught with great conviction. The teacher was the only one to ask questions in class, and when she did, the student called upon to answer would stand up, hands at their sides, and shout out the answer as if addressing a regiment. We were not required to formulate any views of our own, or to discuss, or interpret ideas in any subject. Almost all of our homework was simply memorization, which I was good at, and often came top of the class.

Propaganda seeped into every subject. In our geography lesson we used a textbook that showed photographs of parched plots of land, so arid that the mud was cracked. 'This is a normal farm in South Korea,' the teacher said. 'Farmers there can't grow rice. That's why the people suffer.' Maths textbook questions were sometimes worded emotively. 'In one battle of the Great Fatherland Liberation War, 3 brave uncles of the Korean People's Army wiped out 30 American imperialist bastards. What was the ratio of the soldiers who fought?'

Everything we learned about Americans was negative. In cartoons they were snarling jackals. In the propaganda posters they were as thin as sticks with hook noses and blond hair. We were told they smelled bad. They had turned South Korea into a 'hell on earth' and were maintaining a puppet government there. The teachers never missed an opportunity to remind us of their villainy.

'If you meet a Yankee bastard on the street and he offers you candy, do not take it!' one teacher warned us, wagging a finger in the air. 'If you do, he'll claim North Korean children are beggars. Be on your guard if he asks you anything, even the most innocent questions.'

We all looked at each other. We had never seen an American. Few Westerners, let alone Americans, ever came to our country, but for some reason the threat of the unseen made this warning all the more chilling.

The teacher also told us to be wary of the Chinese, our allies in communism just across the river. They were envious of us, and not to be trusted. This made sense to me because many of the Chinese-made products I saw at the market were often of dubious quality. The lurid urban myths circulating in Hyesan seemed to confirm the teacher's words. One story had it that the Chinese used human blood to dye fabrics red. This gave me nightmares. These stories affected my mother, too. When she once found insect eggs in the lining of some underwear she'd bought she wondered if they'd been put there deliberately by the Chinese manufacturer.

***

One day early in the first semester our teacher had an announcement to make. Training and drilling for the mass games would soon begin. Mass games, he said, were essential to our education. The training, organization and discipline needed for them would make good communists of us. He gave us an example of what he meant, quoting the words of Kim Jong-il: since every child knew that a single slip by an individual could ruin a display involving thousands of performers, every child learned to subordinate their will to that of the collective. In other words, though we were too young to know it, mass games helped to suppress individual thought.

Mass games marked the most sacred dates in the calendar. We practised all year long except during the coldest weeks. Practice was held on the school grounds, which could be especially arduous in the heat of summer, with the final rehearsals in Hyesan Stadium. The highlight of the year was Kim Il-sung's birthday, on 15 April. I played the drums in the parade. This was followed by the gymnastics and parades for Children's Day on 2 June, at which we'd march through the city holding tall, streaming red banners. Then we trained for the anniversary of the Day of Victory in the Great Fatherland Liberation War (the Korean War) on 27 July, at which we'd join with other schools to form massed choirs. Shortly after this were the mass games for Liberation Day on 15 August (which commemorated the end of Japanese rule), and Party Foundation Day, on 10 October. There was little time left over in the year for proper education or private pursuits.

I didn't enjoy these vast events. They were nerve-wracking and stressful. But no one complained and no one was excused. My friends and I were assigned to the card section of the mass games in Hyesan Stadium, which was made up of thousands of children executing an immaculately drilled display of different coloured cards flipped and held up to form a sequence of giant images – all timed to music, gymnastics or marching. Though none of us said it, we all used to worry about the 'single slip' that could ruin the entire display. That filled me with terror. We practised endlessly, and to perfection. Each of us had a large pack containing all our cards, which we displayed in order. We were led by a conductor who stood at the front holding up the number of the next card. When she gave the signal, everyone held up that card in unison. The final pattern in the display formed a vast image of the Great Leader's face with a shimmering gold wreath around it, which the children moved to give it a dazzle effect. We never got to see the visual display that we were creating, but when the stadium was full, and we heard the roar of the crowd, with tens of thousands chanting 'Long life!' over and over – '*MAN–SAE! MAN–SAE! MAN–SAE!*' – the adrenalin was electrifying.

At the end of that first year at secondary school the ceremonies held on the anniversary of the Korean War affected me deeply and made me very emotional. The day began at school with outdoor speeches from our teachers and headmaster. They opened with the solemn words, spoken into a microphone: 'On the morning of 25 June 1950, at 3 a.m., the South Korean enemy attacked our country while our people slept, and killed many innocents . . .'

The images conjured for us of tanks rolling across the border and slaughtering our people in their homes moved us all to floods of tears. The South Koreans had made victims of us. I burned with thoughts of vengeance and righting injustice. All the children felt the same. We talked afterwards of what we would do to a South Korean if we ever saw one.

Despite the endless and exhausting communal activities I had one private realm I could escape to: in books. Reading was a habit I'd picked up from my mother. I had picture books of fairytales, myths and folktales. I had a Korean edition of *The Count of Monte Cristo*, a story I loved – but it had some pages glued together by the censor, and it was impossible to peel them apart. Tales of heroes struggling against oppression were permitted as long as they fitted the North Korean revolutionary worldview, but any inconvenient details got blotted out.

By the second year of secondary school I was reading North Korean spy thrillers. Some of them were so gripping they kept me up late, by candlelight. The best one was about a North Korean special agent operating in South Korea. He lived there with his South Korean wife, never telling her his true identity. He was controlled directly by the head of secret espionage operations, a figure he'd never met face to face but with whom he'd formed a relationship over time. The story climaxes when he discovers that his controller is his own wife. The best stories had endings that were obvious all along and yet took the reader completely by surprise.

***

One evening at the start of my second year at secondary school, I came home to find my mother cooking a special dinner to mark my father's first day in a new job. I had known for a while that he was leaving the air force, but I wasn't talking to him much these days, and taking little interest in what he told me. When he arrived home, I saw him wearing a civilian suit for the first time. He looked smart, and quite different. I was so used to seeing his grey-blue uniform. He was now working for a trading company, which was controlled by the military. He was grinning broadly, and said he would be crossing into China next week on business. He showed me his new passport. I had never seen a passport before, but affected a lack of interest. My mother, however, was in high spirits. A husband with permission to travel abroad was a real mark of status. We were moving up in the world.

The only time I spoke to him over dinner, and not very respectfully, was to ask what he actually did in this fancy new job. He gave some vague, unspecific response. Clearly it was supposed to be some big secret. I rolled my eyes and left the table, which angered my mother. My father remained silent. I knew I had hurt him, but I felt more resentful towards him than ever. This was yet another fact being kept hidden from me. The pain I felt over the truth about my parentage had not lessened at all. I did not realize that in not telling me about his job he was trying to protect me.

My father began crossing into China on business, sometimes staying away for a night or two. It was very fortunate, therefore, that he happened to be at home with my mother on the evening of the fire.

About two months later, I had gone to bed very early, aching and exhausted after mass games practice, and was already asleep next to Min-ho when my mother's cry awoke me, and my father came crashing into the room. Behind him was a flickering orange light, and everywhere a sharp reek of aviation fuel. We saved nothing from the house but the clothes we had on and the portraits my father had snatched from the wall, just seconds before the roof collapsed. All my picture books, my novels, and my beloved accordion and guitar were destroyed.

But there was something else I treasured that was also destroyed by the fire. Something so dangerous to possess that it could have got us sent to a prison camp. Looking back, the fire may have been a mighty stroke of luck.

Chapter 10

'Rocky island'

A few months before the fire one of my best friends had gathered a close-knit group of us together in the schoolyard. I tended to make friends with older girls, from similar backgrounds. This friend was the daughter of the city's chief of police. She'd heard that cassette tapes of illegal South Korean pop music could be bought, very discreetly, from certain dealers.

Soon we were in possession of some of this red-hot criminal contraband. We were among the first in North Korea to hear these new hits.

A small group of us began secretly meeting up on the weekends in the houses of one of us, and when parents and siblings were out we'd dance and sing along to the music of the South Korean singers Ju Hyun-mi and Hyun Chul, twirling around and jiving our hips, keeping the volume low. We made up our own moves. In truth we had very little idea of how people danced to pop. We knew we were not supposed to enjoy the archenemy's music, but we did not realize quite how grave our crime was until news spread around Hyesan that some local women had been sentenced to a prison camp for partying to South Korean pop. One in their group had denounced the others.

After that I listened to the tapes alone at home, lying on my bed.

My favourite was a song called 'Rocky Island' by the singer Kim Weon-joong. The rocky island of the title referred to a woman he loved, and the chorus went:

Even if you don't like me, I love you so much,
Even if I can't wake up, I love you so much . . .

I adored this mush. It was about teenage love, and touched my heart in a way that filled me with longing. It was changing me, making me feel I was growing up. I got nothing like this from North Korean music. Our country had pop music of its own, but with songs called 'Our Happiness in our General's Embrace' or 'Young People, Forward!' I cringed to listen to it.

I taught myself to play 'Rocky Island' on my accordion. I took care to play quietly, keeping the door and windows shut, but one morning while I was practising a hard knock sounded on the front door.

I froze.

One of our neighbours was on the doorstep. He was on his way to work. He told me he had heard me playing.

A pool of cold fear gathered in the pit of my stomach. Was he going to denounce me, or just warn me? But to my great surprise he smiled and told me that hearing that song made him emotional and gave him energy. Then he got back on his bicycle and rode off. It was such a weird thing to say. I wonder now if he knew full well it was a South Korean song and was reaching out to me, giving me a signal, like a secret handshake.

A few months later, by the time the illicit pop cassettes had gone up in flames with the house, I knew all the songs off by heart. The melody and lyrics of 'Rocky Island', especially, would be a great comfort to me in the times ahead.

The South Korean pop songs had given me a vague awareness of a universe beyond the borders of North Korea. If I'd had more awareness in general I might have spotted clues indicating that the world outside was undergoing dramatic changes – changes so great that the regime was being put under stresses it had never experienced before. I was oblivious to the fact that the Russians had allowed communism to collapse in the Soviet Union, 'without even a shot fired', as Kim Jong-il would put it. But this was affecting our country in ways that were starting to become impossible for the regime to conceal. My parents' jobs and business dealings meant that we had enough food. I had not yet noticed that the rations of basic food essentials provided by the Public Distribution System were dwindling or becoming irregular, nor had I paid attention when the government launched a widely publicized campaign in 1992 called 'Let us eat two meals a day', which it said was healthier than eating three. Anyone who hadn't yet figured out a moneymaking hustle of their own was still depending on the state for essentials, and they were beginning to suffer.

As it happened, our next move as a family took us to the very edge of that world outside, as close to it as anyone could go, as if fortune was contriving to make us look outward. Our new house faced directly onto the bank of the Yalu River itself. I could throw a stone from our front gate over the water into China.

Chapter 11

'The house is cursed'

Our new neighbourhood was a cluster of single-storey homes separated by narrow alleys. The house was larger than previous houses we'd lived in, painted white, with a tiled roof, and surrounded by a white concrete wall. It had three rooms, each the width of the building, so that we had to go through the kitchen area to the main room and through that to the back room, which is where the four of us slept.

My mother had paid a lot of money for it. Officially, there is no private property in North Korea, and no real-estate business, but in reality people who have been allocated desirable or conveniently located housing often do sell or swap them if the price is right.

The location of this house was perfect for my mother's illicit enterprises. She could arrange for goods to be smuggled from just a few yards away in China, straight over the river to our front door. For security against the rampant thievery she had the wall around the house built higher, to about six feet, and bought a fierce, trained dog from the military. The entrance was through a gate in the front wall, that we kept heavily locked. We had to pass through a total of three doors and five locks just to come and go. In front of the house was a path that ran along the riverside, five yards from our front gate, along which the guards patrolled in pairs. Uncle Opium and Aunt Pretty dropped by and congratulated my mother. The location couldn't be better, they said.

Min-ho was extremely excited about this new home. It was a warm, mild autumn and the day we moved in he saw boys his own age playing in the river, mixing with Chinese boys from the other side, while their mothers washed clothes along the banks. To most North Koreans, the borders are impassable barriers. Our country is sealed shut from neighbouring countries. And yet here were five-, six- and seven-year-old boys splashing and flitting between the two banks, North Korea's and China's, like the fish and the birds.

The next day my mother went to introduce herself to the neighbours. What they told her made her heart sink to her stomach. She returned to the house looking angry and pale.

'The house is cursed,' she said, slumping to the floor and covering her face with her hands. 'I've made a terrible mistake.'

A neighbour had told her that a child of the previous occupants had died in an accident. My mother thought she'd been lucky to find the place, but in fact the occupants were selling in a hurry to escape the association with tragedy and bad luck. I tried to comfort her, but she shook her head and looked tired. Her superstitions ran too deep to be reasoned with. I half-believed it myself. Many of my mother's beliefs were rubbing off on me. I could tell she was already thinking of another expensive session with a fortune-teller to see if she could get the curse lifted.

My mother quickly furnished the house, once again doing her makeover. People who could afford them had started buying refrigerators coming from China, but my mother was reluctant to attract attention. This meant daily shopping for food, almost all of which she obtained at the local semi-official markets, not from the Public Distribution System. Her director at the government bureau where she worked had recently been sent to a prison camp after inspectors had found food in his home that he had been given as a bribe, so my mother was especially careful. We never stocked up on rice – seldom keeping more than twenty or thirty kilos in the house.

The one luxury we did buy for the new house was a Toshiba colour television, which was a signal of social status. The television would expand my horizon, and Min-ho's, dramatically. Not for the 'news' it broadcast – we had one channel, Korea Central Television, which showed endlessly repeated footage of the Great Leader or the Dear Leader visiting factories, schools or farms and delivering their on-the-spot guidance on everything from nitrate fertilizers to women's shoes. Nor for the entertainment, which consisted of old North Korean movies,

Pioneers performing in musical ensembles, or vast army choruses praising the Revolution and the Party. Its attraction was that we could pick up Chinese TV stations that broadcast soap operas and glamorous commercials for luscious products. Though we could not understand Mandarin, just watching them provided a window onto an entirely different way of life. Watching foreign TV stations was highly illegal and a very serious offence. Our mother scolded us severely when she caught us. But I was naughty. I'd put blankets over the windows and watch when she was out, or sleeping.

We were now living in a sensitive area, politically. The government knew that people living along the river often succumbed to the poison of capitalism and traded smuggled goods, watched pernicious foreign television programmes, and even defected. Families living in this area were monitored much more closely than others by the *Bowibu* for any sign of disloyalty. A family that fell under suspicion might be watched and reported on daily by the local police. Often, subterfuge was used to catch offenders. One morning not long after we'd moved in, a pleasant and friendly man knocked on the door and told my mother that he had heard that the Yankees paid a lot of money for the returned remains of their soldiers killed during the Korean War. He had some bones himself, he said, disinterred from various sites in the province. He wondered if my mother could help him smuggle them across the border.

My mother treated requests for help with extreme caution. She knew how undercover *Bowibu* agents operated, dropping by with intriguing propositions. They had all kinds of tricks. We'd heard of one high-ranking family who had got into serious trouble when investigators turned up at their children's kindergarten and asked brightly: 'What's the best movie you've seen lately?' and a child had enthusiastically described a South Korean blockbuster, watched on illegal video. On this occasion, however, her superstitions were her best defence. She didn't want to be haunted by the disturbed spirits of American soldiers, and told the man she couldn't help.

In mid-November, a few weeks after we had moved to the new house, the first snow had been falling all day in fine grains that stung our faces. We were huddled on the floor for warmth, wearing our coats indoors, when my father arrived home. Each time he returned from China he brought with him small luxuries that were out of reach for most people. Sometimes he came with good-quality toilet paper, or bananas and oranges, which were almost never available at home. This time he was carrying such an enormous package that I failed to affect my usual boredom in his presence. I was too curious to know what it was. It contained gifts for Min-ho and me. Mine was a larger-than-life doll with silky white-blonde hair, blue eyes and a pale Western face. She had the most beautiful dress, of patterned gingham trimmed with lace. She was so large I could barely carry her. I had to prop her up in a corner next to my bed. My mother said she could hear me chattering to her. Min-ho's gift was a hand-held Game Boy video game. His little face was overawed. This was something so new. We knew of no one else who had anything like it.

I can only think of that doll now with immense sadness. I was a little too old for a doll, but it was such a beautiful, generous gift. I realize now that my father felt he had lost me and was trying to reconnect with me, somehow. He knew something had gone badly wrong between us, and he had probably figured out what it was. I certainly did not deserve the gift.

It was the last thing he ever gave me.

Chapter 12

Tragedy at the bridge

I was about to turn fourteen, by the Korean way of measuring age. It was January 1994, the beginning of an eventful and tragic year that made me grow up quickly.

I was now almost as tall as my mother. I was fit and active, playing a lot of sport, which I enjoyed very much – ice skating, becoming good enough to represent the school in a tournament, and taekwondo indoors when the weather was cold. I was a good runner, and had run the Hyesan half-marathon.

My birthday, however, got the year off to a terrible start.

I had long been pushing my luck with my appearance. The teachers had never taken much notice when I didn't wear the school uniform – they knew they could depend on my mother when the school needed cash donations, or fuel for heating. But I was not a child any more, and my nonconformity was becoming conspicuous.

The inevitable happened.

A new teacher had joined the school a few months previously. Her name was Mrs Kang, and she taught physics. She was a young woman, with small, sharp eyes and a shrill voice. On the day of my birthday she wished us good morning, and noticed me immediately. Every girl was in school uniform and all had short hair, no longer than shoulder length. I stood out a mile in my pink Chinese coat and my perm, and a new pair of tall, fashionable boots.

Her eyes froze on the boots, and I knew I'd gone too far.

'Why are you wearing those?' She was addressing me in front of the whole class. 'And for that matter, why aren't you ever in uniform, like everyone else?'

Before I could stop myself the words were out. 'Why do you have a problem? My mother doesn't.'

The room tensed.

'How dare you talk back to me!' She was shrieking, and marching up to my desk. 'You want to look like some rotten capitalist? Fine!' She swung her arm out and slapped me hard across the face.

I put my hand to my cheek. The blood was singing in my ears. I was shaking, and outraged. My mother had never slapped me. I stormed out of the class, and ran home in tears.

That day, for the first time in a long time, I yearned for the comfort and security my father always provided, but he was away again, on a business trip to China. Each time he came home he seemed more and more tired and subdued. My mother said he wasn't sleeping. Something was wrong. He'd told her he thought he was being watched.

I realize now that having the nerve to wear those boots and perm my hair was just a symptom of a deeper and general disillusion I was feeling. I was falling out of love with the 'organizational life' and the collective activities that no one in the country was exempt from. Now that I was fourteen I was no longer a Pioneer, and had to join the Socialist Youth League. This was another important milestone. We were told to start thinking of our futures, and of how we would serve our country. My childhood was over.

Members of the Socialist Youth League had to undergo military training. I had to put on army fatigues and learn how to shoot with live ammunition at a firing range in Hyesan. I hated this so much, and my mother was so nervous about me being surrounded by children with guns, where accidents could easily happen, and sometimes did, that she got me excused by bribing the school authorities with cash.

Ideological indoctrination intensified. As model communist youths we were now expected to deepen our emotional bond with the Great Leader, and start learning about the Party's ideology of *juche* (loosely translated as 'self-reliance'), which promoted our country's isolation and rejection of all foreign influences.

I was now part of a Socialist Youth League 'cell' within my secondary school. Fortunately, I managed to avoid joining the Maintenance of Social Order Brigade – the vigilantes who monitored the streets for citizens whose ideological purity had lapsed. By 1994 there were several additions to the list of banned items. Now the youths were cracking down on anyone caught wearing clothing with Western lettering, which was in vogue in China.

By the time spring came there was no avoiding the revolutionary duty we all had to undertake: the pilgrimage to the sacred sites surrounding Mount Paektu. The mountains of Ryanggang Province were where Kim Il-sung fought as a guerrilla against the Japanese in the 1930s and 1940s. To mark this significance, three of the province's eleven counties were renamed after the great man's wife, father and uncle. Young Pioneers and Socialist Youth from all over North Korea visited this 'outdoor revolutionary museum', with its statues and monuments to the Great Leader's victories, and a nearby village called Pochonbo, where in 1937 he had led a band of 150 guerrillas in an attack on the local Japanese police station. The battle is famous in North Korean history as the great turning point in the struggle for Korean independence, and stunning proof of Kim Il-sung's tactical genius, winning victory in the face of overwhelming odds.

Our guide showed us bullet holes on the old police station, circled in white, and a cell where the Japanese had tortured communist partisans. None of this impressed me. I just wanted to get out of there. With a tremendous effort I had to control my face to hide my boredom.

Only when I finally saw, with my own eyes, the preserved log cabin beneath the pines on the slopes of Mount Paektu, the site of the secret guerrilla base where Kim Jong-il was born, did I feel like a child again, just for a moment. I remembered painting the cabin, and the star in the sky, and the rainbow over Mount Paektu. This magical story still had the power to move me.

The disaffection I was feeling meant that my relationship with Min-ho wasn't getting any better. He was at elementary school in Hyesan. He'd hear from the boys in his year what a cute girl their older brothers thought I was. He must have thought they were talking about someone else. I still wasn't friends with him in the way I should have been. Deep down I wanted an older brother to protect me, not a kid I had to watch out for. He was now seven years old and developing quite an adventurous streak – I strongly suspected him of making secret forays of his own to the opposite bank of the river. He could be dogged, too. Given a chore, he'd get on with it. His school once gave the students an absurd quota of ten kilos each of berries to pick. He was the only one to hit the target. In that sense he was quite unlike me, who would find excuses to avoid physical work and not get my nice clothes dirty. The one thing we both had in common was the Hyesan stubbornness, like our mother's.

A few days after the visit to Mount Paektu I came home from school to find my mother pacing around the house in a state of high anxiety.

'Your father's still not back,' she said, folding and unfolding her arms.

My father was supposed to have returned from his business trip to China the previous day. She said he had seemed particularly anxious before leaving.

Two days went by and still he did not return.

By the third day my mother was a wreck. She could not relax, sleep, eat, or sit still. She tried several times to contact the bureau of the trading company where he worked, but each time was stonewalled and told to wait for information.

Another day passed in a dismal limbo. Min-ho was constantly asking if someone could check where our father was.

Finally, a work colleague from the trading company called at the house.

The news was not good.

My father had been arrested four days ago at the Friendship Bridge as he crossed the border back into North Korea.

Chapter 13

Sunlight on dark water

A group of men from Pyongyang were waiting for my father at the bridge. They were officers of the Military Security Command. This organization is separate from the Ministry of State Security, the *Bowibu*. It is a secret police that watches the military.

Another ten days went by with no news. We knew only that he had been detained while investigations were made into his business conduct. To the outside world my mother presented the hardened, no-nonsense mask she always wore. At home, she became brittle and tearful. She began to steel herself for the worst. She knew that few people ever emerged from such detentions unharmed, or even emerged at all. I had never seen her like this.

It was while she was in this restless state that she told me a family story I had never heard before. It concerned the marriage of Aunt Old, my mother's eldest sister. She had been married before I was born and had three children I did not know about. Her husband had been a Korean-Chinese man who had escaped the Cultural Revolution in China in the late 1960s to what he thought was a communist utopia in North Korea. My mother said he was a kind man with a very forthright and honest nature. My grandmother opposed the marriage because he was a foreigner, but Aunt Old said she would rather die if she couldn't be with him. And so they were married.

After a few years he got sick of the propaganda and said he wanted to return to China. Aunt Old refused to leave home, so he went alone, and was stopped at the border. Had he told the border police he simply wanted to visit family in China and return to North Korea, he might have got off lightly. But his honesty was his undoing. He told his interrogators that he had become disenchanted. They sent him straight to a political prison camp without trial. My grandmother then stepped in to protect the family and fixed it so that Aunt Old could divorce her husband and put the three children up for adoption. This way, the family could avoid the guilt by association with a 'criminal element' that would degrade their *songbun* and blight the family for generations. This is a common arrangement when a spouse is imprisoned.

The three children were each adopted by good families. One of them became an army officer. Aunt Old met him when he had grown up, and told him the story. He broke down and hugged her, swearing that he didn't care about his family background and from then on wanted his real mother and siblings to be his family.

This son travelled to the prison camp to try and meet his father, but was turned away at the gates. There are two kinds of prison in the gulag. One is for prisoners sentenced to 'revolutionary re-education through labour'. If they survive their punishment they will be released back into society, and monitored closely for the rest of their lives. The other is a zone of no return – prisoners there are worked to death. The son feared that his father was in the second type, and was still there.

This story distressed me a lot. On the rare occasions we mentioned anyone we knew who had fallen foul of the authorities we did so without analysis or judgement, or any comment on the fairness of the punishment. We just described the bare facts. That's how North Koreans talk. But now my mother was speaking emotionally of how the gulag had affected our own family.

No one spoke openly of the gulag. We knew of it only through terrifying rumours and whispers. We did not know where the camps were located or what conditions there were like. All I knew about was Baekam County, a less extreme place of punishment not far from Hyesan. We knew a family who'd been deported there from Pyongyang because the father had rolled a cigarette using a square of cut newspaper without noticing that the Great Leader's face was printed on the other side. His whole family was sent to the mountains for a backbreaking life of potato digging on the 10.18 Collective Farm.

Now I was picturing my father being sent to a prison camp. A great fog swirled in my head. The resentment I'd felt towards him was becoming a mess of confused feelings.

While we were waiting for news, five uniformed military officials hammered on our door one evening, entered without removing their boots, and ransacked our home in search of cash and valuables my father had allegedly hidden. They ripped open the walls, tore up the floor and pulled down the ceiling. They left, empty-handed, after an hour of destruction. My mother and I were in shock as we stared about at the damage. Our house was completely wrecked.

About two weeks after my father had disappeared, my mother was told that he had suddenly been released to the hospital in Hyesan. When she saw him she was overwhelmed, and began sobbing freely. His appearance shocked her. He was haggard, with sunken eyes, but he tried to give her a grin. He seemed much older.

The investigation into him was still ongoing, he said. He'd been accused of bribery and abuse of position. A more likely reason was that he had fallen out of political favour, or had put some senior cadre's nose out of joint. He had been interrogated many times, and ordered to write his confession over and over again. Each time, the interrogator ripped it up in his face and told him to start again.

My mother did not ask what else they had done to him. She did not want him to relive the trauma, but she could see that he had been badly beaten, and had not been allowed to sleep. At the hospital he slept for days with the covers pulled over his head.

My father kept everything bottled up, as many North Korean men did. They could not talk about their feelings, or mention the fear and stress they were under. It was the reason I would see terrible drunken fights breaking out among men in Hyesan during the public holidays. My father never drank alcohol, but he turned his feelings inward. He had lost a lot of weight, and had become very listless. We realize now that he had fallen into a severe depression, an illness that is not acknowledged in North Korea. He spent about six weeks in the hospital in Hyesan.

My mother needed Min-ho and me out of the way while she tended to my father, visiting him daily for hours at the hospital. We were sent to the east coast to stay with Uncle Cinema, his wife, and their children, my cousins.

One afternoon, Uncle Cinema came home early. Min-ho and I were in the living room with our aunt and our cousins. He took his shoes off and stepped into the house, closing the door carefully behind him.

'Min-young, Min-ho, I am afraid I have bad news,' he said.

He looked grave and we knew something terrible had happened. He told us that our mother had telephoned him at his office. She said that our father had fallen very ill in hospital, and had died.

Min-ho was devastated. He ran into the bedroom and shut the door.

I walked numbly down to the beach and gazed out into the East Sea. From behind the clouds sharp rays made fields of light on the dark water. A few distant, rusted shipping boats were on the horizon. The sea was calm.

The resentment I had nurtured towards my father had put such a wall between us. Why had I done that? I grew up understanding the importance of family and blood ties. Discovering that my blood did not come from him had shocked me and confused me. I had frozen him out. I was hurt by a secret that had been kept from me.

I thought of how he'd met my mother, all those years ago on the train to Pyongyang. He had loved her so much that he had married her even though she was divorced and had a child by another man. Memories came back to me, dozens of them, of our happy times chasing dragonflies in fields near Anju, and of our family life in Hamhung, of the fun we'd all had together watching my mother eat *naengmyeon*, of how proud I'd been of him when he came to my Pioneer ceremony, how safe I'd always felt with him.

I stared at the sea and the scale of my folly came home to me.

He'd raised me lovingly, as his own child. My selfish feelings had stopped me seeing how much I loved him.

I fell to my knees on the beach and cried bitter tears, clawing with my hands at the sand.

After what seemed like hours, as the sun was setting, I walked back to the house. I knew that I would regret for the rest of my life the way I'd behaved towards my father. Knowing that he'd died thinking that I resented him would only make my bereavement more painful over the years ahead.

***

My father's death was a shock to everyone who knew him. He was still a young man, barely into his forties. No one was with him when he died.

But before my mother had time to react to the blow of his death, she received another devastating piece of news. The hospital death certificate stated that he had committed suicide by overdosing on Diazepam (Valium). This drug was readily available in the markets. He must have gone out and bought it himself.

In North Korea, suicide is taboo. Not only is it considered gravely humiliating to the surviving family members, it also guarantees that any children left behind will be reclassified as 'hostile' in the *songbun* system and denied university entrance and the chance of a good job. Suicide in Korean culture is a highly emotive means of protest. The regime regards it as a form of defection. By punishing the surviving family, the regime attempts to disable this ultimate form of protest.

My mother was jolted out of her grief. She acted at once to protect us all.

She had to get the hospital documentation changed very quickly, and this was a delicate and difficult task, but our futures depended on it. My mother's tact and diplomacy succeeded. It cost her nearly all her hard-currency savings, but she did it. She bribed the hospital authorities. They agreed to change the cause of my father's death to 'heart attack'. The funeral was conducted in haste, before any questions were asked, and before Min-ho and I had arrived back from the coast. We did not even get a chance to say goodbye to him. Even worse, my father's parents had cursed my mother angrily at the funeral, telling her that she had brought ill fortune upon their family.

As a final, gratuitous humiliation, the investigating military authority wrote to inform my mother that my father had been formally dismissed from his post.

After my father's death I felt much closer to Min-ho. It was as if I was seeing him with clear vision for the first time in years. The stupid delusion that had made me withdraw from my father was the same one that had stopped me feeling close to my own sibling. I started to see him for who he was – my brother, as bereaved and as heartbroken as I was.

I no longer felt the same about our house on the river. Within a short time of moving there we'd had a tragedy in the family. It made me think the curse on the place was real, and potent.

We were still trying to come to terms with what had happened, when an event occurred that united the entire country in grief – in such wailing, brow-beating scenes of mass hysteria as the world's media had never before seen. It was an event that reverberates in North Korea to this day.

Chapter 14

'The great heart has stopped beating'

I went to school as usual on the morning of 8 July 1994. Just before lunchtime, our lesson was interrupted when a teacher entered and told us that the school was closing for the day. We were all instructed to return home and turn on the television. This was odd, since there was no daytime television during weekdays.

Instead of going home, I went with a girl friend to her apartment near the school. We turned on the television. Shortly after, the famous news anchor Ri Chun-hui came on, dressed in black. Her eyes were red from crying. She then announced the impossible. Kim Il-sung, the Great Leader, the father of our nation, was dead. The announcement made on the radio was equally dramatic: 'The great heart has stopped beating.'

My friend broke into a wail and couldn't stop. Her crying affected me a little, but it was my mind that was moved, not my heart. How could he die? Incredible as it may sound now, it had never occurred to me, or to many North Koreans, that this god-king, so powerful that he could control the weather, might die. He was flawless and almighty. He existed so far above humankind that a part of me didn't think he was real. We did not even think he needed to sleep or urinate. But he'd died.

A door opened in my mind.

He's an eighty-two-year-old man, I thought. He grew old and weak. He was human after all. I sat there listening to my friend's sobs, but my eyes were dry. I was too raw with grief for my father to spend my tears on the Great Leader.

The next morning the entire school gathered in front of the school building. We stood in long, regimented lines. The sky was a milky blue and the day was warming up uncomfortably. Emotional speeches were made by the headmaster and the teachers, all of whom were choking with tears, to a background accompaniment of piped funeral music. Hour after hour it went on. I had felt sad at first, but after three hours of standing under the hot sun, I was becoming thirsty and tired.

Nobody had ordered us to cry. No one had hinted that if we didn't cry we would fall under suspicion. But we knew our tears were being demanded. From all around me came the sounds of sniffing, sobbing and wailing. It looked as if everyone was beside themselves with grief. My survival instinct kicked in. If I didn't cry like everyone else I'd be in trouble. So I rubbed my face in false distress, surreptitiously spat on my fingertips, and dabbed my eyes. I made a gasping noise that I hoped sounded like I was heaving with despair.

After a long time doing this, I felt I could not stand there for much longer. The sun now was overhead. It was very warm. So I stumbled a little. The teachers thought I was about to faint, so they put me in the ambulance that was there on standby. That was a relief.

The next day there was a similar event joined by all the city's schools at the Victorious Battle of Pochonbo Memorial in Hyesan Park. This time several thousand students and teachers joined in the sobbing and the wailing. The grief seemed to be getting more extreme by the hour. A kind of hysteria was spreading across the city. Our schooling stopped. The steel and lumber mills, the factories, shops and markets closed. Every citizen had to participate in daily mass events to demonstrate their inconsolable sorrow. Day after day a teacher took us into the hills to pick wild flowers to place before the bronze statue of Kim Il-sung in Hyesan Park. After a few days, every flower had been picked, but we had to find them from somewhere. To turn up with one flower was an insult to the Great Leader.

On one of these searches for flowers a swarm of dragonflies flew alongside us in the field.

'Look.' In a voice full of wonder the teacher said: 'Even the dragonflies are sad at the Great Leader's death.'

She was being serious, and we took the comment uncritically.

After the mourning period, as I'd feared might happen, punishment awaited those who had shed too few tears. On the day classes resumed the entire student body gathered in front of the school to hurl criticism and abuse at a girl accused of faking her tears. The girl was terrified, and this time really crying. I felt sorry for her, but my main emotion was relief. As a fake crier myself, I was just glad no one had seen through my performance.

Many adults across the city were similarly accused and the *Bowibu* made a spate of arrests. It wasn't long before notices began appearing, giving the time and place for clusters of public executions.

It is mandatory from elementary school to attend public executions. Often classes would be cancelled so students could go. Factories would send their workers, to ensure a large crowd. I always tried to avoid attending, but on one occasion that summer I made an exception, because I knew one of the men being killed. Many people in Hyesan knew him. You might think the execution of an acquaintance is the last thing you'd want to see. In fact, people made excuses not to go if they didn't know the victim. But if they knew the victim, they felt obliged to go, as they would to a funeral.

He was in his twenties and always seemed to have money. He was popular with the girls, and had followers among the city's hoodlums. His crime was helping people to escape to China and selling banned goods. But his real offence was to continue his illegal activity during the mourning period following Kim Il-sung's death.

He was to be shot along with three others at Hyesan Airport, a common site for executions. The three men were brought out of a van before a large crowd waiting in the glaring heat. Immediately, people around me began to whisper. The popular guy had to be lifted up and dragged to the post by a group of police, with the tips of his feet scraping along in the dust. He seemed half dead already.

Each of the three had his head, chest and waist tied to a stake. His hands and feet were tied together behind the stake. A perfunctory people's trial opened, in which the judge announced that the criminals had confessed their crimes. He asked if they had any last words. He wasn't expecting a response, since all three had been gagged and had stones pushed into their mouths to stop them cursing the regime with their final breath.

Three uniformed marksmen then lined up opposite each of them, and took aim. The marksmen's faces were flushed, I noticed. Executioners were known to drink alcohol beforehand. The noise of the reports ricocheted in the dry air – three shots, the first in the head; the second in the chest; the third in the stomach. When the shot hit the popular guy's head, it exploded, leaving a fine pink mist. His family had been forced to watch from the front row.

Chapter 15

Girlfriend of a hoodlum

When I turned fifteen I began attending a special class for girls only, where we learned to knit and keep house. We should have been learning about sex.

All of us were astonishingly ignorant about men, and about the most basic facts of reproduction. For all its interference in our lives, the Party was extraordinarily bashful when it came to telling us how life itself was made. This was despite the fact that a teenage pregnancy could land a girl in a terrible situation – she'd have to marry immediately to avoid trouble. An abortion would have been difficult to arrange and probably would not even have been suggested. Instead she'd have been forced to give the baby up for adoption, or to a state orphanage.

I believed that I could get pregnant if I kissed a man, or held hands with him. My girl friends thought the same. The boys' ignorance of sex was just as bad. I once saw a group of youths in their early teens near the pharmacy opposite Hyesan Station blowing up condoms as if they were balloons, and kicking them about in the street. If someone had told them what those items were for, they would have run away red-faced.

With such an utter lack of sexual awareness, none of us blossoming girls showed off our maturing bodies, or flirted, or teased boys at school. The North Korean brassiere is shaped like a blouse designed to flatten rather than enhance our breasts. One of the girls in my class had large breasts. Instead of being envied by the girls, she was teased.

I finally learned about the sexual act from an unexpected source. A girl friend from school invited me home one afternoon to watch an illegal South Korean drama on video. When we turned on the recorder, however, we found that one of the adults of the house had left another type of video inside. It took me a minute to figure out what I was seeing. The screen filled with a jumble of limbs and intimate body parts, accompanied by rhythmic grunting and moaning. My friend started chuckling at my shocked face. I had never even seen anyone kiss in a North Korean movie. Pornography, in Party propaganda, was a pernicious foreign corruption. But this 'love-making' video, as she called it, had been made in Pyongyang, for sale abroad and for circulation among elite Party cadres. I would not have believed it if the 'actors' hadn't spoken in such familiar accents. I lost my innocence that day. To my mind, my country did, too.

Like my other friends, when I menstruated the first time I went through three emotions in sharp succession: shock, embarrassment and absolute panic. I had to use my wits to figure out what to do. Incredibly, most of us handled it, without telling anyone or asking our mothers for advice. My mother, the most sensible woman I knew, offered me none, just as my grandmother, I'm sure, had given her none.

It was at the height of my panic during my first menstrual cycle that one of the girls in class told me she'd seen something that had scared her at a public toilet near our school. She wanted to show me. We crept in there to take a look together. The place was dripping, dim, and stinking. Next to the hole of the squat toilet was a bloodied white plastic bag. Inside was a dead baby with a tiny blue-pink face. The mother must have given birth there and fled. The umbilical cord and the placenta lay next to it. I was shocked to the core and didn't sleep that night.

That year, 1995, I dated my first boyfriend. He was four years older than me, and a hoodlum. His name was Tae-chul. He was tall, thin, and wore a Japanese casual jacket, the height of sophistication in Hyesan. He had a conceited little half-smile I found attractive. Every North Korean city has hoodlums. These are not violent criminals, but young people with the kind of personality that attracts followers and who often deal in banned goods. There is quite a lot of low-level crime they can get away with, as long as they do nothing that verges on the political and attracts the eyes of the *Bowibu*.

He had money. He was also in the police academy and was training to be a policeman. Just walking with him thrilled me because of the attention I was getting. In fact, after he waited for me a few times outside the school gate, the rumours started flying about us. This was quite a serious matter, because when the word gets out that a girl has been dating, it's not easy for her to find another match.

I worried about this, but I liked him. I was proud that he wanted to go out with me when so many other girls wanted him. We would go to his house to listen to South Korean pop cassettes and play the guitar and accordion together. Like any other boyfriend and girlfriend in North Korea of this age, we did not even kiss. Holding hands was as far as it went. Even then we were discreet. Our families were not aware of our romance and did not consider it improper for me to be at his house. My mother would have had a stroke if she'd known he was my boyfriend.

That year I found my duties with the Socialist Youth League more oppressive than ever. In spring we had to help plant rice saplings, in the summer we weeded and spread fertilizer, and in autumn came the harvest, which students and workers from all over the country helped with. This mass enterprise, in fields of flying red banners, was the epitome of communist idealism.

In the summer we were also ordered to dig tunnels around our school. The entire country was being mobilized, and everyone was on a war footing. Sirens wailed almost daily, and everybody dropped what they were doing and dashed to and fro in frenzy, practising air-raid drills in case of an attack. America and South Korea were about to launch a nuclear strike, we were told. War could break out at any minute. The thought of nuclear war terrified me. My mother panicked and gave a lot of stuff away. She gave all our spare blankets and pillows to Uncle Poor and his family on the collective farm.

The boys dug frantically with shovels and the girls shifted the earth. I hated every minute of this. If war started while we were at school, several hundred students were supposed to hide in the warren of tunnels. I was worried that our amateur engineering might prove disastrous, and bury us alive. I was sceptical, too, of whether these tunnels were deep enough to protect us from a nuclear strike. Years later I discovered that the propaganda had an element of truth. The United States had actually been considering air strikes against our country's nuclear plants.

After one of these tedious and exhausting days of digging and air-raid drills, I went to my friend Sun-i's house after school. She was in the tight bunch of friends I hung out with, but this was the first time I'd been to her home. Usually she came to mine.

'Shall we eat something?' I said. 'I'm hungry.'

'I'm not sure what we've got.' She sounded vague.

'Anything.'

'We don't have much.'

This annoyed me. *You're always getting snacks at my house.* 'I don't need a meal,' I said.

Sun-i hesitated. She was embarrassed.

'Come here,' she said, leading me into the kitchen. Four pots sat on the stove. She slid the lid off one. 'Look. I can't give you this.'

Inside the pot were thick dark-green objects. She put the lid back on before I could ask what they were, but I could tell it wasn't normal food. On the way home, I realized they might have been corn stalks.

Why would her mother be cooking such a thing instead of rice?

Chapter 16

'By the time you read this, the five of us will no longer exist in this world'

My mother came home from work looking tired and distracted. She hadn't been sleeping much since my father had died and had more lines beneath her eyes and around her mouth. It had been months since I'd seen her smile. But at least she was able to provide for us through her small business deals. We had food and money. Her job at the local government bureau also meant that she had access to farm produce managed by her office. This gave her an opportunity for graft that she was expected to exercise. Soon after Kim Il-sung's death the government had stopped paying salaries. It continued to give out ration coupons through the workplace, but these were becoming increasingly worthless. For some reason there were fewer and fewer goods to exchange for them.

She'd brought home a letter received by one of her colleagues. It was from the woman's sister who lived in North Hamgyong Province, a neighbouring province to the east of ours. My mother wanted to show it to us.

'I need you and Min-ho to know something. People are having a hard time. You ask me for this and complain we don't have that. Not everyone has what we have.'

She handed me the letter.

Dear Sister,

By the time you read this, the five of us will no longer exist in this world. We have not eaten for a few weeks. We are emaciated, though recently our bodies have become bloated. We are waiting to die. My one hope before I go is to eat some corn cake.

My first response was puzzlement.

Why hadn't they eaten for weeks? This was one of the most prosperous countries in the world. Every evening the news showed factories and farms producing in abundance, well-fed people enjoying leisure time, and the department stores in Pyongyang filled with goods. And why was this woman's last wish to eat corn cake – 'poor man's cake'? Shouldn't she want to see her sister one last time?

The realization was slow in coming.

I thought of how offhand I'd been with my friend Sun-i because she hadn't offered me a snack at her house. I was mortified.

Her family was struggling to find food.

A few days later, I witnessed famine for the first time.

I was at the market outside Wiyeon Station in Hyesan and saw a woman lying on her side on the ground with a baby in her arms. She was young, in her twenties. The baby, a boy, was about two years old, and staring at his mother. They were pale and skeletal, and dressed in rags. The woman's face was caked with filth and her hair badly matted. She looked sick. To my astonishment people were walking past her and the baby as if they were invisible.

I could not ignore her. I put a 100-won note on the baby's lap. I thought it was hopeless to give it to the mother. Her eyes were clouded and not focusing. She wasn't seeing me. I guessed she was close to death. The money would have bought food for a couple of days.

'I rescued a baby today,' I told my mother when I got home. I thought she would be proud to know that I had cared while others had walked by.

'What do you mean?'

I told her what I had done.

She dropped what she was doing and turned to me, highly annoyed. 'Are you completely stupid? How can a baby buy anything? Some thief will have snatched that note straight off him. You should have just bought food for them.'

She was right, and I felt responsible.

After that I started thinking a lot about charity. Sharing what we had made us good communists, but at the same time it seemed futile. People had so little, and had to take care of their own families first. I could spare the 100-won note I'd given to the baby and his mother, but I realized it would have solved their problem only for a couple of days. This thought depressed me utterly.

A shadow began to fall across Hyesan. Beggars were appearing everywhere, especially around the markets. This was a sight I'd never seen in our country before. There were vagrant children, too. At first, only in twos and threes, but soon many of them, migrating to Hyesan from the countryside. Their parents had perished of hunger, leaving them to fend for themselves, without relatives. They were nicknamed *kotchebi* ('flowering swallows') and, like birds, they seemed to gather in flocks. One of their survival tricks was to distract a market vendor while accomplices snatched the food and ran off. In a horrible twist of irony they were regularly seen scavenging in the dirt for grains, peel or gristle – exactly how we'd been told the children in South Korea lived. At school, children whose parents were struggling to feed them came less regularly, and then stopped coming altogether. My class shrank in size by a third. Some of the teachers stopped coming, too. They were making a living as market traders instead.

Food was not the only thing in short supply. There was no fertilizer for crops. In the villages children had to bring a quota of their own excrement to school for use as fertilizer. Families locked their outhouses in case thieves stole what little they had. There was no fuel. The steel and lumber mills fell idle. Factory chimneys stopped puffing smoke, and the city streets fell silent and empty during the day. The larches and pines that made the foothills of the mountains so beautiful began to disappear. The landscape was being denuded of trees. People were foraging for fuel as a freezing wind swept down from Manchuria with the onset of winter. Power cuts became more frequent, to the point where the electricity hardly came on at all. To light our home in the evening my mother made a lamp from a pot of diesel with a strip of cotton as a wick. This gave off such a dirty smoke that Min-ho and I would have a circle of soot around our mouths.

One cold morning early in winter, a few weeks before the river froze,

I took a walk in the sunshine along the riverside path and saw what looked like a rag gliding in the slow current. Then I saw that the rag had an upturned human face. The eyes were open. I watched in horror as it passed, heading downriver past my house. Just before dawn, before people on the Chinese bank would notice, the border guards had been retrieving corpses from the water and covering them with straw. They were people who had tried to cross somewhere upriver and were too weak to make it. The current could be fast after it had rained in the mountains.

In early 1996, not long after my sixteenth birthday, I saw a crowd gathered around a middle-aged man at a market outside the city. He was giving a speech, speaking with a Korean-Chinese accent. He had a pot belly and a good-quality padded coat. He looked well off. I guessed he had come from China for the day to visit relatives.

'Why has this suffering fallen upon our people?' he said. Tears were rolling down his plump cheeks. 'People are starving and dying. How could this happen to our country?'

He reached into his breast pocket and took out a wad of blue Chinese ten-yuan notes. An instant tension ran through the crowd. He began handing the notes out to everyone and anyone. As if summoned by a whistle, beggars in rags materialized from everywhere, holding out their hands. The man was surrounded in every direction by outstretched arms. He gave away all his notes.

His question stuck in my mind.

What exactly was happening? There had been no war. In fact everyone had forgotten all about the nuclear strike for which we'd spent so much time digging and practising air-raid drills. Famine had appeared out of nowhere like a plague.

The official explanation for the 'arduous march', as the propaganda obliquely called the famine, was the Yankee-backed UN economic sanctions, coupled with crop failures and freak flooding that had made the situation worse. When I heard this I believed that Kim Jong-il was doing his very best for us in terrible circumstances. What would the people do without him? The true reason, which I did not learn until years later, and which was known to very few people in North Korea, had more to do with the collapse of the Soviet Union, and the refusal of the new Russian government to continue subsidizing us with fuel and food.

Kim Jong-il was now in charge of the country. We listened to a television news anchor quavering with emotion as she described how our Dear Leader was eating only simple meals of rice balls and potatoes in sympathy with the people's suffering. But on the screen he looked as portly and well fed as ever. As a distraction from the economy, which seemed not to be functioning at all, news reports showed him endlessly inspecting the nation's defences and army bases. A war for unification with the South would solve everything, people were saying.

I could tell from their accents that a lot of the beggars in the city were not from Hyesan – they had come from North Hamgyong and South Hamgyong provinces. We'd heard that the situation there was very bad. I did not realize how bad until I made a visit to Aunt Pretty in Hamhung that spring of 1996.

It was a journey through the landscape of hell.

Spring is the leanest season in North Korea, when food stocks from the previous harvest are exhausted and the year's crops have not yet grown. The land was bare and brown. It looked blighted, cursed. On every hill, trees had been felled, and for miles around individual people dotted the open countryside, roaming listlessly like living dead, foraging for food, aimless; or they sat on their haunches along the side of the track, doing nothing, waiting for nothing.

Before the famine, no one could make a journey without a travel permit stamped in their ID passbook, which was scanned by inspectors at the train station. Now there were no controls. Order was breaking down everywhere. Soldiers turned thieves. Police became muggers. The trains ran to no timetable. At each stop there were hundreds more passengers than seats, and the journey became terrifying. At one stop I narrowly avoided being hit by shards of smashed glass as people broke a carriage window to climb straight in and avoid the bottleneck at the doors. The carriage was dangerously packed. Workless, hungry people were travelling in the hope of selling something for food. The crowds became so thick and tight that when we finally reached Hamhung I had to climb over people to get to the door.

On the platform, I looked back and saw there were hundreds of people on the roof of the carriage. People smuggling goods to sell chose to sit on the roof. No official would risk his life going up there to inspect.

At around this time, my mother, on a journey of her own to Wonsan to visit Uncle Cinema, saw a policeman order an old woman down. Her clothing was bulging with some contraband she was hoping to sell. The police were always alert for smuggled goods that they could confiscate for themselves and sell.

'Please don't search me.' She was begging him from the top of the train. 'It's all I have.'

'Get down right now, you old bitch,' the policeman yelled.

The woman asked to be helped down.

The policeman reached up to her. As she took his hand, her free arm shot up and her fist closed over the electrified wire above the train. Both were killed instantly. She must have thought, *If I'm going, I'm taking this bastard with me.*

As I entered the city I thought my memory was playing tricks. The Hamhung where I'd lived as a girl was a buzzing industrial hub, with so many factory chimneys gushing smoke that the air sometimes choked us, but now it was fresh and clear. That great polluting monster, the Hungnam ammonium fertilizer plant, was no longer turning the sky yellow with chemicals. There were almost no trolley buses or cars, no bustle on the sidewalks, just people wandering lethargically, or talking to themselves, hallucinating from hunger.

Aunt Pretty had been making money importing Chinese clothes from Hyesan to Hamhung, and sending back seafood from the coast, but now she was casting about for a new venture as the transport situation became dire. She thought the authorities had taken the decision to cut off the Public Distribution System altogether in North Hamgyong Province, in order to save the rest of the country. I asked why that province.

'Because it has so many people of the lowest *songbun*,' she said.

People were falling dead in the streets. Starvation and necessity, however, were forcing a radical change of mindset. I saw it for myself in Hamhung. People were unlearning lifetimes of ideology, and reverting to what humans have practised for thousands of years – trade.

Black markets, where food was on sale at high, free-market prices, were springing up everywhere – at roadsides, in train stations, in mothballed industrial plants – and the new rising class of entrepreneurs was over-whelmingly female, and of low *songbun*. Very soon a person's *songbun* became far less important than their ability to make money and obtain food. Many women laid their wares on mats along the sidewalk, keeping alert for thieves and *kotchebi*, but some markets had already developed into more permanent-looking sites, with stalls, and awnings fashioned from blue burlap rice sacks of the UN World Food Program. Incredible as it seemed for a city in the grip of a deathly famine, there were opportunities for social advancement and business success for those who had an eye for a chance. During this visit I heard someone say: 'There are those who starve, those who beg, and those who trade.' Coming from Hyesan, I knew many commercially minded people, but in Hamhung, North Korea's second-biggest city, such attitudes seemed new.

The journey back to Hyesan was as nightmarish as the journey out. Many people were riding in the undercarriage, or clinging to the outside of the train, or sitting on the roof beneath the electrified wires. When I arrived at Hyesan Station a man was lying on the platform with the top of his head so badly smashed that part of his brain was exposed. He was still alive, asking in a quavering voice whether he was going to be all right. He died a few moments later. He had been riding in the undercarriage and had been hit by the edge of the platform as the train came into the station. During the famine, such accidents became common.

That year, 1996, the culture of our country changed noticeably. In the past, when visiting someone's home, I'd be welcomed by the greeting: 'Have you had rice?' This was a gesture of hospitality, meaning: 'Have you eaten? Join us.' But with the food shortages, how could anyone give the old greeting with sincerity? It wasn't long before it was replaced by: 'You've eaten, haven't you?' Many were too embarrassed or proud to admit they were starving and wouldn't take food even when it was offered. When Min-ho's young accordion teacher started coming to the house, my mother would ask if he'd like lunch. She could afford to maintain the old etiquette.

'I've eaten, thank you,' he would say, politely bowing his head, 'but a bowl of water with some *doenjang* would be nice.'

My mother obliged, but thought this odd. Nobody drank water with the soybean paste used to flavour soup. Each time, the teacher gulped it down in seconds. After a month of lessons, he stopped coming. My mother heard he had starved to death. She was stunned. Why hadn't he accepted her offers of food? He'd valued his dignity more than his own life.

One afternoon that summer Min-ho and I came home after school to find a thief in the house. He was a scrawny soldier with pitted skin, no older than about nineteen. He was trying to carry the Toshiba television set, but his arms weren't strong enough. Soldiers had been robbing houses all over Hyesan, and they were usually turned over to the police. But my mother just gave him some money and told him to buy food.

As the famine deepened, rumours of cannibalism spread throughout the province. The government issued stark warnings about it. We heard that an elderly man had killed a child and put the cooked meat into soup. He sold it at a market canteen, where it was eaten by eager diners. The crime was discovered when police found the bones. I thought these killers must have been psychopaths, and that ordinary people would never resort to such crimes. Now I am not so sure. Having spoken to many who came close to death during that time I realize that starvation can drive people to insanity. It can cause parents to take food from their own children, people to eat the corpses of the dead, and the gentlest neighbour to commit murder.

Across the country the travel permit system had collapsed, but entry into Pyongyang was still tightly controlled. That summer I received permission to visit Uncle Money and his wife. It was my second long train journey in the worst imaginable year to travel.

I was nervous about the visit. In fact I was braced for scenes similar to those I'd seen in Hamhung. But to my great surprise, all was normal in the Capital of the Revolution: well-fed people were going about their business; the vast boulevards had electrified streetcars, and traffic; I saw no beggars or hordes of vagrant children. The power stations were puffing smoke. The loyal class who lived here seemed insulated from what was happening in the rest of the country.

After I'd laid flowers and bowed at the feet of the bronze colossus of Kim Il-sung on Mansu Hill, so large it made me feel like an ant, my uncle and aunt took me out to Ok-liu-gwon, the most famous noodle restaurant in the country. The place was packed out, with people waiting for a table. Clearly, no one was going hungry. My uncle had power and influence. We went straight to the front of the line and were admitted without having to wait.

Uncle Money was a large man with a large personality, which seemed fitting to his position as the wealthiest member of the family. His house had its own sauna. I'd never seen such a luxury in my life. I counted five televisions. Some were still in the boxes, to give as bribes. At dinner in his dining room one evening I was served Western food for the first time – some kind of pasta dish.

It didn't look like real food.

Uncle Money laughed at the expression on my face. 'Most people will never have a chance to eat this in their lives. If you don't try it now maybe you never will.'

Uncle Money's wife wore such fashionable clothes she did not look North Korean. She was a manager at Department Store Number One in Pyongyang, which was regularly featured on the television news, showing shelves laden with colourful produce. But when I visited her there she told me that the goods on the shelves were for display only, to impress foreign visitors. The store had no stock to replace what was sold.

I told her I'd hoped to buy a present for my mother, like the small makeup set I'd seen beneath a glass counter.

My aunt winked at the shop assistant, who took it out and gave it to me.

As I travelled back to Hyesan, I thought the whole visit had seemed like a strange dream. I could not believe Pyongyang was in the same country where people were dying on the sidewalks in Hamhung, and vagrant children swarmed in the markets of Hyesan. In the end, though, not even Pyongyang stayed immune. The regime could not prevent famine coming to the heart of its own power base.

Chapter 17

The lights of Changbai

The boy shouted his answer. 'I want to be a tank driver.'

Our teacher beamed approvingly. 'And why do you want to be a tank driver?'

'To defend our country from the Yankee bastards.'

The boy sat back down. It was my final year at secondary school, and we were each being asked about our careers.

Like all obedient Socialist Youth we were telling the teacher what she wanted to hear. When we'd been taught for as long as we could remember how the Respected Father Leader had dedicated his entire life to the people's cause, and how great a burden he had shouldered to keep our country safe from its enemies, even a kindergarten kid would have known it would not have pleased the teacher if I'd put my hand up and said: 'I want to be a pop star.'

You would expect between school friends a more honest conversation about our hopes for the future, and what we wanted to do with our lives, and that did happen, to an extent. But by the time we were ready to graduate, we had learned to trim our expectations in line with our *songbun*. Our choices fell within a certain range. In my class, the few of us with good *songbun* either took the university entrance exam or, if they were boys, went straight to military service. A few were able, through family connections, to land good jobs with the police or the *Bowibu*. More than half the students in my class were in the *songbun* 'hostile' category. A list of their names was sent to a government office in Hyesan, where officials assigned them to mines and farms. One girl from this group took the test to enter university, and passed, but was not permitted to go.

My good *songbun* meant I could plan. My dreams were private and modest. I wanted to be an accordionist. It's a popular instrument in North Korea and a woman who could play it well had no difficulty making a living. That would be my official career, but, like my mother, I also wanted to trade, start an illicit business, and make money. I thought this would be exciting. I also knew that it would be the only way to ensure that my own family, when one day I had children of my own, would have enough to eat.

My mother fully supported the accordion career choice, and found a musician from the theatre in Hyesan to give me tuition. She said my father would have been pleased, as he'd always enjoyed accordion music. This made me cry.

I was seventeen years old. In just a few months, in January 1998, I would turn eighteen. This thought weighed heavy. At eighteen, we were adult citizens and received our official ID passbooks. The pranks and misdemeanours that children could get away with became serious crimes once we turned eighteen. And there was one prank I was increasingly tempted to commit, before it was too late.

In the winter of 1997, a school friend who lived near our house asked if I'd like to slip across the river with her to the border county of Changbai, in China. Her mother, like mine, had trading contacts there. She had already crossed a few times, so she knew what she was doing.

The idea thrilled me. My plan after the winter vacation was to try for a place at Hyesan Economics School, which ran two-year courses. It was harder to get into than a four-year university course. Graduates were expected to work for state-run companies, of course, not in illegal private trade. Grades didn't matter much. Money and influence were what counted. I wanted to study there and start a business trading in imported goods. So why not take a sneak look at Changbai? Changbai, to me, represented business.

By then, Min-ho had crossed illegally many times. Young boys often did. He wanted to play with the Chinese boys on the other side. Sometimes, when the guards weren't looking, he'd slip across to visit

Mr Ahn and his wife, or Mr Chang, my mother's trading contacts, whose homes were nearby. If he could do it, why couldn't I?

From my house I marvelled at the halogen lights and neon signs of Changbai across the river, which never suffered power cuts. At school, the teachers had always told us that the Chinese were envious of us and worse off than we were. I had believed this for years, even though evidence to the contrary was everywhere before my eyes, from the abundant Chinese products on sale in our market to the fashionable Chinese business people walking about Hyesan. In the end it was something Aunt Pretty said that made a light come on in my head. She told me that hungry people headed to Hyesan because there was always more food at border towns.

Food from China? Did the Chinese have more food?

During the famine Hyesan was in darkness every evening, but the clouds over Changbai glowed sodium amber from so many city lights. I started noticing that not one of the Chinese people I saw – not the border guards on the other side, who looked awesome in their green uniforms, or the children playing in the river – looked thin or hungry. They were clearly doing better – much better – than we were. This realization began to dislodge one of my longest-held core beliefs – that our country was the best in the world.

I had no spoken Mandarin at all, but I knew enough Chinese characters to make sense of some of the subtitles when television programmes had them. I had been watching illegal Chinese programmes for a few years now. But even when I couldn't understand, I was still fascinated.

South Korean pop stars regularly appeared on Chinese TV. Acts like Seo Taeji and the Boys and H.O.T., a hugely popular boy band, performed before audiences of screaming girls. I'd never seen anything like them. I could understand the Korean but I didn't know what on earth they were singing or rapping about. Their fashion, hair and dance moves made them seem like aliens to me, too weird to be interesting. I was more intrigued by the Chinese TV dramas. Every character seemed to live in a beautifully furnished home, complete with housekeepers and drivers, and kitchens filled with such luxuries as microwaves and washing machines. My mother washed our clothes in the river. *Do the Chinese really live like this?* I became more and more curious.

My friend was anxious to cross over with me as soon as possible.

The river was frozen solid. Naively, I expected my mother to give her consent. She always encouraged me in everything I did. But when I asked her she became very stern.

'Absolutely not.'

I was put out. 'No one'll know.'

'Do not ever, ever cross the river,' she said. 'It's a serious crime.'

'Min-ho goes.'

'He's too young to be punished. Anyway, he's a boy and a boy needs to learn how to stand on his own two feet. You're a woman now. You'll be eighteen next month.'

My spirits sank. I must have been the only teenager in the world who didn't want to be eighteen.

'I'm not eighteen yet.'

My mother told me that made no difference. Women had to be more careful than men in their attitude to everything in life. There was no persuading her about this. She said only starving parents would agree to let a daughter go to China. I had no reason or excuse to do something so dangerous.

'Well, one day I'm going,' I said, trying to have the last word.

'You will not,' she said, almost in a shout. 'Don't you ever leave our country. Do you understand?'

As if to mollify me, a day or two later she came home with a very stylish pair of shoes for me. 'I could have bought seventy kilos of rice for what I paid for those,' she said. She so wanted me to be gracious, and grateful, but could not help spoiling me.

I understood why she was refusing me, but I couldn't stop longing to go. I wanted to see something of the world, and for me China was the world. Most of all, I wanted to see if what I had been watching on television was real.

Lying on my mat, I thought about that time all those years ago in Anju when I'd run out into a thunderstorm to wait for the terrifying lady in black to come down with the rain. I thought of the day I'd pushed my way through that crowd beneath the bridge to see something a seven-year-old girl should never have seen, a man hanging by the neck. My curiosity had always been greater than my fear – not a good trait to have in North Korea, where fear keeps your senses sharp and helps you stay alive. Part of me knew very well that crossing into China was highly risky. It could have serious consequences, and not just for me.

But I was still seventeen. And in a few months, I would be starting college. After that, there would not be another chance.

Now was the perfect time.

Chapter 18

Over the ice

The Yalu River in front of our house was just eleven yards wide and not deep – waist height for an adult in the middle. Before people started fleeing North Korea during the famine, the border wasn't strictly controlled. By my late teens, however, it had become heavily guarded. River life had all but disappeared. Any activity along the bank invited intense suspicion. The kids now played elsewhere. Border guards had started closely watching the women who climbed down the bank to fetch water and wash clothes, in case they were receiving contraband or waiting for a moment to cross. By that time the women who actually were trading had come to discreet understandings with the guards, and were paying them off. The river ran more quietly than before, as if it were depressed by its role as a prison fence.

Not long after we had moved to the river, the guard whose beat it was along the fifty yards outside our house came to befriend us. He would regularly drop by for a chat and my mother would give him something to eat and drink. His name was Ri Chang-ho. He was six years older than me, tall, and very handsome, like the soldier in the propaganda posters. In fact most of the border guards were good-looking, chosen to represent our country to the foreigners on the Chinese side. Their *songbun* had to be from the loyal class. These young men were privileged, but they were often lonely and far from home.

Chang-ho was good-natured. Military duty didn't suit him. He didn't like being ordered about, and was frequently assigned menial duties as punishment for something or other. When they were off duty, border guards had to remain on base, but he would slip out, and often came to our house. He was charming, but I sometimes found him a little simple. He once told me that as part of his training, he had been shown a documentary film about weaponry.

'We have the most amazing weapons, Min-young.' His voice was excited, like a little boy's. 'We can beat South Korea. And the Yankees. I can't wait till we're at war. It'll be over in no time.'

I knew that I could trust Chang-ho. On a cold night in spring the previous year, when I was sixteen, I was returning home around midnight from a friend's house. It was late for a girl to be out alone. As I approached my house, I made out his silhouette sitting at the side of the road.

'What are you doing there?' I was surprised.

'I've been waiting,' he said.

'What for?'

'For you. I was worried.'

He was like the big brother I never had. I was too naive to recognize his interest in me. He took a letter from his coat and asked me to deliver it to his mother in Hamhung. He knew I was about to make a train journey there to visit Aunt Pretty.

'Don't open it,' he said, with an odd, private smile.

In Hamhung, I found the address and delivered the letter to his mother, and she read it in front of me. She, too, gave me an odd smile.

'Do you know what it says?' she asked.

'He said it was private.'

She seemed to find this amusing, and treated me very affectionately, giving me snacks and juice bought from a dollar store. She was an attractive woman. I could see where Chang-ho got his looks.

When I got back to Hyesan Chang-ho told me with a broad smile what he'd written in the letter – 'Mother, I wish to marry this girl so please treat her well.'

I had not seen that coming. I glared at him in shock, and his face fell.

'I'm too young to marry,' I said flatly, taking a step back from him.

I felt immediately sorry for him. It was a declaration of love I could have handled a lot more sensitively. To his great credit, he took the rebuff in his stride, which made me like him even more. We remained friends, and he continued dropping by the house.

He was still patrolling the border the following year as I plotted my sneak visit to China. By now, my school friend had given up waiting for me to convince my mother, and had gone across on her own. This had disappointed me, but it made me more determined than ever to go, even if it meant going alone. The more I thought about it, the more daring my plan became. Why slip across just for a few hours? Why not visit my father's relatives in Shenyang? It was a longer journey, but perhaps Mr Ahn or Mr Chang would take me. I'd still be back home within four or five days. I decided I'd ask Mr Ahn. He was friendlier than Mr Chang.

I started preparing the way. I told Min-ho that if I didn't come home one evening it was because I had crossed the border to visit Mr Ahn and his wife. We could see their small house among the trees in Changbai from our riverbank. Min-ho went quiet when I said this. I could see he wasn't happy with the idea. He was ten years old now, almost old enough to feel protective of me.

The date I chose was in the second week of December. I was resolved to leave after dinner. There was little I could take. I had no Chinese currency, and I could hardly let my mother see me leave the house with a bag of spare clothes.

That evening my mother was cooking an unusually elaborate meal. 'Why've you made so much food?' I said.

She had prepared much more than we normally ate. The kitchen was warm and smelled wonderful, of spicy stew and marinated pan-fried meat. She had even made bread in the steam pot. Her back was towards me as she stirred the pan.

'I just want to give you both a nice meal,' she said simply.

My heart missed a beat. I don't think she'd guessed what I was about to do, yet it felt like a farewell supper. That evening I ate as much as I could. After the bowls were cleared, I put on my coat, as if it had just occurred to me to go out.

'Where are you going at this time?' she asked.

'Just to a friend's house,' I said, without looking at her. 'I'll be back in a few hours.'

She put on her own coat and walked me out to the front gate holding a kerosene lamp.

'Don't stay out long. Come home quickly.'

She smiled at me.

Over the years to come, I could never shake the memory of that moment and the look on her face in the glow of the lamp. I saw love in her eyes. Her face showed complete trust in me.

I turned away guiltily.

I heard the gate clang shut behind me. *This is it*. My heart began to pound. It was a clear night, and so cold the air burned my nose and turned my breath to plumes of vapour. I tightened my scarf, and zipped my padded coat up to my chin. I stood still for a moment and listened. Dead silence. Not even a breeze to stir the trees. There was no one about. I looked up, and the vault of the sky was lit with stars.

I began to walk. My footsteps seemed very loud. Eventually, there, about ten yards ahead, I could make out the figure of Chang-ho in his long coat, patrolling the riverbank with his rifle on his back. Luckily, he was alone.

There was just enough light to see by. The river beside me was a winding road of ice – pale and translucent, as if it were absorbing the starlight.

I called Chang-ho's name in a low voice. He turned and waved, and switched on his flashlight.

Before he could say a word I said: 'I'm crossing over to visit my relatives.'

I saw his eyebrows shoot up. I'd never mentioned relatives to him before. He thought about this, and shook his head slowly.

'No,' he said dubiously. 'Too dangerous.' His mouth turned down with concern. 'You could get into big trouble. And how would you get to where your relatives live? You don't speak Chinese. And you're alone.'

'I know people just there who'll help.' I nodded in the direction of Mr Ahn's house. He stared at me for several seconds. It was as if he was seeing a different person.

'All right,' he said slowly. 'If you're sure.' He was extremely reluctant about this. 'Don't be longer than a couple of hours.'

'I'm hardly going to be long if I'm wearing these,' I said, pointing to my feet. He shone his flashlight onto my expensive new shoes, gleaming in the beam. I'd worn them thinking they would help me blend in on the other side.

Suddenly we heard a twig snap underfoot on the other bank and our heads turned. A dark outline of a figure was lurking on the other bank, obviously a Chinese smuggler waiting for a contact to exchange goods.

'Hey,' Chang-ho called over to him. The figure looked as if he was about to run away, so he must have been surprised when Chang-ho's next words were: 'Would you help this lady across and take her to where she needs to go?'

There was a pause. Then a faint voice called back. 'Sure.'

It was just a few slippery steps. I'd be across in under a minute.

For the first time I was scared.

If any of the other guards saw me they'd have no hesitation in dragging me back, even from the Chinese bank, where they were not supposed to tread. This was the first time I had ever done something so flagrantly, criminally illegal.

I didn't feel guilt now – just a rushing, hair-raising danger.

I stepped onto the ice, one foot then the next, wobbling and sliding in the new shoes. Ahead of me the Chinese stranger had emerged from the shadows of the trees to help me, holding out his arm.

My mother would be fine, I told myself. Later tonight Min-ho would tell her where I'd gone. By the time I returned she'd have forgotten her anger. I'd only be away for a few days. I was so sure of this that I didn't even look back.

So why did I get the feeling that my life was about to change for ever?

PART TWO

To the Heart of the Dragon

Chapter 19

A visit to Mr Ahn

The door opened, casting a wedge of yellow light across the frozen ground.

'Good evening, Mr Ahn,' I said, bowing my head.

Mr Ahn's tall figure filled the doorway. He frowned. It took him a moment to recognize me.

'Hello there.' He was most surprised. 'Min-young, isn't it?'

My teeth were chattering now, and I was regretting my fashionable new shoes. My toes were already swollen and numb. He invited me in. He was a large man with a few strands of hair ribbed across the top of a bald head, and enormous bulging eyes. A face like a jolly fat fish, was Min-ho's joke. My mother knew him through connections of my father's among the border guards. They said he was the nicest and the most trustworthy of the Chinese traders. I much preferred him to Mr Chang, his grouchy next-door neighbour, my mother's other occasional business partner.

The interior of Mr Ahn's house was warm and inviting. He and his wife lived with their daughter, who was my age, and their son, who was Min-ho's age. They were Korean-Chinese, and their accent more sing-song than mine. Seeing them together around the low table on the floor, I knew this was a close-knit, loving family. Mrs Ahn was very small and slight compared with her husband, with quick, nervous movements, like a bird's. After she had given me hot tea and they'd asked about Min-ho, whom they liked very much, they looked at me expectantly. What on earth was I doing here?

I explained that I wanted to visit my relatives in Shenyang for a few days.

'I was wondering if I could spend the night . . . and if you could help me get there tomorrow. I don't have any money. My relatives will pay you back.' I lowered my eyes. I had not thought this through. It had been years since I'd seen my relatives from Shenyang. I felt my face redden. 'Or if they don't, my mother will, when I get back.'

Mr Ahn frowned again and scratched the back of his neck. He must have known then that I didn't have a clue what I was doing. After a while he said: 'Do you know how far it is to Shenyang?'

I had only the vaguest notion of this city. I thought it was nearby, maybe an hour away on the bus.

'It's an eight-hour journey,' he said, watching his words sink in. 'And the bus is dangerous because you don't have ID and you don't speak Mandarin. There's a police checkpoint along the way.'

This was another serious matter I had not fully considered – the possibility of getting caught. Any North Koreans found illegally in China were handed over to the *Bowibu*.

'It's all right.' The stricken look on my face amused him. 'I can take you, if you really want to go. But we'll have to get there in a taxi.'

I realize now what an extraordinary imposition I was making on him and what a kindness he was doing me. I thanked him, but he held up his palm. He'd been trading with my mother for years, he said. He valued her custom and trusted her.

In the morning, after we'd eaten breakfast, Mrs Ahn began cooking a huge pot of *nooroongji*. This is the rice at the bottom of the pot that gets a little burned and is crisp on the outside.

'I make this for the North Korean visitors,' she said. 'They stop by here at night. Some of them we know. Others are strangers. It happens all the time. If I make this, it's easy just to add some water and heat it up.'

She told me about two strangers who had knocked on the door a year ago. They were emaciated and very weak. They ate a whole potful, enough for twenty people. 'It was awful to watch. They were like wild animals afraid the food would be taken from them. I knew they were eating too quickly. They had to rush outside and puke it all up.'

I could see that the Ahns were not rich. Their home was not like the ones I had seen in the Chinese TV dramas. They had no servants, or a microwave, or a bathroom with gold taps. In fact, it wasn't as nice as our house. But they had plenty of food.

That morning, Mr Ahn showed me Changbai. It felt most odd to be walking among buildings I'd been seeing all my life from the other side of the river, as if I'd passed through a mirror. It was a small town, with pharmacies, window displays filled with ladies' shoes of many styles; cosmetics shops, and food everywhere – in cheap canteens, in super-markets; in colourful packages displayed in kiosks; in the hands of school kids with spiky hair, eating in the street.

Mr Ahn gave me cash to buy some warm winter half-boots and a light-green Chinese-style padded winter coat. These would make me look more Chinese. I had already cut my hair in the style that was fashionable then for girls in China – like men's, long at the front and short at the back.

The next morning we set off as the sky was lightening. Mr Ahn sat next to me in the back of a new taxi car. This in itself was a thrill. I had seldom been in a civilian car. This one had a sound system for the radio. The road ran for a short distance along the river, the border itself. I could not take my eyes from the view of Hyesan. It had snowed heavily overnight, giving the houses domed roofs, like white mushrooms. I could see the Victorious Battle of Pochonbo Memorial in the park, its statues wearing wigs of ice, and my elementary school. The city seemed lost in time. Every building was weathered and grey. Only the snow-clad mountains in the background looked new – brilliant against the neon-blue tint of the dawn.

Two North Korean guards in long coats were patrolling the path along the far bank, watching the women, padded and muffled against the cold, who had climbed down to the river and made holes in the ice to fill their pails.

Rabbit-fur for the soldiers who keep us safe; scrap iron for their guns, copper for their bullets.

Behind them, hundreds of squat houses poured *yontan* smoke from stovepipe chimneys, creating a low haze. Through the trees I caught a glimpse, just for a second, of my house with its tall white wall. The gate was shut. It made me wistful.

I'll be back soon.

At the same time I was feeling a mounting elation, like bubbles rising in my chest, a sense of freedom and anticipation – that now I could do anything. In the darkness at the edge of the ice I had taken a terrible risk, but now look where I was. I had done it. I felt brave, and proud.

For a few minutes the snow everywhere seemed to blanket and silence the doubts in my head. But soon an internal self-criticism was in session. *I notice that Comrade Min-young is feeling happy. I would like to remind her that she doesn't have the first idea about what's going to happen next.*

Then I had a vision of my mother's face, of the love and trust in her eyes as she'd said: 'Don't stay out late,' and pictured her scolding Min-ho for not having told her earlier where I'd gone. My thoughts became less elated – I felt pangs of guilt, and selfishness and stupidity.

I'll be back soon.

The road curved to the right, the trees became thicker, and Hyesan disappeared from view.

Chapter 20

Home truths

The road twisted and turned through the Changbai Mountains. We passed sparse villages of squat, tile-roofed houses along the way. They didn't look much different from those in North Korea. But after a few hours' distance the villages were larger and looked more prosperous. Gradually they merged into towns, and the towns into suburbs. The two-lane road became four lanes. Soon the traffic was a broad, slow-moving river of steel and glowing red taillights. We were caught in an ant-like crawl of thousands of cars, more than I had ever seen. Far from being bored, my eyes were everywhere, taking this in. Every vehicle looked new. There were none of the heavy green military trucks, the most common vehicles around Hyesan.

We stopped for lunch at a service station at the side of the freeway, which had photographs of mouthwatering dishes displayed in illuminated signs. In North Korea, there were only state-owned restaurants, which saw no reason or need to entice customers or make any effort to sell; and private, semi-legal ones operating furtively in markets or in people's homes. But here the restaurants were advertising themselves brightly, inviting me to stop and look. I ordered egg fried rice and the waitress brought a huge plateful. *Chinese people eat so much.* I looked up at Mr Ahn. He laughed heartily at my expression. He was enjoying my reactions to everything.

We approached Shenyang in the late afternoon along an eight-lane expressway. Nothing had prepared me for my first sight of the city. Huge towers of steel and glass rose on either side, their tips aflame in the last light of the sun. The taxi stopped at a crossing as the lights turned red, and hundreds of people crossed the road. Every one of them was dressed differently. No one was in uniform. I glanced up and saw a soaring billboard of an underwear model.

I had not known that Shenyang, the capital of Liaoning Province, is one of the largest cities in China. More than 8 million people live there. It made Pyongyang look like a provincial backwater.

We reached the neighbourhood where my relatives lived, and after stopping several times to ask for directions, found the address. It was in a large, glitzy apartment complex. Each block was twenty storeys high. Mr Ahn and the taxi driver came with me in the elevator up to the eleventh floor. I rang the doorbell and felt a flutter of anxiety. I had no idea what to expect.

My Uncle Jung-gil opened the door and looked from me to Mr Ahn to the taxi driver.

'Uncle, it's me, Min-young.'

It took him a second to absorb this, and then his face was agog, like a cartoon character. Aunt Sang-hee joined him in the door. She was as astonished as he was.

My 'uncle' was in fact my father's cousin. His family had fled Hyesan during the Korean War and he had grown up in Shenyang. He had visited us in Hyesan twice, but not for several years. He had seemed wealthy to us, a little plump, very outgoing, and always laden with gifts. He was now in his late forties.

I introduced Mr Ahn, and explained that it was my vacation and I wanted to see China before I started college. My uncle paid the enormous taxi fare and the driver left. After chatting for a while, Mr Ahn said that he was going to do some shopping and return to Changbai. We said our goodbyes.

My uncle and aunt made me feel instantly welcome. I was family – it made no difference to them that they had not seen me in years. Their apartment was modern and spacious, with small elegant spotlights set into the ceiling. This was like the homes I'd seen in the TV dramas. Floor-to-ceiling windows gave sweeping views onto a dozen tall apartment buildings identical to theirs. The sky had turned a deep orange. Lights were coming on in the other towers, making them look like jewel boxes. Beyond them, all the way to the horizon, hundreds more towers, glittering in the dusk, were being built or had been newly completed.

My uncle asked my aunt to pop out and buy some ice cream. She came back with every variety she could find.

'Try these,' she said. 'Some of them are new.'

We opened them all and I took a spoonful from each. They were the most heavenly flavours I had ever tasted. Jasmine flavour, green tea, mango, black sesame, a luscious fuchsia variety called taro, and a Japanese one called red bean. *Red bean.* Flavours I had not imagined possible. Oh, how this made me want to stay in China.

My uncle was tall, and slimmer than I remembered him. As a girl I'd thought he looked plump because I had grown up in a country where there were no fat people, but compared with the large and rounded Chinese people I'd been seeing everywhere, I saw that his face had the boniness of someone who had endured decades of hardship. Wealth, for him, had come late in life.

I had been so caught up in describing my journey and enjoying the ice cream that we had not yet got onto the subject of family. My uncle asked after my father.

The spoon stopped halfway to my mouth. He did not know that my father, his cousin, was dead.

When I explained what had happened, my uncle's mood darkened. 'How dare they do that to him?' he muttered. He pressed me for details. He wanted to know everything about my father's arrest, the charges, the interrogation. I didn't want to talk about this. When I'd finished he brooded in silence for several minutes, then, to my great surprise, he stood up and launched into a tirade against my country. Years of bottled resentment were suddenly on his lips.

'You know all the history they teach you at school is a lie?' This was his opening shot.

He started counting off the fallacies he said I'd been taught. He said that at the end of the Second World War the Japanese had not been defeated by Kim Il-sung's military genius. They'd been driven out by the Soviet Red Army, which had installed Kim Il-sung in power. There had been no 'Revolution'.

I had never before heard my country being criticized. I thought he'd gone crazy.

'And they taught you the South started the Korean War, didn't they? Well, here's some news for you. It was the North that invaded the

South, and Kim Il-sung would have lost badly to the Yankees if China hadn't stepped in to save his arse.'

Now I knew he'd gone crazy.

'Were you shown the little wooden cabin on Mount Paektu where Kim Jong-il was born?' His tone was heavy with sarcasm. 'It's a complete *myth*. He wasn't even born in Korea. He was born in Siberia, where his father was serving with the Red Army.'

He could see from my face I did not believe a word of this. He might as well have been telling me the earth was flat.

'He's not even a communist.' My uncle had worked himself up into a rage. 'He lives in palaces and beach condos, with brigades of pleasure girls. He drinks fine cognacs and eats Swiss cheeses – while his people go hungry. His only belief is in power.'

This rant was making me uncomfortable. At home we never mentioned the personal lives of the Leaders. Ever. Any such talk was 'gossip', and highly dangerous.

But my uncle was far from finished. He was pacing the room now. 'Do you know how Kim Il-sung died?' he said, pointing at me.

'A heart attack.'

'That's right, and his son drove him to it.'

I looked to Aunt Sang-hee for help, but her expression was as serious as my uncle's.

'Kim Jong-il killed him. By the end of his life his father was a power-less old man who'd been turned into a god. Kim Jong-il was running the country. His father had no influence left except in foreign affairs.'

My uncle's theory was this: just before Kim Il-sung died, former US president Jimmy Carter had visited him to open the way for a summit with sitting US president Bill Clinton. As his legacy to Korea Kim Il-sung was willing to make the peninsula nuclear-free, and told Carter that North Korea would give up its nuclear weapons programme. This incensed Kim Jong-il, who set about blocking the summit. The two had a blazing row. Kim Il-sung got so worked up that his heart failed.

I refused to believe this nonsense. But at the same time parts of it rang true. I'd heard rumours at school that beautiful girls were selected for the Dear Leader's pleasure, and I'd seen for myself on the television news that he hadn't been fasting on simple meals of rice balls during the famine as the propaganda claimed. In truth I didn't know what to think. And so a shutter came down in my mind. My response, as a seventeen-year-old girl, was to enjoy the ice cream. What my uncle said about my country had a depressing and a repelling effect on me. I did not want to know.

Uncle Jung-gil ran a trading company. He had started off by selling pharmaceuticals to South Korea but his business had diversified and prospered. He drove a new Audi. Aunt Sang-hee was a pharmacist. They had a grown-up son who lived in another province. Both of them were talkative and extroverted, and loved dining out, dancing and socializing.

Before they took me on my first night out in Shenyang, they suggested I assumed a new name. This was for my own protection. The name they concocted for me was Chae Mi-ran. I liked it. It seemed fun to use an alias. When my uncle and aunt's friends dropped by, I was introduced as Mi-ran. I was visiting from Yanbian, they were told, the Korean region of China where many people speak Korean as a first language and may not speak Mandarin so well. The friends gave a knowing 'Aah' and accepted this explanation.

Shenyang was a revelation. In North Korea, streets are dark and deserted at night. Here, the city came alive at sunset. The sidewalks of Taiyuan Street heaved with shoppers and young people my own age on a night out, boys and girls mixing together, stylish and laughing. Music boomed and throbbed from cars and bars. Everything seemed suffused with a kind of super-reality, as if I'd come from a world of black and white into one of Technicolor. It was magical – an illusion enhanced by the myriad sparkling lights in every window display, restaurant and lobby, and on the fir trees that stood everywhere. Aunt Sang-hee explained that they were Christmas trees, a Western custom that had caught on in China. Each evening we dined somewhere new. 'What're you in the mood for?' my uncle would say, clapping his hands together. 'Chinese, Korean, Japanese, European? Or something else?' One restaurant had fish swimming in a tank illuminated an electric blue. I chose the one I wanted to eat. Menus overwhelmed me with choice. I ate ice cream every night.

Aunt Sang-hee showed me how to work the karaoke machine in the apartment. At first I sang South Korean ballads with the volume turned low and the door closed, until she yelled from the next room: 'Turn it up, I like that one.' In this country, there was no secret music.

After that they took me, along with a large crowd of their friends, to a noisy karaoke bar, another new experience for me. I could not believe I was singing my beloved 'Rocky Island' in public, and got a round of applause. I had never enjoyed a night out so much.

When, at the end of four or five days, Aunt Sang-hee said: 'Can't you stay a while longer?' I took no persuading.

During the day, while my uncle and aunt were at work, I had to stay inside. But even that was fascinating. I could freely watch any television I wanted without having to close the curtains or keep the volume down or worry about the neighbours. This was pure freedom.

Before I knew it, a month had shot by and I had celebrated my eighteenth birthday in Shenyang. I could not delay my return any longer. My uncle said he would drive me back to Changbai. These weeks had been such a whirl of discovery and enjoyment that I had given little thought to the implications of turning eighteen.

The day before our departure, the home phone rang in the kitchen. My uncle answered it. His face tensed, then without a word he passed the phone to me.

Behind the crackle and hiss on the line the voice was faint. 'Min-young, listen to me . . .'

It was my mother.

'Don't come back. We're in trouble.'

Chapter 21

The suitor

I didn't know how she was calling. We didn't have a home phone. She would not have called from her workplace because the *Bowibu* monitored the line. Wherever she was calling from, it was dangerous. She was speaking quickly. She wasn't angry; she had no time to tell me off, or for any chitchat.

'The day after you left, they started a census for the next elections,' she said.

I felt myself break out in a sweat.

Every so often the authorities registered voters in order to find out who was missing and why. I had turned eighteen and was old enough to vote in North Korea's 'elections', which always returned Kim Jong-il, with a hundred per cent approval.

'The inspectors wanted to know where you were. The *banjang* was with them. I said you were visiting Aunt Pretty in Hamhung. The *banjang* doesn't know it's not true, but you know how gossip gets around. There's already a rumour that you're in China.'

It was Chang-ho, my friend the border guard, who'd told her where I'd gone. 'She'll be back soon,' he'd said cheerfully. He'd always had more looks than brains. My mother had almost fainted. For the next few days she'd been in an agony of nerves. She knew she had to do something. So a week after telling the census inspectors I'd gone to Hamhung, she reported me missing to the police.

'The rumour that you've been in China may be too strong for me to take care of if you suddenly reappear. You're young. You have your future ahead of you. I don't want you to live your life with this stain on your record.'

What did that mean? That I could not go back at all?

Her voice was tense, urgent.

'Our situation will be dangerous for a while. Don't contact us. The neighbours are watching us. We'll sell the house and move. I don't know where, but you know what I mean.'

I understood. My mother and Min-ho would have to move to a neighbourhood where people didn't know us and would accept the story that the family had a missing daughter.

'I have to go,' she said abruptly.

There was a click as she hung up. The line went dead. The call had lasted under a minute.

I handed the phone back to my uncle in a daze. I was perspiring as if I'd been for a hard run. There was something desperate about the way she'd ended the call, without even a goodbye.

When I told my uncle and aunt what she'd said they looked at each other.

'Well, then, you should stay in China,' my aunt said gravely. They were taken aback. They knew I had nowhere to go.

I didn't want to be a burden, I said, but they reassured me. Things would work out, somehow. My aunt turned to stare out of the window. They were still digesting this news.

I am ashamed to admit that my first emotion, when I was alone in my room, was relief. I was just glad that I didn't have to go back. I thought life in Shenyang was a marvellous vacation.

Over the years to come, when my loneliness would become unbearable, and the full realization of the trouble I had brought upon my mother sank in, the memory of that relief would make me so guilty that I would lie awake at night. If I'd known that when reality began to bite, and I began to miss my mother, Min-ho, and my uncles and aunts in Hyesan so much that the feeling was almost a physical pain, I would have disobeyed her and gone straight back to Hyesan.

Now that I was to stay indefinitely in China, I had to learn Mandarin. And I had the best teacher – necessity. You can study a language for years at school, but nothing helps you succeed like need, and mine was clear, and urgent. If I didn't want the apartment to become my prison, I had to become as fluent in Mandarin as any Chinese girl my age.

My uncle started me off with a kindergarten book that I studied alone during the day and practised in conversations with him and my aunt at night. I soon progressed to children's stories. I watched hours of television daily. As China has so many ethnic groups for whom Mandarin is a second language, most TV dramas and news had subtitles in Chinese characters. Not only was it more interesting to learn this way, but I didn't have to limit myself to kids' shows because I already had a basic grasp of characters, having learned them at school. I had my father to thank for that. Back then I hadn't seen the point of learning them, but my father had been adamant. As a result, Chinese characters became one of my best subjects.

Being free from all other distractions, I made fast progress in basic Mandarin. Recognizing a word in a subtitle that I had just learned was always a *Yes!* moment of satisfaction for me.

For six months I did little else apart from sneaking out for the occasional walk, and my days became monotonous. Each morning I felt more and more homesick. Eventually the day came when I stared out at the rain, seeing the other apartment towers disappear up into cloud like unfinished sketches, and it dawned on me.

I will never go home.

Over the next few days this realization took such a hold that I thought I was losing my sanity. It was a disaster, and I had not seen it coming. *I'm never going to see my mother or Min-ho again.*

My mind's eye endlessly reran the taxi ride along the river and that final second when I'd seen my house through the trees. *Why didn't I ask the driver to pull over and let me out?* I couldn't stop thinking of that last phone call from my mother. How desperate she'd sounded, and we didn't even say goodbye.

I was trapped in a foreign country with no identity. My aunt and uncle were being good to me, but our family connection was so distant it was beginning to make me uncomfortable. I would not be able to trespass on their kindness for ever. The day would come when they'd want me to go.

What if I were to go home now?

No, I couldn't. I had come too far. It was too late.

My cousin had left a guitar behind when he moved away. I started playing the songs I used to sing in North Korea. These would make me cry. I cried every day, so much that it became impossible to conceal from my uncle and aunt. They were sympathetic but I could sense they were getting fed up with me. I didn't blame them.

At about this time, I had the first nightmare. I dreamed that my mother had been arrested by the *Bowibu* and sent to a labour camp, one of the political zones of no return, and had died there. Min-ho was now an orphan and a beggar. I saw him – so vividly in my dream – walking alone along a desolate dirt track. He was in rags and barefoot. His features had turned mean and he was obsessed with food, like a feral dog. I felt paralysed with guilt. The dream changed scene. Before she died, my mother had written to me. It began: *My dear daughter, I'm so sorry that I went first and that I couldn't take care of Min-ho . . .*

I woke up gasping for air. When I realized it was a dream I started to sob and became hysterical. The noise woke my aunt. She ran in to see what was wrong, and held me as I cried. It had been so lucid, this dream, that I was convinced something very bad had happened. There was no way to know. The next day I was subdued. I felt bereaved.

The following night I had the second nightmare. I had sneaked over the frozen river and was walking alone through a deserted Hyesan. It was night-time, and nothing was lit. It was like a city of the dead. I went to my house. Through the window I could make out my mother and Min-ho huddled together. My mother was weeping and Min-ho was comforting her. They had no money and no food. It was all my fault. I could only watch. If I entered the gate the neighbours would see me and inform on me. I walked to the river to find Chang-ho. I felt guilty about him, too. I saw him patrolling the bank but I couldn't approach him, so I hid in some trees and watched from a distance. Suddenly, *Bowibu* agents emerged from the shadows all around me. I ran for my life back across the ice to China, with the sounds of whistles and police dogs behind me. Then I woke up.

These two dreams would replay over and over again. The same scenes played on a loop, hundreds of times, night after night.

Any feeling that I was living a liberated life of excitement and discovery in Shenyang had vanished. From that summer of 1998, I had entered a long lonely valley. I deserved my fate. I had brought this upon myself.

If the chance came now I would do it, I thought. *I would go back.*

By now I knew that North Korea was not the greatest country on earth. Not one of the Korean-Chinese friends of my uncle and aunt had a good word to say about the place, and the Chinese media seemed to regard it as a relic, an embarrassment. Shenyang's newspapers openly lampooned Kim Jong-il.

I didn't care about any of that. My country was wherever my mother and Min-ho lived. It was where my memories were from. It was where I'd been happy. The very things I'd regarded as symbols of our back-wardness I now missed the most. Burning *yontan*, kerosene lamps, even Korea Central Television with its Pioneer ensembles playing accordions. The simplicity of life. One thing was for sure – I'd never known true misery until now.

One morning when my uncle and aunt had gone to work I called Mr Ahn's number in Changbai, hoping he could pass a message to my mother. His phone was no longer in service. I got a dead signal each time I tried. In the end I called his next-door neighbour, Mr Chang, the other trader my mother knew.

He was very angry to receive my call.

'Why are you calling me?'

'I want to send a message to my mother.'

'What are you talking about? I don't know you.'

'Yes, you—'

'Don't ever call this number again,' he shouted, and hung up. I thought perhaps he'd been drunk and so I tried again the next day. This time, the line was dead.

My lifelines to Hyesan had been cut.

Aunt Sang-hee became desperate to pull me out of my despair. I was becoming a serious worry to her. I had no role in life, and she could see I was becoming depressed. She began to hatch a plan that she thought would be the solution to my situation.

I knew nothing about it until one evening when the doorbell rang. I was in my bedroom, as usual, playing sad songs on the guitar. She knocked softly on the door, and told me I had a visitor.

My heart leapt. My depressed mind was making all kinds of irrational connections. I thought maybe it was someone from Hyesan.

I followed her into the living room.

A tall young man I did not recognize was standing on the rug, holding a bunch of pink azaleas. He was in his mid-twenties and looking sweaty and ill at ease in a jacket and tie.

My aunt beamed. 'Mi-ran,' she said, using my alias, 'this is Geun-soo.'

'It's my pleasure to meet you,' he said, using the honorific form of address. He bowed, and presented me with the azaleas, but his eyes did not meet mine.

Chapter 22

The wedding trap

Geun-soo, my aunt explained, was the son of her good friend Mrs Jang, a member of her Korean-Chinese social circle. He was gangly and so nondescript I'm not sure I could have picked him out in a crowd. He had the sallow complexion of someone whose pursuits all took place indoors, and an adolescent sheen to his skin.

There was an awkward pause after the introductions were made. I looked at my aunt. To my mortification, she said: 'Now, why don't you youngsters go out for an ice cream?'

In an ice-cream parlour near my uncle and aunt's apartment, I saw that Geun-soo was even more uncomfortable than I was. To put him at his ease I suggested we share a tub of my favourite, the heavenly purple taro. He seemed to relax a little. He was twenty-two, he told me, and had two older sisters. He'd graduated from a university in Shenyang, but seemed in no hurry to find a job. His family ran a successful chain of restaurants, and had money. He spoke with great deference about his widowed mother, more than I would have expected from a young man. It made him seem filial and kind, which I liked. He admitted that he enjoyed nights out drinking with his old college buddies. I thought he must be daring and fun. I knew no young people in North Korea who drank.

This was the first of many dates with Geun-soo. Over the following months he would take me for walks in Beiling Park during the day, or to noodle bars, or out to a *noraebang* bar, the Korean version of karaoke, in the evenings. He was harmless, but I soon began to find him glib and uninspiring. I felt no emotional bond.

No matter how hard I challenged him to an interesting discussion, even to the point of provoking him, he seemed unable to offer a firm opinion on anything. We often spent our dates in silence. I got the feeling that when he wasn't seeing me he spent his days playing video games. He also had such a devotion to his mother that I began to dread meeting her. He seemed content for her to decide everything for him.

Geun-soo knew that I was North Korean, but believed my name was Chae Mi-ran. I saw no reason to reveal my real name to him. In fact I was getting so used to being called Mi-ran it felt as if I was shedding the name Min-young like a former skin. I went along with the dating and would occasionally hold Geun-soo's hand. The relationship wasn't serious; it was pleasing my uncle and aunt; it helped to keep me distracted as the Western New Year passed again, then my nineteenth birthday, then the Chinese New Year, and to ward off miserable thoughts that it was now well over a year since I'd last seen my mother and Min-ho.

I should have seen the warning lights when Geun-soo began urging me to improve my Mandarin and correcting me on points of etiquette.

When he took me to meet his mother, I was made to feel the significance of the occasion. The family apartment was far larger and more luxurious than my uncle and aunt's. Mrs Jang greeted me in the hallway. I had never seen such a rich lady. She was elegant and very slim. Her hair was pulled back in a mother-of-pearl barrette; she wore an Hermès scarf around her neck, and beautiful Japanese pearl jewellery.

'Welcome, Mi-ran,' she said. Her smile was tepid.

I could guess what she was thinking. A North Korean girl was beneath her son. Yet I also knew from Geun-soo that she did not approve of him dating Chinese girls, a cultural prejudice against the Chinese shared by many ethnic Koreans.

Mrs Jang was a pragmatic, calculating woman: she was willing to put her misgivings aside because she thought a North Korean girl would make a compliant and obedient wife. After all, I was an illegal, and hardly in any position to complain. She also knew that I was raised in a culture that revered elders. I would be submissive to her, my mother-in-law. Although her conversation was excruciatingly polite I watched her looking me up and down as if she were inspecting livestock.

Over the next few months, whenever I was taken to Geun-soo's home,

Mrs Jang began to talk about my future with her son. The family would open a new restaurant for him and me to manage together, she said. Not long after that, without anyone asking me what I felt about the idea, she was mentioning marriage. Her son was a little too young to marry, she told me, but out of consideration towards her he wanted to provide her with grandchildren as soon as possible.

I began to feel caught in a gathering wave. Geun-soo had not proposed marriage to me. In fact, I wasn't even sure how he felt about me. I found it difficult to picture him getting aroused and passionate about anything. Perhaps he became livelier when he went out drinking, but it was clear that he was keeping that side of his life separate from me. He was passive in all his mother's schemes.

My dates with him started to become stifling. He kept repeating the need to improve my Mandarin, and would correct me often. His main concern seemed to be that I should not embarrass his family by making mistakes when I spoke. I felt as if I had been enrolled in a training programme to join his family, without once having given my assent. My situation was becoming deeply awkward because my uncle and aunt saw marriage as the solution to my problem, and to theirs. My five-day visit had already turned into a stay of nearly two years.

One afternoon toward the end of 1999, when I was at Geun-soo's home, Mrs Jang came home laden with department-store shopping bags and mentioned, quite casually, that she had given my birth details to a fortune-teller, who had recommended a propitious date in the summer for our wedding. And she had found a home for us in a nearby apartment, she said. She would soon start choosing our furniture.

That evening, lying on my bed, I was forced to examine – really, truly examine – whether I had any options. I tried to think calculatingly, like Mrs Jang. Regardless of my feelings about the feckless Geun-soo, I asked myself whether this marriage would help me, or trap me. I knew I had a desire to be a businesswoman, and to travel. But if I were to marry now and have children, I'd have to put any career on hold. On the other hand, my position was precarious. I could not stay at my uncle and aunt's much longer. I had no prospects, least of all of becoming a businesswoman. The alternative was a life on the run.

And if I'm caught?

Arrest, repatriation, beatings, prison camp. The ruin of my family's *songbun*. A spasm of terror ran through me.

No matter which way I looked at it, I had no choice.

So I tried hard to convince myself. *Geun-soo's all right. A girl could do a lot worse. If I married him I'd have a comfortable life without fear, and a Chinese ID.* I spent weeks thinking these thoughts, arguing in silence with myself.

There was just one problem, however, and it was a major one. I wasn't choosing any of this. It was all happening to me.

Through connections, Geun-soo's family obtained a new identity for me. He even showed me the ID card and let me hold it. I recognized my face, but not the name. It was a new name, another one I had not chosen. I was to be a Korean-Chinese called Jang Soon-hyang. As I was too young to marry – the legal marriage age in China is twenty – they'd made me older.

'You'll get it after the wedding,' Geun-soo said with a smirk, and picked it out of my hands. Even he could tell I was having misgivings – more so when I learned that my new name meant 'the person who respects elders, and makes a good wife by following her husband and listening really well to him'.

The millennium passed, then another birthday. My uncle gave me a Motorola cellphone as a present, so that I could chat with Geun-soo whenever I liked, he said. The wedding plans gathered pace.

Mrs Jang sensed that I was feeling pressured by her will. She tried to reassure me. 'After you're married, we'll take care of you,' she said, squeezing my hand with her bony fingers and rings. 'You won't have to worry about a thing.'

It was kind of her to say that. It emboldened me to ask the question I wanted to ask. I don't know why I thought I had to ask her permission.

'When I'm married would it be all right to visit my family?'

I thought my new Chinese ID would mean I could visit North Korea legally.

We were sitting around the kitchen table at her home. Mrs Jang and Geun-soo's two sisters stared at me in horror.

'Oh, no, no, no,' she said, as if there'd been some gross misunderstanding. 'You can never go back. Do you understand?' Her voice carried an edge of warning. 'They might find out who you are. Then we'd all be in trouble. We've had to break rules to get your ID as it is. In fact, it's too dangerous even to contact your family again.'

She saw the shock on my face and she gave a thin, quick smile, like a sudden crack in ice.

'After you marry, you will have a new family. You will join our family.'

When I told Geun-soo what his mother had said, I was still emotional. He knew how badly I wanted to see my mother and Min-ho again. I thought this was his moment – to comfort his future wife, show understanding, tell me we'd find a way to achieve it, somehow, and not to worry. Instead he said blandly: 'My mother's right. It's for the best.' He wasn't even looking at me. He was playing a video game.

I was stunned. He and my future in-laws were closing down any talk of my seeing my family again. If I even managed to contact them, I would have to keep it secret from those closest to me.

I looked at Geun-soo's face, pale in the reflected light of the video game, and knew I could not marry this man.

Whatever happened next I would be on my own, but I didn't care. I would find a way to fly in life. I didn't know how, but I would take my chances.

My uncle and aunt were talking excitedly about the wedding at almost every mealtime. I could not bear to tell them of my decision, or to witness their disappointment. I was fearful, too, that Mrs Jang might feel so angry and humiliated by the loss of face that she would report me to the authorities as a fugitive. I had no one to talk to. The situation left only one door open.

Escape.

It was the summer of 2000. The wedding was just weeks away. I thought hard about when I would make my move. It was a phone call from Geun-soo that decided the matter for me. He told me that his mother, without asking us, had booked our honeymoon at a luxurious beach resort at Sanya, on the South China Sea.

That did it. I would leave straight away.

I threw some clothes into a bag, and waited until my aunt and uncle had left for work. I took the elevator down to the lobby and smiled at the caretaker. The blood was rushing to my temples. A memory flashed across my mind of my foot stepping onto the ice of the Yalu River. I walked calmly out of the apartment building, took the chip out of my cellphone, and dropped it in a trash can.

Chapter 23

Shenyang girl

The cab driver's eyes regarded me in the mirror, waiting for me to say where to go. I was in an agony of hesitation. I had no plan. For the first time in my life I had no one to turn to.

Shenyang is a vast metropolis. I could go anywhere, but my gut feeling told me to stay away from the district known as Xita, or West Pagoda. This was Shenyang's Koreatown, where most of the city's ethnic Koreans lived and ran businesses. If anyone searched for me, it would be there. I told the driver to head to a district I did not know, on the opposite side of the city, where no one would find me. I would have to speak Mandarin, but after two years of study, my ability was adequate. I felt I could handle things.

But once we were on the freeway and passing through unfamiliar districts, I was again filled with doubts.

Although it was risky, the best chance of finding a job and someone to help me would be in Xita, among Koreans. I had been there several times with my aunt and remembered seeing an informal job market where people hung about, waiting to be offered a casual day's work. And I needed to find work, fast. My uncle had been giving me some modest living expenses, but I had only saved enough to last me a couple of days. I told the driver to change direction and head to Xita.

Among the crowd of jobseekers I didn't know whether to appear eager or nonchalant. I'd been standing there only a few minutes when a woman approached me and spoke in Mandarin.

'Hello,' she said brightly. 'Are you looking for a job?'

She was middle-aged, but with very girlish makeup, and a cotton dress that showed bare shoulders.

'Yes.'

'I'm the manager of a hair salon and need another stylist. Are you interested?' Her voice was girlish too. 'You'll be trained. And the lodgings are free.'

I could not believe my luck.

'It's on the edge of the city. We can go by cab. It'll take about thirty minutes.'

Her name was Miss Ma. On the way there, she asked me many questions. I felt she was trying to befriend me. I told her I was from Shenyang and that my 'father' owned a trading company that did business with South Korea. She expressed surprise that a girl from such a family would want a job in a hair salon. I tried to give the impression I was rebelling.

I noticed that Miss Ma's nails were painted a cyclamen purple, which I thought rather far out for a woman her age, and she wore a thin gold trace chain around her ankle.

We arrived at a drab suburb of shops and apartments. It looked more like Changbai than Shenyang. The hair salon was unlike any beauty parlour I had known. The left side was lined with black leather sofas and on the right were a half-dozen barber's chairs facing large mirrors. Two of the chairs were occupied by middle-aged men having their hair shampooed.

This is a men's hair salon?

Another man of about fifty was sprawled on one of the sofas reading a newspaper and smoking. He tapped his ash into a paper cup. I noticed something peeping above his shirt collar: the blue head of a serpent tattooed on his neck. Miss Ma greeted him and his eyes followed me without smiling. Without my needing to be told I knew this man was the boss.

Miss Ma led me down into the basement and pointed out six small 'therapy' rooms with smoked-glass doors. She told me this was where I would be working. Her tone was less friendly now. There was a stale yellow light. It smelled of damp and male sweat. She opened the door to one of the rooms, and I heard myself gasp.

Inside, lit only by a tea light, a young woman in a skimpy slip was sitting beside a man lying on a futon on his stomach. He was naked but for a white towel around his waist. Coming from prudish North Korea, I had never been in an environment where men and women mingled naked, let alone touched each other. She was massaging one of his arms.

What is this place?

'Here, why don't you massage the other arm?' the girl said.

Without another word Miss Ma closed the door and left.

I didn't even know what massage was for, let alone how to give one. The man was very fat and shining with sweat, as if he'd just come out of a sauna. In the dim light he looked like some sea mammal that had washed ashore and begun to rot. I touched him with extreme reluctance. I couldn't see his face. After a few seconds, he said: 'Who's this? She's hopeless.'

'She's new,' my co-worker said. 'We're training her.'

The girl gave me an imploring look, as if I was getting her into trouble. She was about my own age, small and pretty, but with a damaged look in her eyes.

After a while the man heaved himself up, took a good look at me, and invited both of us to join him in a karaoke bar a short drive away.

'I don't think we're allowed to do that,' I said.

'Don't be silly,' my co-worker laughed. 'Of course we are.'

Upstairs, the man with the blue serpent tattoo stood to open the glass doors for us, and flagged down a taxi.

I hadn't eaten anything and my stomach was churning with nerves. I was worried that events were going to take an even weirder turn in the karaoke bar, but the fat man lost interest in me after I twice declined an alcoholic drink. It seemed to deflate whatever plans he had for a night with two girls. My co-worker, however, joined him in several shots of *soju*. I sang a few Chinese songs. He sang some himself. By the time we took a taxi back it was dark.

My co-worker took me to a building at the back of the hair salon. We climbed several flights of narrow stairs to a door with multiple locks. She opened it, turned on the light, and I saw the filthiest room I had seen in my life. In the corner something scuttled and vanished. Five bunk beds were crammed into a tiny space. Ten girls were living here. It stank of body odour and drains. A line of drying panties was strung between bunks; clothes were strewn across the beds. I peered into the bathroom, and pressed my hand to my nose and mouth.

This is what I've escaped to?

I was very tired by now, and weak from having eaten nothing but a few bar snacks. I said: 'If it's all right with you, I'll stay tonight because it's late. But I'll leave in the morning. I don't think I'm going to take this job.'

I'll never forget the look that came into the girl's eyes. I'd seen it many times in North Korea. She was afraid.

'This is not the kind of place you can just leave,' she said.

'What do you mean?'

Her voice fell to a whisper. 'They won't let you.'

I lay awake all night on a stained mattress. I was too scared to sleep. It was very humid and the room had no ventilation. Was this my fate as an illegal? To live in places like this? How could they make me stay against my will? They couldn't chain me. I was trying to make sense of the fear in my co-worker's eyes, and the answer presented itself. *They'll harm me if I try to leave.*

I had been a complete fool. Miss Ma had guessed I was an illegal the moment she saw me.

The woman had tricked me to get me here. I would need to employ the same tactic to leave. I would have to trick her back.

The next morning, the other beds were still empty. Whoever they belonged to had slept elsewhere. My co-worker and I went to the salon. I was relieved to see that the brute with the blue serpent tattoo was not there. Miss Ma was sitting behind the cash register, looking gaudily dolled up.

I walked towards her. I needed to put on an act, and a good one.

'We had such a time at the karaoke,' I said. I held my hand to my head as if I had a hangover, and gave a look of comic mock-despair.

'Good.' She gave a small, sour smile. 'That's what you're here for. How much did the gentleman tip you?'

He hadn't given me anything. 'The money's in my jeans in the dorm,' I said. 'I was in no state to count it last night.'

'Never leave money there. Always bring it straight here.'

'Sure. Sorry. When do I meet the other girls?'

'They'll be here when they're ready.'

I crossed my fingers for luck. 'Before it gets busy, I'm going to pop back to Xita and get my things.'

Her eyes hardened. All of yesterday's friendliness had gone. 'What do you need? I will provide it.'

'Oh, no,' I laughed, 'I wouldn't ask you to provide a guitar. That's all I want to fetch, and some personal photos. The guitar won't get in the way. In fact, everything will fit underneath the bunk.'

I pretended to worry that she thought my stuff would take up too much space.

'You'll be late for your first booking if you go anywhere.'

She's hesitating.

'I'll make up for it later with overtime, and I won't waste your money on a taxi,' I said. 'I'll go by bus and pay for it myself. I'll be back here by ten.'

She huffed and puffed. She was annoyed now, and glanced toward the window. I wondered if she was looking for the man with the blue serpent tattoo. 'Be quick. We're fully booked today.'

'Understood,' I said, giving her a cheery salute, as if to say, *You're the boss.*

I walked out of the glass doors.

When I was around the corner and out of sight I ran along the sidewalk toward the cab rank where we'd been dropped off the previous night after the karaoke.

I stopped dead in my tracks.

The driver of the first free cab was leaning against his car and talking to the man with the blue serpent tattoo, who had a newspaper under his arm. I turned on my heels and walked back the way I had come, hoping he had not seen me. This meant that I had to walk back past the glass front of the hair salon. If Miss Ma saw me she would know I was not going to the bus stop. I hung back for a moment and tried to walk past with some other people, as if I was with them. I was halfway past the salon when I heard her shout from inside: 'Hey!'

I ran – down one street after another. I didn't know where I was. When I saw the amber light of a free cab coming toward me I flagged it down like a madwoman.

I jumped in, and sank low into the back seat. This time there was no hesitation. 'Xita. Go, go, go.'

Chapter 24

Guilt call

I had not slept and had hardly eaten in thirty-six hours, running on pure adrenalin. I had no possessions. My bag had been left behind in the dorm. In the cab I counted the last of the cash in my wallet. It was enough to pay the driver and buy some fried noodles at a market stall. After that, I was in serious trouble. I had to find a job today.

Back in Koreatown, I decided to try the restaurants, which seemed a safer option than the casual job market. After walking into a dozen of them to ask for work, and having no luck, I caught sight of my reflection in a window. I looked hollow-eyed, hungry and desperate. Just a yard from my face, however, was a notice in Korean attached to the inside of the glass. It was advertising for waitresses. I was in front of a restaurant called Gyeong-hwoi-ru, a large and busy establishment, with about thirty round tables and at least ten waitresses I could see gliding about in the traditional *chima jeogori* dress. The lunchtime rush was on: huge trays of hot food going in one direction, empty plates in the other. I composed myself, and went in.

'I want to be a waitress,' I said to the lady at the drinks counter who looked like she might be the manager. She wore formal business clothes.

'You're a student looking for vacation work?'

'No, I'd like a full-time job.'

She fetched a form and a pen. 'Name?'

'Jang Soon-hyang,' I said, using the name from the identity Geun-soo's family had obtained for me. 'I'm Korean-Chinese. From Yanbian.'

There was a pause as she wrote this down, and I felt my stomach turn to water. It had not occurred to me till now that I would need ID to find work. If her next question was to ask for my ID, the game was up.

She seemed to spend a long time filling out the form. 'I can give you a job. We have a dormitory for workers who need it. It's two minutes away.'

I felt relief wash over me. Nowhere in the world could be as squalid as the dorm I'd just come from.

'When can you start?'

'Today,' I said, tapping the counter in a show of eagerness.

The woman gave me a curious look. 'Isn't there something you'd like to know?'

You don't need to see any ID? 'No, sounds great.'

'You're not interested in your pay?'

I'd been so desperate for a lifeline that I had not asked the most basic question.

'It's three hundred and fifty yuan a month,' she said. The equivalent of about forty US dollars.

In North Korea, I could survive six months on a sum like that. It seemed a generous wage to me.

The lady smiled. 'And meals are free.'

My first day as a waitress in the Gyeong-hwoi-ru Korean Restaurant nearly ended in catastrophe. My very first customers were a table of Han Chinese businessmen in suits. One of them asked me for the check, and some chewing gum.

I brought them to him.

'What's this?' He looked up at me.

I sensed abuse coming. I'd already noticed this was common in restaurants here. Some people thought that if they were spending money they had the right to be as rude as they liked.

'I didn't ask for this.'

'I'm sorry, sir. You asked for gum?'

'I said cigarette, not gum.' His eyes narrowed.

He must have said the Mandarin word *xiang yan* (cigarette) but I'd heard *kou xiang tang* (gum). The lady manager came over to us.

'Is something the matter?'

'Yes,' the man said, pointing at me in front of his colleagues. 'She's from North Korea.'

The colour drained from my face.

'She's from Yanbian,' the manager said softly. 'She didn't catch your meaning.'

'Bullshit. People her age from Yanbian speak Mandarin perfectly well these days. She didn't understand me. She's North Korean.'

'She's Korean-Chinese,' the manager said, with a firm smile. 'I do apologize for the mistake. Let me bring you each a packet of cigarettes, with our compliments.'

This seemed to calm him down and he dropped the matter.

Later the manager told me that some customers behaved like pigs in order to get something for free. She told me not to feel upset.

She had not suspected that the man was right.

I fell into a routine. I arrived for work at 8.30 a.m. to set tables, fill salt shakers and soy sauce bottles, and waited on tables all day until the last customers left at 10 p.m. The restaurant was open every day and the waitresses got one day off each month. It was hard work, but I didn't mind. I was proud that I'd solved my problem by myself, even if my situation was still far from secure. For the first time in my life I had some independence. I had some money of my own. My Mandarin improved rapidly. I returned to the dorm after work each evening so exhausted that I'd drop off straight away. I got used to the nightmares. They still repeated, on an endless loop, night after night.

The four waitresses who shared the dorm were friendly and talkative, but I was guarded about what I revealed, especially to the two who were from Yanbian. One slip, and they might easily guess the truth about me. Despite this, one of these girls intrigued me, and we became friends. Her name was Ji-woo. She was putting herself through a business studies degree at Dongbei University in Shenyang, and paying her way with waitressing. This impressed me so much. The only other young person I'd met in China who'd been through higher education was Geun-soo, but he'd been such an indifferent student he couldn't even describe for me what he'd studied. Ji-woo was fun and intelligent, and like me, loved fashion. I wanted to learn what she was learning about business models, but her textbooks seemed so difficult. Several times I was tempted to tell her my secret, but each time a warning voice in my head said, *Don't.*

I was getting used to another new name. Ji-hae, Min-young, Mi-ran were behind me. My name was now Soon-hyang and I wore it like a new bud.

After a few months waiting tables, I was assigned to the cash register. I was good at handling money. My monthly wage was now 500 yuan ($60). My goal was to save enough for the journey to Changbai. From there I would try to make contact with my mother and Min-ho.

I was enjoying the job. The people who came to the restaurant fascinated me. I found myself observing customers, trying to guess their stories. I started to see that the world was far less conventional than I'd ever imagined in North Korea. People were complex and diverse. Many lifestyles and choices were possible.

As my life became more settled, the memory of how I'd run away from my uncle and aunt's troubled me. I'd fled without even leaving them a note. They had been kind to me. How could I have been so disrespectful? I realized that a note would have required explaining my feelings, and I was not accustomed to doing that. Few North Koreans are.

After about six months, in December 2000, I called them from a street phone. Aunt Sang-hee answered. 'Mi-ran,' she said in a gasp. Even she had forgotten my real name. Once she'd got over her shock I could hear the conflict in her voice, between relief, concern for me, and wounded pride.

'You humiliated us,' she said. 'You're our family. Running away like that made us all look bad.'

'I'm so sorry. I couldn't go through with it.'

She wanted to know where I was. I told her I was waitressing and doing fine. She invited me to visit, but I sensed that the hurt I had caused was still raw. I would leave it a while.

'Don't you want to know what happened to Geun-soo?' she said.

'I don't want to know.'

'You must call the family to apologize.'

I brooded about this for two days, but I knew I had to do it. Several times I started punching in the number only for my courage to fail me at the last second. Finally, I made the call. Mrs Jang answered. I couldn't talk at first. My mouth had gone dry. She was about to hang up when I said: 'It's Mi-ran.'

'Oh, my God.' There was a long pause. 'Where are you?'

I could picture her gesturing furiously to the sisters. *It's her.*

I thought she would be hissing with fury, but her voice was cool and controlled. To my great surprise she said: 'Please come back, Mi-ran. For my son's sake. He's not the same. He's been very depressed since you left.'

Geun-soo is depressed over me? 'Could I talk to him?'

He was weeping when he came to the phone. He sounded drunk and couldn't form his words properly.

'Please come back,' he said. 'I still have the honeymoon tickets. We can go away.'

These were the first strong sentiments I'd ever heard from him. I felt very sorry for him, and dismayed. I'd had to abandon him before he was able to figure out how he felt about me. But it was too late. I could not go back. The clearest desire in my mind was to reconnect with my family. He and his mother would be a barrier to that.

I kept saying over and over how sorry I was. I had humiliated him and insulted his family.

When the call ended, I slumped against the wall next to the pay phone and buried my face in my hands. I had brought great misfortune upon Geun-soo.

Our Respected Father Leader commands that we respect our elders and honour our families. I have noticed that Comrade Mi-ran does nothing but hurt the people closest to her. Would she agree that she is a person of bad character?

Yes. That's what I was. A bad person.

I had no one to talk to, no one who might have told me that, for my own wellbeing, the choice I had made did not make me bad.

Instead, this scathing self-assessment sank in, and a part of me turned cold. When I was crying in my uncle's apartment, missing my mother, my heart was there. But now something inside me had hardened and the tears had stopped.

I no longer liked myself.

I swore that I would do penance for the harm I had done Geun-soo. For weeks I thought about how I might do this. In the end, I decided that my punishment would be never to marry. I would not add to the hurt and insult I had caused him by marrying someone else.

Whenever people asked when I would marry, I got into the habit of saying: 'Never. It's not important to me.'

Chapter 25

The men from the South

In January 2001, two sleek young men came into the restaurant at lunchtime. They were friendly and asked me about Shenyang. They had perfect teeth, I noticed.

That day we were short-staffed so I was waiting tables. I was laying out *banchan* dishes in front of them when one of them spoke in a low voice.

'You wouldn't know any North Koreans, would you?'

I avoided their eyes. 'Why do you want to know?'

They put their business cards on the table and told me they were filmmakers from one of South Korea's main television stations.

'We're making a documentary,' one of them said. 'We want to find a North Korean defector trying to reach South Korea. We'll pay the brokers' fees to make sure they get there, and any other expenses.'

I was taken aback. The North and the South were mortal enemies. The Korean War had ended in 1953 with a ceasefire, not a peace treaty. The two countries were still at war.

'How can a North Korean go to South Korea?' I said. This was the first I'd heard of such a thing.

'Many come these days,' the man said.

I told them I'd ask around. I walked away intrigued.

Am I the one you're looking for?

Each day the two men came in for lunch. I was seriously considering telling them my secret, but my instinct was urging extreme caution. This could be a trap. Before I did anything rash I needed some facts. I told Ji-woo, my dorm friend, what the South Koreans had said to me, sounding as casual as I could. What she said in response came as a massive surprise. South Korea considered all North Koreans to be South Korean citizens, she said. Any who succeeded in reaching Seoul were given a South Korean passport and quite a large allowance to help them resettle.

This got me thinking. I knew from my uncle and aunt that South Korea was not the 'hell on earth' portrayed by the Party's propaganda. My uncle had visited the South on business and told me it was even richer and freer than China. I thought he was exaggerating. In truth I had given very little thought to South Korea. I had been so focused on learning Mandarin that I had not even watched South Korean soap operas on the cable channels. I also still believed that the North's problems were all down to the Yankee-backed UN sanctions. Going to pro-Yankee South Korea would be a betrayal of my own country, wouldn't it? What's more, I remembered that on the rare occasions someone had defected *to* North Korea, the Party propagandists had held a press conference. If I defected to the South, wouldn't I have to do the same, in front of a bank of microphones and flashing cameras? That could get my family into terrible trouble.

I was still undecided when, after a week, the two South Koreans stopped coming to the restaurant. They must have found what they were looking for.

Uncle Opium had once told me you get three chances in life. I couldn't shake the feeling that I had just let a major one go flying past my ears.

That evening I went on a night out with the dorm girls. We ate skewered lamb from a market food stall, then went to a café for bubble-milk tea. The girls chatted about their private lives, family worries, boyfriend problems. Each one of them wanted a better life. One of them, a Korean-Chinese girl from Yanbian, gave me a sideways look and said: 'You never say much about yourself. You're not an orphan, are you?'

For months I had dreaded the curiosity of others, but after the missed opportunity with the filmmakers I was feeling reckless. It was my extreme caution that had caused me to miss the chance. I was sick of lying.

'No, not an orphan,' I said. I had a habit of pausing before I spoke, to give myself a second to weigh the consequences. This time I came straight out with it. 'I'm from North Korea.'

The girls looked at each other. Ji-woo, the most savvy of the group, said she'd had no idea. Suddenly they were intensely interested. So I told them my story. We were in the café until closing time.

For the first time I became curious about other fugitive North Koreans in Shenyang. So many were in hiding that every few months the police launched a city-wide sweep to catch them and send them back. At a birthday party for one of the waitresses, I heard a girl whose Mandarin was so halting that I guessed she was North Korean. I introduced myself. Gradually and discreetly, I got to know several other North Korean girls, all of them, like me, hiding in plain sight.

The girl I'd met at the birthday party was called Soo-jin. She had the oval face, large eyes and full, bow-shaped red lips considered very beautiful in North Korea. She too was a waitress. I began to enjoy long chats with her on the phone once or twice a week. She was living in Shenyang with her South Korean boyfriend. *Living with a South Korean boyfriend.* I was scandalized when she told me that, and thrilled.

But after a few weeks her calls suddenly stopped. When I called her phone, I got a *number discontinued* tone. I sensed disaster in it.

Six months later I thought I spotted Soo-jin in the street in Koreatown after dark, but I wasn't sure. I called her name, and a face turned toward me with a hunted look, like an animal caught ferreting in trash. It was her. Her features had grown thin and drawn. I could see her shoulder bones poking through her T-shirt.

Far from being happy to see me, her eyes were darting about, as if she thought she was being followed. She said the police had come to her apartment and asked for her ID. She didn't have one. They arrested her and processed her at the Xita Road Police Station, then deported her back to North Korea. She was imprisoned for three months in a *Bowibu* holding camp. Hygiene was non-existent and each meal consisted of ten kernels of corn. New arrivals quickly contracted diarrhoea, which, with starvation rations, killed many in a matter of days.

On her release she was made to sign a document vowing never to escape again. She knew that if she was caught a second time, she would not survive the punishment. Scars from kicks and beatings were livid on her legs. She said that China was too dangerous for her now. She was determined to get to South Korea.

Soo-jin was desperate to keep a low profile. She was convinced that she had been betrayed by a mutual North Korean friend of ours in Shenyang called Choon-hi, who she believed had been let off by the Chinese police in exchange for becoming an informer.

Soo-jin squeezed my hand. 'Soon-hyang, be careful.'

I watched her go. I never saw her again.

What Soo-jin told me spooked me and made me paranoid about informers. How many knew I was North Korean? I kept going over and over this. Whom had I told?

Even then, I didn't see disaster coming.

A week later, the receptionist at the restaurant called my cellphone at about ten in the morning. It was my day off and I was in the dormitory. Two good-looking young men were in the restaurant, she said, sounding upbeat. 'They've asked for you by name.'

My heart leapt. No one ever asked for me by name, but I had given my name to the two South Korean filmmakers.

'Ask them to wait,' I said. 'I'll be right there.'

I put on some makeup, and rushed to the restaurant.

At that time of morning there were few customers. The receptionist pointed to a table. Two men I did not recognize stood up.

'Soon-hyang?' one of them said.

'Yes.'

They opened their jackets to reveal their warrant badges.

'Police. You're coming with us.'

Chapter 26

Interrogation

The two plainclothes officers escorted me outside to an unmarked BMW. I felt hazily detached from reality, as if this were some bad daydream. They did not cuff me. They seemed relaxed, as if they'd done this many times. One of them was extraordinarily handsome I noticed, like a movie actor. A third man was sitting in the driver's seat. I sat between the two men in the back.

'Where are we going?' I said.

The handsome one answered. 'Xita Road Station.'

The car's air con was chilling me. My teeth began to chatter. *It's over*, I thought. There was no possible way out of this.

As we sped through the familiar streets of Xita I thought of the awful trouble my family would be in once the *Bowibu* found out I'd been in China. It was my mother and Min-ho I was fearful for, not for myself.

I deserved this. I had done this to myself.

I linked my fingers in my lap, and for the first time in my life, I prayed. I belonged to no faith, so I prayed to the spirits of my ancestors. *If this is another nightmare, let me wake up.* I prayed to the spirit of my dear father. *If you can, please help me now.*

The car pulled over in front of the station. The officers walked either side of me into a reception area lit by fluorescent lighting. It was busy, with people in uniform and civilian clothes coming and going. To the left I saw what looked like a temporary holding cell with floor-to-ceiling bars. At least thirty people were crammed into the space, leaning against the wall or sitting on the floor. Men and women together, silent, with blank, resigned faces. Some of them were very thin. They stared at me. They *looked* North Korean. I felt no pity for them. I felt nothing.

In a few minutes I'll be joining you.

We passed a desk where a one- or two-month-old baby lay wrapped in a blanket. It was crying, and unattended.

My legs turned to straw. The two policemen led me upstairs.

On the second floor, we entered a large, bright conference room. Twenty or so police officers in pale-blue shirts stood about, leaning against the wall. All watched me as I came in. The handsome officer politely offered me a chair facing a desk, then sat behind it between two other male officials. The scene was surreal, and like a dream. Relaxed, yet menacing.

The handsome officer introduced himself as Inspector Xu. He was to be my interrogator. It was happening here. I was surrounded.

Focus, I told myself. *Pay attention only to what is crucial – the three men behind the desk. Forget the others watching me.*

Inspector Xu was not the only one asking the questions. The other two also took turns to interrogate me in Mandarin.

What is your family name? Where were you born? Your parents' names? Their occupations? Their precise address? The names of your siblings?

I told them I was the daughter of Uncle Jung-gil and Aunt Sang-hee in Shenyang and gave all their details.

'I need your family's home phone number,' one of the officials said.

Sirens went off in my head. I could not risk them phoning my uncle and aunt.

'We don't have one now. My parents cancelled it because they're staying in South Korea for a while.'

Which elementary school did you attend? What was the headmaster's name?

My mind dredged up every shred of information I could recall from conversations with Geun-soo and his sisters about their schooling in Shenyang.

Your secondary school? Which one?

My heart was beating wildly but I forced myself to remain calm. My body went into a kind of emergency operating mode. It was almost as if I was not there.

They're watching to see if I'm lying. Don't show them. Speak clearly and with confidence. Nervousness began to show in my fingers. I was clutching my hands together in my lap. They would notice that. I stilled my fingers.

Back to your parents. What is your father's date of birth? Your mother's? And then, casually, as if asking the day of the week: 'When is Kim Il-sung's birthday?'

April 15th. A question any North Korean could answer without thinking. 'I have absolutely no idea,' I said.

The questioning moved on to a new phase. Inspector Xu asked me when I would get married. I thought there might be a trap in the question.

'Not for ten years yet,' I said. My laugh sounded fake. 'I'm too young.'

The police standing behind me observed the whole scene in silence. No one came into the room; no one left.

Inspector Xu was watching me carefully, twirling his pen in his fingers.

Next he slid a copy of the *Shenyang Daily* across the desk, and told me to start reading the first article. It was about a traffic pile-up on the Shen-Da Expressway.

By this time, my Mandarin sounded natural. I was fairly sure that I spoke without a trace of a North Korean accent.

After a minute or two, he said: 'Enough.'

I noticed that so far nobody had entered any of the answers I had given into the computer on the desk.

They've got doubts. They think I may be Chinese.

Next was a written test in Chinese. One of the interrogators dictated from the newspaper, and stood behind me as I wrote down his words.

When I'd done that one of them said: 'Where's your ID?'

'It's at home.' When Geun-soo had shown me the ID card his family had made for me, I had memorized the ID number. I gave it to them. The ID system was still paper-based. Checking the number would require a call to another station, which would have to retrieve a file.

If they think I'm North Korean, they'll start checking properly now. Then that's the end.

Instead, the atmosphere in the room lightened. The suspicion was draining from their faces. Inspector Xu smiled for the first time. 'So, when are you really getting married?'

I laughed again. 'When the best offer comes along.'

One of the interrogators flipped his notebook shut. I heard him say to the other: 'False report.'

So, someone had reported me.

Inspector Xu stood up. 'You're free to go,' he said with a sweep of his arm toward the door. 'Sorry to take up your time. We had to follow procedure.'

I walked to the door in a daze, under the eyes of all the police in the room, and just like in a dream, I expected to hear: 'Ah, one last thing . . .'

The door closed behind me. I rushed down the stairs, across the reception area, and past the holding cell. I could not bear to look at the people locked in there.

I walked out into the sunshine and the bustle of the street. Once I was several blocks away from the station I slowed and stopped for a minute on the sidewalk. It was a clear, warm morning. Business was carrying on as usual in Xita. Pedestrians flowed around me. I looked up. An airplane was tracing its way across the blue, like a tiny silver minnow.

Thank you, my dear father, with all my heart. Thank you for making me study Chinese for all that time at school.

Chinese characters take years to master. That final test had dispelled the last doubts in their minds.

My father had saved me.

I knew now that time was running out for me in Shenyang. I could not stay. It was too dangerous. Until I figured out where to go, I would hide. I would move out of the dorm. But to where? Nowhere in the city was safe from the police.

As I walked my relief began turning into depression. I was already hiding beneath so many lies that I hardly knew who I was any more. I was becoming a non-person. The experience I'd just had was deeply dehumanizing. A police bureaucracy, with its correct procedures and trick questions, and inspectors in pressed shirts, thought it reasonable and right to send people from my country to a *Bowibu* torture cell for beatings with wire cables.

I clasped my hands to my head. *How could I have been so stupid, telling anyone I was from North Korea?* Now I had no one I could trust. And nowhere I could feel protected.

The moment I thought that, an idea occurred to me.

If the net for catching escaped North Koreans was cast from the Xita Road Police Station, then I would move right next to it. No one would imagine that a fugitive would live next to the very place where the round-ups were planned. The darkest spot is right beneath the candle.

A few days later I rented a one-room apartment next door to the Xita Road Police Station. In fact, the distance from the entrance of my new apartment building to the station was about five steps. From my window, I could see some of the police from the interrogation room coming and going in their dark-blue uniforms. I was so close that I figured they wouldn't bother with my block, even on one of their most thorough round-ups.

Two weeks after I had moved there, I was returning home after a long day at the restaurant. I was so tired it was an effort to climb the stairs. I felt in the bottom of my bag for the keys to my door. The stairwell had no light.

Suddenly I heard the sound of a rapid movement in the darkness to my left, as if something were rushing toward me. Before I could react, a massive blow struck the back of my head. The explosion in my ears stunned my brain.

My vision went blank, then I blacked out.

Chapter 27

The plan

I opened my eyes to a diffuse white light. I was lying on my side on a bed. Pain pulsed from the back of my head. I felt nauseous. A soft-spoken female voice asked me to look at her. I turned my eyes slightly and saw a lady in a green surgical mask. The gash in my head required ten stitches, she said. I was being given an anaesthetic and would be going under for about half an hour.

If I don't wake up no one will know who I am, I thought.

The girl with many names and no identity.

My eyes began to droop.

It was a couple of days before I could piece together what had happened. My neighbour in the apartment block had heard a noise in the stairwell. She found me lying on the concrete floor. A widening pool of blood was flowing from the back of my skull. The attacker had smashed a full one-litre beer bottle over my head and had run off.

Someone had been waiting for me in the dark, intending to attack me with such violence that the blow might have been fatal. Whoever it was didn't take my wallet, or the keys out of my hand to rob my apartment.

I had been very lucky that my attacker had not drunk the beer first, the hospital staff said. The glass of an empty bottle would have done far more damage. They urged me to report to the police as soon as possible. I said I would, but I had no intention of talking to the police.

My old dorm friend, Ji-woo, thought the family of my jilted ex-fiancé was behind the attack. Mrs Jang might have been seeking to avenge the family's honour for my humiliation of Geun-soo before the wedding.

This thought troubled me very much. But the more I considered it, the less likely it seemed. The manner of the attack, and the choice of weapon – a one-litre bottle of beer! – wasn't something the family would stoop to. I credited Mrs Jang with more class.

The timing, just two weeks after my police interrogation, suggested that it was more likely to be connected to the informer who'd told the police I was a North Korean, and who provided them with my name and place of work. This is speculation, but the informer might have suffered consequences for wasting police time with a 'false' report, and was taking revenge.

Once I was on the mend, I went back to work at the restaurant, but I was no longer enjoying the job. The comfort of my routine had been shattered. I was now mistrustful of everyone. I became paranoid whenever a customer tried to chat with me.

I missed my family more than ever. I longed for my mother's affection. I wanted to cry in her arms after what had happened to me. I longed for Min-ho's company. There was not an hour of the day when I did not think about them. Before the police interrogation, I had started to make friends in Shenyang, but now I kept to myself. Once again, I was alone.

In my new neighbourhood, I found myself using the same laundry as some of the policemen. Sometimes I saw the handsome Inspector Xu. He didn't recognize me. One of the regulars in the laundry was a Korean-Chinese officer who always smiled at me. I tried to think whether he'd been in the background when I'd been interrogated, but I wasn't sure and I couldn't ask. He seemed nice. His name was Shin Jin-su and he held the rank of sergeant. He was a little older than me. Not good-looking, but impressive in his uniform. One evening in the laundry he asked if I'd like to have dinner. My instinct was to smile and decline, but after all that had happened in the last few weeks, I was frightened and cynical. A voice in my head said: *Why not?* A policeman ally could be useful.

We began dating. It was the autumn of 2001. Our dates were nothing fancy. We'd go to a McDonald's or a KFC. One evening, he seemed tired but in high spirits. 'I'm exhausted,' he said. 'And starving.' He was stuffing a Big Mac and fries into his mouth and wiping the grease from his lips with the back of his hand.

'Why?'

'Rounding up North Koreans since dawn.' His mouth was full. 'We caught so many I had to skip lunch.'

He described how some of them cried and begged when they were cornered, and seemed to think I'd find this as funny as he did. 'Please don't send me back,' he said, putting on a high-pitched North Korean accent.

I had to control my face to hide my anger. *The woman you're looking at is one of them, you bastard.*

I knew I had no real affection for him, that I was using him for protection. But far from being clever, I realized I was courting danger.

I would have to end my relationship with Police Sergeant Shin Jin-su. But while I sat there listening to him boast about his role in the round-ups, it gave me satisfaction to know that I finally had a North Korean plan of my own.

Almost four years had passed since that final call from my mother. On each anniversary of that date a valve in my heart would open and flood me with sadness. But as the fourth anniversary approached, in the winter of 2001, I had hope for the first time. Four years of frugal living meant that I had saved enough to pay a broker to find my family in Hyesan. Even if a reunion with them could not be arranged, I was desperate to get a message to them. To tell them I was alive, and thinking of them every day; to ask them if they were safe; to say that I loved them very much.

I had no choice but to travel to Changbai, turn up at Mr Ahn's house, and hope the Ahn family still lived there. Their phone number had not been in service for years.

That is why I also formed a Plan B.

A wealthy Korean-Chinese businessman who came to the restaurant for dinner most weeks often chatted to me. He was generous and much liked by the staff. One evening he noticed that I seemed low. He was relaxing after dinner with a cigarette and a whisky. On an impulse, I told him I had relatives in North Korea that I needed to speak to. 'Why didn't you tell me sooner?' he said. 'I have contacts, I know people.'

He discreetly introduced me to a Chinese broker with experience of getting people out of North Korea – those who could afford his fee.

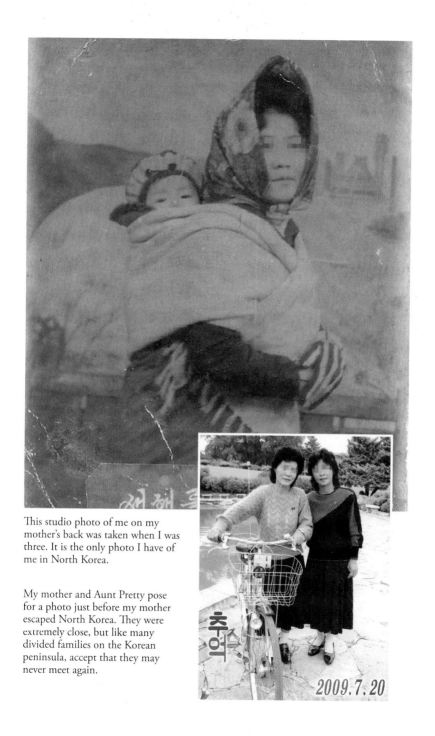

This studio photo of me on my mother's back was taken when I was three. It is the only photo I have of me in North Korea.

My mother and Aunt Pretty pose for a photo just before my mother escaped North Korea. They were extremely close, but like many divided families on the Korean peninsula, accept that they may never meet again.

2009.7.20

These towers in Pyongyang were completed in time for the centenary of Kim Il-sung's birth in 2012, the year in which North Korea was to become 'a strong and prosperous nation'. They house high-ranking members of the Workers' Party and their families.

However, even for families of the 'loyal class', housing can be poor.

Portraits of Kim Il-sung and his son, Kim Jong-il, are formed by thousands of children holding up cards in unison during a mass games display. In the stadium at Hyesan my classmates and I rehearsed for hours in the card section without being allowed a toilet break. We had no choice but to urinate in our clothes.

Citizens bow before the colossal bronzes of Kim Il-sung and Kim Jong-il on Mansu Hill, Pyongyang, a major shrine in the cult of Kim. Foreigners visiting the capital are brought here and are asked to bow. In this way the regime creates the impression on ordinary North Koreans that the Kims are respected and admired the world over.

A propaganda painting of Kim Jong-il adorns a float in a parade. He is depicted on a rainswept terrace gazing into the dawn. The symbolism here is that he steered the country through tempestuous times towards a bright future. A slogan on a float in the background says 'Regeneration through self-effort!'

A slogan on a public building in Hyesan reads 'Unification of the Fatherland. Our Great Leader Kim Il-sung is always with us.'

Factory workers in Hyesan march to work behind their unit
leader. Children set off to school in the same way.

A picture from Changbai, China, across the border into Hyesan, North Korea. The river separating the two countries is very narrow here, and when it is frozen over, it is easier for North Koreans to escape. Because North Korean train schedules are so irregular, numerous people have died on the stretch of railroad tracks in the distance, jumping off to avoid an oncoming train.

In China a woman and a girl attempting to enter the Japanese consulate to seek asylum in South Korea are dragged out of the compound by the police. Due to international pressure, China later allowed the group to leave for South Korea. Since then, China has intensified security around foreign embassies. China regularly repatriates defectors to North Korea, where they are severely punished.

Our family at Navy Pier in Chicago. It was my mother's first visit to
America and she was frequently surprised by America's development,
and that many people were so friendly. She had been taught the opposite.

My mother and brother experiencing their first water fight. They said
this was the most fun they had had in years. North Korea is a conservative
society, so a water fight among family members is almost unheard of.
My mother and brother have vowed to have a rematch in the future.

Testifying at a special session of the United Nations Security Council in April 2014. The session was historic, as it was the first time the Security Council specifically focused on North Korean human rights abuses.

LEE HYONGSEO

Meeting the US ambassador to the United Nations, Samantha Power. Ambassador Power has been a strong advocate for the Responsibility to Protect (R2P), and endeavours to promote human rights.

He was a small, tough man who seemed honest. He spoke in the cautious manner of someone with a realistic attitude to risk. But I also thought I would not want to get on the wrong side of him. He asked me what I wanted to achieve. 'A reunion with my mother and brother,' I said. I reasoned that having this second channel would increase my chances of success.

Plan B would turn out to be a disastrous mistake.

Chapter 28

The gang

The frail woman who opened the door was Mrs Ahn. In four years she had aged a decade. She clasped her hands to her mouth when she saw me, and told me on the doorstep that Mr Ahn was very sick – bedridden, and unable to stand without help.

His 'jolly fat fish' face was unrecognizable. It was contorted in pain. He had difficulty speaking.

Mrs Ahn explained that North Korean border guards had caught him delivering contraband on the Hyesan side of the river, bundled him into a sack, and took him to their station. They said they knew he helped people to escape, and beat him black and blue. They knew he wouldn't say a thing to the Chinese police because he was a smuggler. 'He should never have gone back over there after that,' Mrs Ahn said. But he did, and was almost caught a second time when the guards spotted him. They aimed a shot at him as he fled back over the river, and he suffered a gunshot wound to his arm. On top of his injury, he now had severe diabetes.

This was shocking enough, but her next piece of news horrified me. Their next-door neighbour, Mr Chang, who had been so angry that time I phoned him, had been convicted of selling North Korean women as brides and prostitutes for Chinese men. That explained his reaction to my call. He was under investigation by the Chinese police at the time. He died soon after starting a ten-year prison sentence, and his wife had gone insane. *Mr Chang was a human trafficker?* To think that I had almost knocked on his door that night after crossing the river, but instead chose Mr Ahn.

Mrs Ahn had no news of my family. Min-ho had not visited in years. Cross-river trade had gone quiet for a long while, she said, since an event that had occurred two years ago, in 1999. The Party chief of Hyesan had complained to Kim Jong-il that the city was becoming a hotbed of capitalism, and a brutal crackdown was ordered by Pyongyang. Many traders were arrested and executed in people's trials at Hyesan Airport.

I felt sick suddenly. I had never thought that my mother and Min-ho might be dead.

Mrs Ahn's kindness had not changed. She said she would get one of the smugglers to search for my family and, if he found them, arrange for Min-ho to come over the river to meet me in Changbai. I said I would pay the smuggler a fee.

It was dark when I had arrived, and dark when I left early the next morning. I did not see Hyesan across the river, but I sensed its presence. I smelt it. The *yontan* smoke, and fresh-cut lumber. The unearthly stillness.

All I could do now was return to Shenyang, go back to work, and wait.

On a freezing-cold Saturday morning a few weeks later, I was in my apartment when Mrs Ahn called. She said the smuggler had located my family, and Min-ho had crossed the river. What she said next made me almost scream in her ear. 'He's standing right here.'

There was a fumbling sound as she handed over the phone.

'Hello?' a voice said.

I held my breath. *Who is this?*

'Nuna, it's me,' the voice said, using the Korean word a boy uses for an older sister. Something was wrong. It sounded nothing like Min-ho. I turned to the window. I was picturing my brother in the reflection of the glass. When I'd last seen him he was a boy of ten. Now he was fourteen. 'Nuna, trust me,' the voice said. 'Do you remember the time I sneaked over here in the school vacation and couldn't get back because the river flooded?'

Finally I exhaled. *It's him.* I began to giggle stupidly and cry at the same time. I felt such a surge of love for him.

'Your voice is so changed,' was all I could manage to say.

'So is yours.'

***

On the way to the train station I withdrew all my savings and converted it into US dollars. It came to about $800. Some of this I would use to pay to Mrs Ahn's smuggler as a fee; the rest I would give to my brother and mother. I thought dollars would be handier for them to use as bribes in North Korea. I took the train from Shenyang to Changchun, then the bus to Changbai. It was expensive, but much quicker.

On the fast, silent train, watching the hills slip by, my mind was filling with elated thoughts of seeing Min-ho, when my phone rang again.

A man's voice said: 'My men have found your family.' It was the Chinese broker. That took the smile off my face.

I had almost forgotten about Plan B.

It seemed the most absurd bad luck that both channels had worked and I would now have to pay for both.

'When will you come to Changbai?'

'Tomorrow,' I lied.

When I arrived at the Ahns' house, a young man was sitting at Mr Ahn's bedside. He stood up when he saw me.

Whenever I thought of Min-ho, I saw the smooth-faced kid brother with the cute grin. This young man looked nothing like him. He was taller, and fuller, but I recognized my mother's face in his. He was staring at me with intense curiosity. Then he gave that grin I remembered, as if to say *See? Not a kid any more.* To him, I appeared very strange. I was wearing tight jeans and had brown highlights in my hair, a style truly alien in North Korea. We studied each other across Mr Ahn's living room, taking each other in, as if across an expanse of years.

'It's really you,' I said.

'Yes.' He spoke with a man's voice.

Then we both laughed at the same time, came together, and I hugged his face to mine. I could not believe I had my brother in my arms.

Before I'd even had a chance to ask about our mother a knock sounded on the front door.

Mrs Ahn opened it. Four men were outside. I knew the moment I saw them that I had trouble.

They were dressed in black jackets and jeans. One of them had face piercings. These were not locals from Changbai. They were from a gang.

'Are you Soon-hyang?' one of them called, spotting me behind Mrs Ahn. He had a shaved head. 'We're the ones who found your family.'

The Chinese broker hired these thugs?

I stepped outside to face them and tried to keep the alarm out of my voice. 'I'll be in touch with you tomorrow,' I said.

'No, you have to come with us now,' the shaven-headed one said. 'Don't worry. Everything will be fine.'

Mrs Ahn looked shocked.

I left my phone and my bag, and went with them. Min-ho wanted to come. I told him to stay. I had to handle this.

The men took me to an unfurnished apartment in a block on the other side of Changbai. The shaven-headed one led me into a bare room, and closed the door. He stood so close I could feel his breath, and spoke directly into my face.

'We found your family. Your mother said your brother had already left to meet you at that old man Ahn's house. Whether you needed us or not makes no difference to me. We've done our part. Now you pay.'

'How much?'

'Seventy thousand yuan.'

My blood froze. That was almost $8,500 and many, many times more than I had.

'I don't have that kind of money.'

'Your rich-ass businessman friend in Shenyang is paying,' he said. 'The broker was clear about that.' He handed me a cellphone. 'Call the businessman. Tell him to transfer the money.'

My heart sank to my stomach. As misunderstandings went, this one couldn't be bigger.

'This has nothing to do with the businessman,' I said. 'I'm the one who has to pay. He was just being helpful. I hardly know him. I can't ask him for money.'

'Then you have a problem.'

'What problem?'

'I'll put it this way. If you don't pay, we'll take you back to North Korea.'

Chapter 29

The comfort of moonlight

Sympathetic people I'd met in China would sometimes express their bewilderment that the Kim dynasty had been tyrannizing North Korea for almost six decades. How does that family get away with it? Just as baffling, how do their subjects go on coping? In truth there is no dividing line between cruel leaders and oppressed citizens. The Kims rule by making everyone complicit in a brutal system, implicating all, from the highest to the lowest, blurring morals so that no one is blameless. A terrorized Party cadre will terrorize his subordinates, and so on down the chain; a friend will inform on a friend out of fear of punishment for not informing. A nicely brought-up boy will become a guard who kicks to death a girl caught trying to escape to China, because her *songbun* has sunk to the bottom of the heap and she's worthless and hostile in the eyes of the state. Ordinary people are made persecutors, denouncers, thieves. They use the fear flowing from the top to win some advantage, or to survive. And although he was Chinese, and not from North Korea, I was seeing a prime example in this criminal in front of me, standing inches from my face. He had it in his power to rescue people, to be a hero. Instead he was using the terror of the regime to benefit himself and add to the misery of others. He had me on a cliff edge. *Pay me, or I push.*

I said it again. 'I don't have that kind of money. If you can reduce the fee, I'll see what I can do. But if you can't, there's nothing I can do.'

I felt utterly resigned. He must have seen it in my eyes, because he left me alone and conferred with the others. The apartment had cheap plaster walls. I could hear most of what was spoken in the next room.

'If you want money from her, you can't touch her,' one of them said.

Shaven-head came back into the room. He said I would have to stay here until a solution was found. He would send to Mr Ahn's for my bag.

I hoped the neutral look on my face hid my panic. My phone and all my cash were in that bag. I did not want them to get their hands on the cash – or I'd have nothing to give Min-ho and my mother, or to Mrs Ahn for the smuggler's fee.

I asked Shaven-head if I could use his phone. He told me to talk in front of him so he could hear what I was saying.

I called my own phone's number but no one at Mr Ahn's answered it. I called it again. And again. Shaven-head lost interest and went to talk to the others.

Come on. Please. Someone answer.

Min-ho later told me that he and Mr Ahn had heard the phone ring but couldn't see what to press to answer it. Neither of them had seen a cellphone before. Finally, they figured it out. Min-ho answered.

In a low, urgent voice I told him to leave the wallet in my bag but take out all the cash, pay Mrs Ahn the smuggler's fee, and go as quickly as he could back across the river to Hyesan.

One of the gang returned with my bag. Min-ho had done as I had asked.

Later that day Shaven-head lowered the gang's fee to 60,000 yuan ($7,250) and told me not even to think of leaving until it was paid.

There was no lock on the room where they kept me, so they took turns to guard me outside the door, while the others slept in the room connected to the only exit. Escape was impossible.

That evening one of them brought back a takeaway meal of skewered lamb and dumplings. My hope was that if I held out they would continue to lower the fee. I was too ashamed to play the only card I had – calling my uncle and aunt in Shenyang. I thought I would rather face my fate in North Korea. After the disrespect I had shown them, how could I ask them to pay a fortune to a criminal gang?

I played for time, telling Shaven-head I was messaging people, appealing to various contacts to see if I could raise the money.

By the third evening they'd had enough of takeaways and took me to a local restaurant, where I was wedged between two of them in a dining booth. I can't imagine what other customers thought I was doing with these thugs. The gang knew that an illegal like me wouldn't try anything stupid, like calling for help. If I did, I'd be in even worse trouble.

From their accents I knew that the one with face piercings was Han Chinese. He scared me the most. Violence crackled about him like static. I tried to avoid his eye. He kept looking at me in a way that made me feel naked. Two of the others were Korean-Chinese. They were more normal in appearance. I gathered that they were from a gang based in Yanji. They also dealt in fake leather goods and amphetamines. They were respectful toward Shaven-head. I couldn't place his accent. Dandong, maybe.

Later, after they'd closed the door on me in the bare room, they opened beers and toasted each other with shots of *soju*. I heard the constant flick of a lighter and guessed they were smoking a drug. Whatever it was, it wasn't calming them. The talk became competitive and aggressive, and soon turned ominously coarse. My stomach began to knot.

Then the one with the face piercings reminded them that they had a twenty-one-year-old girl in the next room.

There was silence for a moment. I heard him say: 'What's she going to do?'

Please no.

Until this moment I'd been in that strange calm emergency mode I'd been in at the Xita Road Police Station, keeping my fear under control, as if I wasn't quite there. Now I was losing it. My breathing became shallow. My body began trembling and refused to stop. If they entered the room now I would start screaming.

I heard movement, as if they were getting up off the floor. I pressed myself into a corner. I would beg and plead.

They were talking again. Face-piercings asked why the hell were they treating me so well. One of the Korean-Chinese said: 'She's like our client. If you mess her up we might lose the fee.'

One of the others murmured agreement. Shaven-head remained silent. There was another toast of *soju*. Face-piercings seemed to back down. The conversation moved on.

All night I remained crouched in the corner with my arms around my knees, not daring to move, watching the moon's progress across the windowpane, silken and faint behind cloud, like a moth cocoon. It was the same moon my mother and Min-ho could see. I told myself that if I stayed in its light I would be safe.

Safe. I thought of my policeman boyfriend in Shenyang, Sergeant Shin Jin-su. I wondered what he'd do if I asked him for help, if I told him the truth about me. The thought of the shock on his face almost made me smile.

At first light I called my uncle in Shenyang. It was the first time I had spoken to him since fleeing his apartment. My voice was fragile with fear and shame. I asked him to help me. I told him I would devote my life to repaying him.

He said: 'I'll do it at once.' He would transfer the money to the gang's account.

I tried to thank him but the words choked in my throat. He had my father's genes, and the same love and generosity my father had shown me.

We had to wait two days for the money to clear. I noticed that the two Korean-Chinese took turns to guard me in the next room, not Face-piercings. They didn't trust him. I was grateful to them for that.

After almost a week as their prisoner, the gang took me with them to the bank in Changbai, and withdrew the money.

Face-piercings' eyes shone when he saw the thick wads of red 100-yuan bills in an envelope. He clasped the others by the shoulders and pulled them toward him. 'Oh, we did well.'

Shaven-head took me to the coach station. Before he left he held out his hand and said: 'Give me your fucking phone.'

I gave it to him.

When he'd gone, I reached into a hidden pocket in the lining of my long winter coat and retrieved some money I had hidden there in a tight roll. I used it to buy a bus ticket for Shenyang.

On the journey back, I rested my head on the cold glass of the window and stared out at a world of white, an empty dimension. Sixty thousand yuan – a fortune representing ten years' wages at the restaurant – and a week's imprisonment with the threat of rape, and all I'd achieved was a three-minute reunion with Min-ho.

But I had made contact with my family. I knew they were alive and not in prison. And they knew that I was alive, and that, somehow, I was fine.

With the stress of my ordeals, not to mention the debt that would take me decades to repay, I fell sick once I got back to my apartment, and developed such painful mouth ulcers I found it hard to eat or drink. I was anxious and paranoid. I wanted to get out of Shenyang. Fast. I had an idea of where I would go, but, thinking of what my mother would do, I visited a fortune-teller for good luck.

'If you move . . .' the lady said, pausing for effect, 'you should go south, to a warmer place.'

'Such as Shanghai?' I did not care that I was prompting her with the response I wanted.

She pronounced her next words with an air of profound wisdom, as if she hadn't heard me. 'The best place for you would be Shanghai.'

That was all the confirmation I needed.

I gave notice on my apartment. I quit my job at the restaurant. I was about to call Police Sergeant Shin Jin-su to arrange a final meeting and tell him our relationship was over, but changed my mind. He'd soon figure that out for himself.

Just days into January 2002, I packed everything I had into two light bags, bought a one-way ticket to Shanghai, and boarded the fast train.

Chapter 30

The biggest, brashest city in Asia

I took the train with a Korean-Chinese acquaintance of mine named Yee-un, who was also moving to Shanghai. She was a waitress I'd met once or twice. I noticed that she avoided the subject of her past, which was fine by me. I told her nothing of mine. I guessed we were both running away from something. She was good-natured, with a blunt manner and a foghorn voice. I liked her. When we talked of how we would get by in Shanghai we both had the same thought at once: we could share an apartment. The moment we agreed on it I felt the tension and anxiety that had been in me for weeks begin to dissolve. Sharing with Yee-un meant I would not have to cope with everything alone all over again. We were both almost penniless, but now starting anew didn't seem so daunting.

We were laughing over the fact that we'd be eating nothing but instant noodles until we found work when I saw a forest-green police uniform and cap enter the far end of the long carriage, and people reaching for jackets and wallets.

They were holding up their IDs. Beads of cold sweat broke out on my brow.

I knew that these checks sometimes happened on buses and trains, but until now I'd been lucky.

The policeman was examining each one with a nod, moving along the rows, coming closer.

He was fifteen yards away. *What to do?* My chest felt as if it were stuffed with hot wool. Panic was rising in me. Yee-un's mouth was moving. I heard her voice as if it were underwater.

'Soon-hyang, I said are you all right?'

'Bit travel-sick,' I said, and shot out of my seat.

I locked the door of the toilet and waited, listening to a rushing, keening noise as the train entered a long tunnel and picked up speed. When I emerged after almost an hour, I peeped into the carriages to the left and the right. The policeman had gone.

I found Yee-un asleep in her seat. For the rest of the journey I sat upright and alert, my stomach clenching with nerves.

The train approached Shanghai Station at dawn. Against a feathered peach sky I glimpsed the faint outlines of towers half a kilometre high, the skyline of Pudong. Maybe it was because I was hearing snatches of Shanghainese and other dialects around me in the carriage, but it didn't feel like I was even in China any more.

Many of the passengers disembarking with huge holdalls and rucksacks were people like Yee-un and me. Young migrants, some of the thousands arriving every week in the biggest, brashest city in Asia to start new lives, to be someone, make fortunes, create new identities, or to hide. Back in Shenyang I'd sometimes felt like a special, secret visitor. Here I was utterly insignificant. This realization was alienating and exciting at the same time. Here, perhaps I could be anyone I wanted to be.

The year I arrived, about 17 million people were living in this megalopolis, of which the ethnic Korean population was small, about 80,000. About a third of those were South Korean expatriates; the rest were Korean-Chinese, as I was pretending to be.

Yee-un and I headed straight to a district called Longbai, where there was a small, prospering Koreatown. By the end of the same day it was our great good fortune to find a cramped, shabby, two-room apartment for a modest monthly rent without any deposit required. It had a tiny hotplate, a leaking sink, and a view onto a construction site where illegal drilling and hammering went on through the night.

We didn't care. We both felt we'd been given a new chance.

You get three chances in life. This time, I'd seized one.

My plan was to get a job in a restaurant until I found something better. Again, everything seemed to happen at once. Nothing stood still in Shanghai. Within a day Yee-un and I both got work in the same nearby restaurant. I was at the counter; she waited tables.

To mark this new start I changed my name again. This time I decided to call myself Chae In-hee. My fifth name. I had told too many people in Shenyang I was North Korean. I needed to bury the name Soon-hyang.

Yee-un was incredulous. 'Eh? Why? What's wrong with Soon-hyang?'

'The fortune-teller said this name would bring me luck.'

I had become an accomplished liar, even to the people who thought they were close to me.

By day the skyscrapers of Lujiazui were grey and blurred in a haze of smog. By night they were glittering displays of colour and crystal, each with a distinct character of its own, their summits forming atolls of light in the clouds, their bases competing for attention with vast moving images, of a soccer ball kicked into goal by a Nike shoe, of Coca-Cola being poured into a glass of sparkling LED bubbles.

One evening not long after I arrived, I went window-shopping along the exclusive strip on Huaihai Lu, wandering through the golden glow of displayed diamond jewellery and luxury Western-brand watches. I realized that I wasn't simply in another country; I was in another universe from the one where I'd grown up. Money was the obsession here, and celebrity and fame. I had dreaded the curiosity of others about my past, but in Shanghai no one cared where you were from, as long as you weren't illegal. Fortunes were being made overnight in property, stocks and retail. The city opened doors to those with nerve, ambition and talent. It was uncaring and cruel to those with no right to be here.

If I was to get out of waitressing I needed what every illegal in the city craved: a legitimate ID card. The absence of this small vital item was what barred me from opportunity. Without an ID, there was no chance of better-paid, more meaningful work.

Over the next few months I made discreet enquiries among the wait-resses in Koreatown. Many illegals were drawn to the glamour of Shanghai, and restaurants were often where they found their first jobs. Some of these girls must have obtained IDs, somehow. A few of them admitted to me that their IDs were fakes, but I was wary of acquiring a fake. It was a dangerous thing to possess if the police checked it. The safest option was to buy a real ID from someone. For that I would need a broker.

The first broker I met, a contact of one of these waitresses, asked for the equivalent of $16,000. I told him to forget it. The second one asked for even more. The predicament reminded me of the gang in Changbai. Anyone who knew I was an illegal was going to take advantage – they would fleece me for as much as they could get and feel little motivation to help me.

To avoid the gangsters, I needed a better tactic. I needed to make up a story.

A mild fresh spring turned to the torpor of summer in my first year in Shanghai. I was cooling off after work in an ice-cream parlour with Yee-un when a man at the next table tried to flirt with us. He was a Korean-Chinese in his thirties, with his own shop in Koreatown. He was slightly tipsy, I realized. Somehow, the conversation got onto his aunt.

'She's a marriage broker for women wanting to marry South Korean men,' he said. 'Can you believe that?'

Instinctively, I sensed a possibility. 'I wish I could study in South Korea,' I said. Yee-un turned to stare at me as if I'd grown a second head. 'But I'm too old for a student visa. I need to make myself a few years younger, somehow.'

'With a new ID,' he said, finishing my thought. Perhaps he was trying to impress two pretty girls in an ice-cream parlour, but he was suddenly eager to help.

'Let me ask her for you. Let's see what she says . . .'

He took my phone number.

Weeks passed, summer stretched far into September, and then to a mild and pleasant autumn, and I forgot about the man in the ice-cream parlour. Then, in November, near the end of my first year in the city, an unfamiliar number called my phone.

It took me a minute to figure out what the woman at the other end was on about. It was the aunt of the man from the ice-cream parlour.

She asked me to visit her in Harbin. She would sort me out with a new ID.

'Thank you,' I said. *Harbin . . . where is that?*

'A thousand miles from Shanghai, in the far northeast, that's where,' Yee-un said when I asked her. She had a good laugh about that.

I lied to the manager of the restaurant, saying that my mother was sick in hospital and that I had to see her. I bought a train ticket to Harbin. The journey to the northeast took almost two days. I arrived from the mild Shanghai winter totally underdressed for the snowed-under, below-freezing northeast. I stayed in Harbin just two hours, long enough to meet a tiny lady so muffled in furs she looked like some woodland animal, have an official photo taken, then catch a train back.

A month later an envelope arrived through the mail at my apartment. I opened it and held in my hands my own ID card. My new name was Park Sun-ja.

Sun-ja. I sighed. My sixth name.

The identity had belonged to a Korean-Chinese girl who, the lady in Harbin told me, had a mental illness. Her parents wanted to raise money for her care by selling her ID. It had cost me all the money I had saved in Shanghai, but now I was legal, or at least I could pass for legal with little fear of discovery.

As if sensing my new status, within days the city was lifting the curtain onto a much brighter side of life.

Chapter 31

Career woman

About a week after receiving my ID, I found a job that paid almost four times what I earned as a waitress. I became an interpreter and secretary at a South Korean tech company that made compact discs and LED lights. Its office was in Koreatown. My boss was one of the South Korean directors, and part of my role was to accompany him on visits to clients and manufacturing plants. I noticed that the Chinese looked up to South Koreans and addressed them respectfully. I had usually known them to scowl down their noses at North Koreans.

Everything had happened so fast. Overnight I had gone from waiting tables to sitting in boardrooms, interpreting in negotiations, learning how a modern company operated, and the culture in which business was conducted. I was meeting clients and buyers from Taiwan and Malaysia, and mingling socially with South Korean co-workers. The friends I'd made while waitressing knew me as In-hee. In my new job I used the name on my ID card and documentation, Sun-ja. I would have to take care that these two worlds never collided.

The company's products were manufactured in a plant that was modern even by Shanghai standards. The process was kept entirely dust-free. To enter we passed through a special machine that blew contaminates from our clothing.

The South Koreans treated me well. I could not bear to imagine their reaction if they'd known I'd grown up in the bosom of their archenemy. At times this felt surreal. We were all Koreans, sharing the same language and culture, yet we were technically at war.

***

I began to relax and enjoy life a little. I felt financially more secure, though there was still the enormous debt to my uncle, which I repaid in monthly instalments. I started to dress as nicely as I could afford. I noticed how the businesswomen I saw along Nanjing Lu judged their clothes well, and carried stylish accessories. I took driving lessons and got my driver's licence. The rent on our apartment became too high for Yee-un. She moved out, and I kept the place to myself.

I felt more confident. I no longer lived in the shadows.

The cloud in my sky was the absence of my family. It was now more than five years since that last call from my mother. That ache of longing I felt had not lessened. After the ordeal with the gang I was frightened of returning to Changbai. I had no plan. A sense of profound resignation crept over me. The path that led back to my mother and brother was becoming darker and fainter with time. I wasn't even sure I'd find it again. I was twenty-two years old. If I'd stayed in North Korea I'd have graduated from Hyesan Economics School by now. I'd probably have a government job in Hyesan, like my mother, a house on the river, and a network of trading contacts shared with my uncles and aunts. Would that have been so bad?

I pushed such thoughts from my mind.

I now felt safe enough with my new identity to eat at two restaurants in Shanghai that were owned and operated by North Korea. One of them, near my home in Koreatown, was the Morangak; the other, in the downtown Jianguo Hotel, was the Pyongyang Okryugwan, where I went often. These restaurants were foreign-currency earners for whichever bureau of the Party in Pyongyang operated them. The waitresses were selected for their loyalty, their *songbun* and their beauty. Because they were popular with South Koreans, I suspected also that they provided cover for *Bowibu* agents spying on overseas Korean communities.

The first time I walked into the Pyongyang Okryugwan and sat down I felt I was back home. The waitresses spoke Korean with the strong accents familiar to me, and wore their hair in the conservative fashion of North Korea, almost unchanged since the time of the Korean War. They were polite but reserved when engaging with customers. They knew they were each being watched by their co-workers. They were forbidden to form friendships with any customer. I guessed that at night they were confined to a dorm and not permitted to go out into the city.

One particular waitress often served me and, against the rules, became quite familiar with me. She was from Pyongyang. One time she astonished me by saying that she hoped to have a boob job done in Shanghai.

'You can leave here to have it done?'

She lowered her voice. 'I haven't asked yet, but it might be possible.'

That surprised me. Some rules could be bent, but I didn't think that was one of them. As soon as she mentioned it I found myself searching her face.

'You've had your eyes done,' I exclaimed.

She had double eyelids, a popular procedure among Korean women to make their eyes appear larger.

'Yes.'

'Here?'

'In Pyongyang.'

I almost dropped my glass. The elite in Pyongyang had access to beauty surgery? It seemed almost obscene given the poverty and hunger of most of the population.

Clients visiting my company from South Korea would often ask to be taken to these restaurants, and the behaviour of some of the men made me uncomfortable. There is an old Korean proverb, 'south man, north woman', meaning that the most handsome men are in the south of the peninsula, the prettiest women in the north. The proverb seemed borne out by the beauty of the waitresses, whose sheer unavailability turned some of the men into romantic idiots. They would become besotted, returning night after night to see a girl they had fallen for. I witnessed some of them handing over small, elegant gift boxes of jewellery from the luxury-brand stores. To my great surprise the waitresses would smile coyly and accept the gifts. I figured that the restaurant allowed this and confiscated them on behalf of the North Korean state. Not only were these men unwittingly donating valuables to Pyongyang, they were placing the women in a compromising and potentially dangerous situation. I don't think any of them understood the risk for a North Korean woman should they actually get what they wanted. But one of them was to find out.

One evening in my second year in Shanghai I arrived at the Pyongyang

Okryugwan to find it closed. The next morning the gossip was all over my office – a waitress had run off with one of my company's South Korean clients, a friend of my boss the director. Rather unwisely, the man had hidden the woman in his apartment. The North Koreans reported the disappearance to the Shanghai police, who questioned the staff, quickly identified the customer, and went straight to the man's apartment. Both were deported, he to South Korea and she to North Korea and her fate. I never found out for sure who the waitress was, but I had an awful intimation it was the friendly one who'd wanted a boob job. Two months later the restaurant reopened with completely new staff.

By my second year in Shanghai I sometimes forgot that I was North Korean. My friends were all Korean-Chinese or South Koreans from my workplace. I socialized with them as one of them. I spoke fluent Mandarin with a Korean-Chinese accent. My ID documents stated that I was Korean-Chinese. I was enjoying my work and felt that I was finally on life's upward curve. No one in the city knew my true identity.

I was jolted out of this insouciance by an unexpected encounter.

It was during my lunch hour on a busy street in Koreatown. A loud, man's voice behind me said: 'Soon-hyang?'

I froze. But then I could not stop myself from turning around to see who it was. I recognized him at once, the friendly businessman from the restaurant in Shenyang who'd put me in touch with the Chinese broker, someone who probably knew full well I was from North Korea. He was smiling, waiting for me to acknowledge him.

'You've mistaken me for someone else,' I said and walked away.

Fear breathed on me like a draught of night air. I took this as a warning not to get complacent. I was not so safe from my past. It could catch up with me at any time. For days after that I avoided Koreatown at lunchtime.

Just a few weeks later, I was recognized again, in a much more serious incident.

It was at a house party I was taken to by a colleague from work. She told me it was the birthday celebration of a charming man from Shenyang whom she knew only vaguely. When we arrived at this man's apartment, the music was booming and the drinks flowing. I was led across a crowded room to meet the host. When I saw him I blanched. I knew him. He owned a restaurant in Shenyang. I'd met him several times and had even been on nights out with him and others. I racked my brains for an excuse to turn and leave. But it was too late. He'd seen me.

'Soon-hyang,' he said. His eyes were wide with astonishment. 'I don't believe it.' He was genuinely happy to see me. 'What are you doing here?'

My work colleague gave me a puzzled look.

'Soon-hyang? No,' I said, laughing. 'That's not me, but it's lovely to meet you.'

He thought I was pulling his leg. It took me several minutes to persuade him that I was not this person Soon-hyang. My work colleague was listening to all of this. If anyone at my workplace realized I was not who I said I was, questions would be asked, and my documents examined.

Eventually he scratched his head and said over the noise: 'Well, I have to tell you that I know a girl in Shenyang who looks exactly like you. You must have a twin. I'm sure this is a secret only your mother knows.'

I had just about got away with it, when a fresh group of guests arrived. 'Soon-hyang!'

A woman was waving at me from across the room, and pushing her way through toward me.

It was a strange feeling, being exposed so publicly. A kind of exhilaration mixed with a sickening contraction in my stomach.

'Soon-hyang! I don't believe it, it's been a long time.' She hugged me, right in front of the man I'd just lied to. 'I didn't know you were coming.'

She was another acquaintance from the restaurant trade in Shenyang, a woman I'd met many times. There was no possible way I could repeat the lie to someone who so obviously knew who I was. Over her shoulder my eyes searched for my work colleague. She was caught up in a conversation with someone and had not heard this drama over the noise of the party. But the man from Shenyang, whose party this was, was staring at me in bewilderment. His eyes were saying, *Why would you tell a lie like that?*

I had to say something to him.

'I'm sorry,' I said with my head lowered. 'Please don't tell anyone.'

I wished I could tell him why I had lied about my name, but I couldn't. I went home filled with self-loathing. *Wherever I go, even in a country as big as this, the truth will catch up with me.* All I could do was stay one step ahead of it by lying and deceiving. In bed that night I cried for the first time in a long time. What I missed most was a North Korean friend I could confide in and trust, someone who would understand why I'd behaved in the way I had; who would tell me that it wasn't my fault, that she would have done the same.

As if in answer to a prayer, fortune sent me one.

Her name was Ok-hee, and I'd known her briefly back in Shenyang. She too had been a waitress, and belonged to the small circle of North Korean friends I had started making. I had barely got to know her when the police interrogated me. After that I had kept a low profile and shunned everyone, especially North Koreans.

It was actually me who saw her first, outside a cosmetics store in Koreatown. She was extremely surprised to see me. She was a slim quiet girl, with a charming habit of inclining her head and twirling her hair when spoken to. Over a cup of bubble-milk tea she admitted to me that her ID was a fake. Her greatest fear was that her poor Mandarin would let her down and expose her. She too was fleeing the authorities in Shenyang.

Ok-hee would become a great friend to me in China.

Chapter 32

A connection to Hyesan

Not long after meeting Ok-hee, I got a call out of the blue from Min-ho. What he told me transformed my life.

I was doubly surprised to hear him, not only because I'd been losing hope of ever speaking to my family again, but because I'd always thought that I would be the one making contact. It hadn't occurred to me that this might be in his power, too. He was speaking from Mr Ahn's house in Changbai.

After my initial elation, my spirits began to slide when he explained the reason for the call. He and my mother had money problems, he said. The cash I had given him in Changbai had been used up.

'Used up?' I was dumbfounded.

'Yes. Will you send some more?'

I had given them 5,000 yuan. A farmer in China makes 2,000–3,000 yuan a year. I figured the money would last them quite a while, even if they didn't earn anything themselves. After years in the Chinese workforce, I had developed an emotional attachment to money. My earnings were my hard work and long hours; my savings were comforts deferred. North Koreans have no way to relate to this. In the outside world, they believe, money is plentifully available to all. Min-ho seemed to think I just had to go to a money shop and get more. There was no point telling him that I had just paid a great deal for my ID, that my rent was high, and that I had a huge debt to repay after the disaster with the gang.

I sighed, and said: 'I'll see what I can do.'

He was vague about where the money had gone. I guessed that my mother must have had bribes to pay. It was only later that I found out that she had been helping my uncles and aunts.

At the end of the conversation, almost as an afterthought, he dropped another bombshell. This piece of information changed everything for me.

'Oh, and could you send me a cellphone?'

He said that people in the border area had started using cellphones to make calls to China, using the Chinese network. It was highly illegal, of course.

This took a moment to sink in.

The next day I bought a Nokia and a chip and sent it, along with 1,000 yuan in cash, for Mr Ahn to send to Min-ho.

The first time I called the Nokia, Min-ho answered. Something like this only happened in a happy dream. *He's passing the phone to my mother.*

'Min-young?' I hadn't been called that name in a long time. 'Is that you?'

I was hearing her voice, but it sounded strange and ethereal, as if she were speaking from another world.

'Omma,' I said, using the Korean word for mother.

'Yes?'

'Is it you?'

Just as with Min-ho when I heard his voice on the phone, the suspicion flitted across my mind that this wasn't her, that it was some kind of trap. 'Can you tell me what time of day it was when you last saw me?'

She laughed, and the laugh was warmly familiar.

'You left the house just after dinner, at seven o'clock on the fourteenth of December 1997. And you had those bloody fashion shoes on.'

Now I laughed. 'How do you remember so exactly?'

'How could I forget the night my little girl left me?'

She remembers the exact date and time. A lump rose to my throat. I felt horrible. *My omma.*

Then it was her turn. She too wondered if I was an impostor. My accent was no longer North Korean. She asked a few questions to which only I would know the answers. After I'd answered the last one, she tried to say something but choked on the word *daughter*. She was unable to speak. Then I too began to cry. Streams of hot tears rolled down my cheeks and onto my lap. We held our phones to our ears, a thousand miles apart, listening to the pent-up silence for several minutes without saying a word.

When I reflect on the pain I had caused my mother, I know it is something I cannot fully know. I may never fathom it completely, although maybe, when I have children of my own, I will begin to understand a part of her despair.

Hearing my mother's voice brought me right back to original truth, as if a mooring had been pulled tight. For years my sense of identity had drifted. In Shenyang I had sometimes thought of myself as Korean-Chinese; in Shanghai I even sometimes thought of myself as South Korean. Her voice reactivated something strongly in me to do with identity. All the lies I'd spun around myself fell away. I was born and raised in Hyesan, on the banks of the Yalu River, in the province of Mount Paektu. I could not be anything else.

She told me that she had visited several fortune-tellers over the years since I'd been gone, 'I don't know where my daughter is but I miss her.' She couldn't say I was in China.

'She is not in our land.' Every one of them said that.

One said: 'She is like the one tree growing on rock on the side of the mountain. It's hard to survive. She is tough and she is smart. But she is lonely.'

'She is well, do not worry,' another said. 'She is living like a noble-man's wife in China.'

She told me she had even invited a shaman to the house to perform traditional ceremonies for my good fortune and safety in China. My mother reached out to me in the void like this, half believing and briefly comforted.

'My daughter,' she said to me.

We got into a routine of calling every weekend. Each time, my mother would call me and I would call her back. We'd talk for one or two hours. Sometimes, we spoke for so long I would fall asleep. Her voice was so comforting. The charges for these calls came to about 150 yuan ($20) a month, but sometimes it would be 300 yuan for a single call.

I had been away so long that it took weeks to catch up on all that had happened in Hyesan.

When my mother had reported me missing, the police were highly suspicious. She had to bribe them. After that, as I'd dreaded would happen, she and Min-ho were placed under close surveillance, by the *banjang*, the neighbours, and the local police. She and Min-ho moved house to a neighbourhood in Hyesan where nobody knew them. At work she received a promotion. This was not a sign of favour, but a way of bringing her into closer contact with the authorities, so that she could be more closely watched. One day a colleague whispered to her that he had been ordered to provide weekly reports on her for the past three years. He warned her to be careful. After that, she quit her job at the government bureau and got involved in the same business as Aunt Pretty – sending Chinese goods on the train for sale in Pyongyang and Hamhung.

My mother admitted that she had started to have negative thoughts about the Party and system. But she used highly coded language. In all of our conversations, she made the assumption that the *Bowibu* might be listening. The secret police were trying to catch cellphone users but they did not yet have the technology to detect signals.

The *Bowibu*, in fact, had already paid her a visit. I found the incident she described particularly unsettling.

My mother arrived home from work to find two plainclothes *Bowibu* officers waiting in the house with Min-ho. The one in charge started to ask about me.

'He was extremely polite,' she said. 'It was chilling.'

He asked to see my photograph, and she showed him the family album. He leafed carefully through every page. 'She's very beautiful,' he said, and then: 'Would you describe for me again how she went missing?'

My mother told him what she'd reported to the police at the time.

He then made an extraordinary offer. If I was indeed in China, he said, and I paid 50,000 yuan (more than $6,000), I could come home to North Korea, have my old life back, and not face charges.

He sounded very conciliatory, but my mother baulked at the idea of me returning and publicly admitting where I'd been. It felt like a trap. She stuck to the story that I had gone missing.

My mother was convinced that she could get me home to North Korea without me having to admit anything, and she badly wanted me to come home. She had already spoken to the authorities about what would happen if I were to come back.

'They said that, as you were not an adult when you left, you committed no crime.'

'But the records will show I've been officially missing for years.'

'We can pay to have the record changed. Look, you're at an age when you should think of getting married. You have to marry in North Korea.'

'Would it be safe to go back?'

'I'll make it safe for you.' She was adamant.

We had this conversation many times. Returning to Hyesan, being united with her and my uncles and aunts, was a dream. But could I really cross back secretly and then report to the authorities as my mother was suggesting, saying that I was a child when I left and had committed no crime? The more I thought about it, the more I was tempted to make the decision to go home, and have the life I should have had. But a small insistent voice in my head was stopping me. A part of me knew that she and I were deluding ourselves. Returning now, after so many years away, was insanely dangerous.

On one occasion, my mother called me with an alarming question. Normally we spoke on the weekends, but this time her call came during the day while I was at work.

She sounded excited. 'I've got a few kilos of ice.'

'*What?*' I sank down in my seat, out of sight of my colleagues.

She wanted to know if I had connections in China who could sell it.

Ice, or crystal methamphetamine, had long replaced heroin in North Korea as the foreign-currency earner of choice for the state. It's a synthetic drug that is not dependent on crops, as heroin is, and can be manufactured to a high purity in state labs. Most of the addicts in China were getting high on crystal meth made in North Korea. Like the opium of the past, crystal meth, though just as illegal, had become an alternative currency in North Korea, and given as gifts and bribes.

'Omma.' My voice was a furious whisper. 'Do you know what that is? It's highly illegal.'

'Well, lots of things are illegal.'

In her world, the law was upside down. People had to break the law to live. The prohibition on drug-dealing, a serious crime in most countries, is not viewed in the same way – as protective of society – by North Koreans. It is viewed as a risk, like unauthorized parking. If you can get away with it, where's the harm? In North Korea the only laws that truly matter, and for which extreme penalties are imposed if they are broken, touch on loyalty to the Kim dynasty. This is well understood by all North Koreans. To my mother, the legality of the ice was a trifling matter. It was just another product to trade.

She said one of the big local traders brought it to the house because he knew I was in China and wondered if I could sell it there.

'Give it back to him. Never get involved. There are bad people in that trade, and they won't care if you're caught.'

She never asked me again.

Sometimes, neither she nor Min-ho would call for two or three weeks. At those times, I couldn't focus on anything. I became convinced they were in a *Bowibu* cell. I'd just stare at the phone and will it to ring. I'd made a special ringtone for their calls. It was a Korean comedy rap that went *kong kong da, kong kong da*. I'd start hearing the ringtone in my dreams and even imagine I'd heard it while I was awake. I would constantly check the phone. Then, weeks later, it would ring. My relief was overwhelming.

'Power cuts,' my mother might say. 'I couldn't charge the phone.'

This happened regularly, but each time I could never suppress my panic and paranoia.

On a weekend evening in spring 2004, I was enjoying a long chat with my mother. I had my feet up. The television was on in the background as usual, with the volume low. As we talked, I was distracted by news footage on the screen. Ok-hee was with me in the apartment. She noticed it too.

'Omma, I'll call you back,' I said.

I grabbed the remote and turned the sound up.

The footage replayed in slow motion. A group of men, women and children were making a desperate bid to rush past some Chinese guards and enter a gate. It was the South Korean embassy in Beijing. Somehow they had distracted the guards, who were now lunging toward them and grabbing them to prevent them reaching South Korean diplomatic territory. One or two made it through, but a guard caught one woman by her coat and pulled her to the ground. The violence he used was shocking. He picked her up by her waist and carried her off. One of her shoes was left on the ground.

The news anchor said they were North Koreans seeking political asylum.

Asylum?

Ok-hee and I stared at each other.

Chapter 33

The teddy-bear conversations

Over the following months, the television news showed similar events unfolding outside other countries' embassies in Beijing, and even at a Japanese school. Sometimes none of the North Koreans made it through the gates, and they were hauled away by police and plainclothes agents. The howls of despair on their faces affected me deeply. These desperate bids for asylum were being filmed by a human-rights organization to highlight China's inhumanity in refusing to treat escaped North Koreans as asylum seekers.

I thought of my uncle's tirade against North Korea when I'd arrived in his apartment in Shenyang over six years ago, and the bizarre truths he'd told me about the Korean War, and the private life of Kim Jong-il. I'd refused to believe him. Ever since, I'd closed my mind to the reality of the regime in North Korea. Unless it directly affected my family, I had never wanted to know. I thought the reason people escaped was because of hunger, or, like me, out of an unexamined sense of curiosity. It had never occurred to me that people would escape for political reasons. I remembered the two South Korean filmmakers I'd met in Shenyang, who'd offered to pay the brokers' fees for a defector trying to get to South Korea. I'd had cold feet because I thought I'd be treated as an exotic arrival from the North who'd have to give a press conference. Until now I'd had no idea of the sheer numbers – thousands each year – trying to escape, or that most of them did not want to live in China, but in South Korea.

The cellphone had transformed my life by reconnecting me with my family. Now, so too did the internet, linking me to what the world was saying about North Korea. I started discreetly researching online from cybercafés. My searches were narrow in scope to begin with. The first intriguing fact I learned was that so many North Koreans were now reaching South Korea that none of them had been asked to give a press conference in years.

I had been in Shanghai more than two years now. In that time I'd learned a great deal about South Korea from my colleagues. I regularly watched South Korean TV dramas. Some of them were such addictive viewing that Ok-hee and I would dash home to my tiny apartment and watch them together, lying on my roll-out mat. But I had never imagined myself *in* South Korea, until I saw these desperate people storming embassy gates. They were risking their lives. The reward had to be worth it.

The more I thought about it, the more the idea of living among South Koreans excited me. I was Korean and so were they. In China, however fluent my Mandarin, however official my ID, I would always be, at heart, a foreigner. This soon became the main topic of conversation between Ok-hee and me. The idea had taken a powerful hold over her, too. Could we go to South Korea together?

I knew I would do nothing so heroic as storming an embassy gate. With my Korean-Chinese ID I thought I could simply apply for a visa and fly to Seoul. From reading online, however, I learned that a visa wouldn't be easy. The South Koreans would need to be convinced that I would return to China and not stay illegally.

Ok-hee had contacts with other North Koreans living secretly in Shanghai. (She was the sole North Korean I knew in the city.) It was she who found a broker. This man had a simple suggestion: she and I should pose as South Koreans who'd lost our passports. We would report the loss to the police, then go to the South Korean embassy in Beijing to apply for new ones. The broker would prepare the necessary documents. He wanted an advance of 10,000 yuan (about $1,400) from each of us on his fee. After a long discussion in a café in Longbai over cups of melon soya milk tea Ok-hee and I decided we'd go for it. We gave each other a high five. I went to bed that night with a sense of destiny.

The next day, however, as we stood in line at the bank to withdraw our money for the broker's fee, Ok-hee was even quieter than usual, and continually twirling her hair. I knew her well enough to see that she had the jitters.

'I'm not sure this is going to work,' she said. 'The fortune-teller told me it was not in my fortune this time to leave the country.'

'It'll work,' I said. I felt confident.

'I think we only have a fifty per cent chance. It could go either way.'

Her fear was that the broker would either take our money and disappear, or the documents he produced would look so phoney it would be too risky to use them.

I told her she was being paranoid. I thought our chances were good. If all went well, we'd soon begin a new life. I could still call my family, using the Chinese network, and even travel to Changbai when I had a South Korean passport. Naively, I thought that if we didn't like South Korea, I might still eventually return home. I was still young. My mother was still trying to persuade me back.

In fact, Ok-hee's fears and superstitions were well founded. Fortune, as I would soon find out, was not smiling on this venture.

I started to wind up my life in Shanghai, and get rid of my possessions. There was something final about this that I found unsettling, and it was mixed with deep feelings of guilt. I knew that my mother would be dead set against me going to South Korea.

Over the following days, these thoughts sent my spirits into a downward spiral. It was the result of a routine medical check-up that tipped me into depression. I was told my blood sugar level was dangerously high. In my despondent frame of mind I became convinced that I was about to die. Like the time I was in the hospital in Shenyang after the attack, I thought that if I died now, alone in my apartment, no one would know who I was. My mother would spend the rest of her life trying to find me. The little money I had in the bank would never reach her.

I stopped thinking about South Korea. I stopped caring about anything. I lay awake on my mat at night, watching the fluorescent lights blinking in the new office block built barely five yards from my apartment. My thoughts turned suicidal. I did not feel able to talk to anyone, not even to Ok-hee.

I bought a small teddy bear for company. Because I worried that I might faint and die while I was eating, I sat the bear at the table where he could watch over me. At first, we didn't talk. But one evening after work I started talking to him as if he were a baby, in long babbling conversations. To ward off the loneliness of the apartment I set a timer so that the television came on thirty minutes before I got home. I criticized myself for wasting money on electricity, then ignored the criticism. Throughout that month, convinced that I was about to die alone without ever saying goodbye to my family, I was utterly broken.

I decided to blow my savings on expensive clothes. *Just for once, I'll live the good life*, I thought. I couldn't tell my mother that I was sick. Adding to her pain wouldn't remove any of mine. I planned to keep up my calls to her until the last moment. I thought long and hard about how to explain the coming silence, and decided to tell her I was leaving for another country and wouldn't be able to call North Korea any longer.

After a month living like this Ok-hee and other friends became so worried that they urged me to get another blood test. This time the results were normal. Apparently the blood sugar spike in the first test was to do with not having had any sleep the night before. I was given the all-clear, and all I had to show for myself were some overpriced clothes.

The self-pity and despondency lingered on in me for a few weeks, until an event in Hyesan shocked me out of it and pulled me back together.

Chapter 34

The tormenting of Min-ho

As part of my preparations to leave Shanghai, I had sent some money and almost all of my belongings to Mr Ahn's house in Changbai. After the shipment had arrived there, I travelled to Changbai myself, my first visit since the ordeal with the gang.

I arrived on a clear night in early October 2004. Standing beneath the trees on the riverbank, I stared across at North Korea. The mountains were black against the constellations. Hyesan itself was in utter darkness. I could have been looking at forest, not at a city. It was almost as if the sky was the substance. The city was the void, the nothing.

My country lay silent and still. I felt immensely sad for it. It seemed as lifeless as ash. Then, in the far distance, an ember – the headlights of a lone truck moving down a street.

Mrs Ahn greeted me with the news that Mr Ahn had died. He had struggled to recover from his injuries and had been very ill with diabetes. This affected me more than I expected. She invited me in. I saw his walking sticks and my eyes became heavy with tears. I had grown up with him always there, just across the river, a kind man my mother trusted. He had become my lifeline in China – the only connection I had to my family, to my past, to my real self.

Mrs Ahn helped me arrange the items I wanted to send across. They were everyday things, but they were rare and of great value in North Korea. I put my iron, hairdryer, some jewellery, vitamin pills, Chanel perfume, and all the other bits and pieces into two large blue sacks, and a smaller white one. I rolled up all of my cash, in US dollars and Chinese yuan, and put it in the small white sack. I called Min-ho and asked when I should send it.

'Tomorrow during the day.'

'In broad daylight?'

'Don't worry. The guards will be all right.'

Mrs Ahn hired two smugglers to carry the sacks across the river. When they returned, they said Min-ho had been waiting for them. Everything had gone smoothly. I breathed a sigh of relief, paid them their fee, and waited for Min-ho's call.

No call came.

Nor did he call the next day. I walked along the riverbank, studying Hyesan. This was my first proper look at my old home since I'd left all those years ago. In the week I'd spent as a prisoner of the gang I never got a good view of it. The only traffic was a couple of military jeeps, and an ox pulling a cart. I'd never seen one of those in the city streets when I'd lived there. I could see a smiling portrait of Kim Il-sung on the side of a distant building, the only dash of colour. Everything looked dilapidated and poor. Nothing had changed. In China, nothing stayed the same. Everywhere was such a frenzy of construction and reinvention that a city could be unrecognizable within a year.

I could not stand still. With each passing hour my desperation mounted. Something had gone wrong. I waited two more days in Changbai, staying in a cheap hotel, the only place I had found open when I'd arrived so late at night. I couldn't sleep from worry, and because the walls were so thin I heard men talking in the next room. They had strong North Korean accents. I didn't know if they were *Bowibu* agents or smugglers, but it added to a presentiment I felt in my stomach, of dread and impending disaster. On the fourth day, after still no word from Min-ho, I returned to Shanghai.

A week later, just as I was leaving work to go home, my phone rang. It was Min-ho.

'Nuna, what did you send?'

No greeting, just this blunt question.

'An iron, a hairdryer, some vitamin pills, other stuff,' I said.

I went through the list without mentioning the money. I asked him why he hadn't called. He ignored my question and asked again: what had I put into the sacks?

'I just told you.'

He hung up. I could make no sense of his call.

The next morning my phone rang again. A man spoke.

'I am a friend of your mother's,' he said. His voice was deep and reassuring. He didn't have a Hyesan accent. 'There's been a small problem because of the items you sent. I want to take care of matters for her, but I need to know how much money was in the sack.'

It was a curious twist of fate that I could be paranoid and suspicious of the most innocent and well-meaning people, but when real danger spoke mellifluously into the phone I did not suspect a thing.

'Thank you for helping her,' I blurted. I'd often wondered if my mother might meet another man. She was not yet fifty. I thought this might be a boyfriend.

'You're welcome. Now, you sent a hairdryer, didn't you?'

'Yes.'

'And an iron?'

'Yes.' He went through the list of items.

'What about the money? How much was in there?'

'I can't remember how much now,' I said. 'My mother will know. You'd better ask her. I really appreciate your help.'

'Not at all,' he said, and ended the call.

A week later, Min-ho called again. I was in a Koreatown supermarket doing my grocery shopping.

'You did well, Nuna,' he said.

'What do you mean?'

'Our calls for the past week have been recorded.'

I stopped still, in an aisle of globe artichokes and pak choi.

'That man you spoke with was a senior army commander. He was calling from a conference room. The phone was on speaker so that others in the room could hear.'

Others?

He explained how he had borrowed a car in order to pick up the sacks at 2 p.m. Everything had been arranged with the border guards. But as he was loading the sacks into the car, a ranking army officer appeared in the distance on a bicycle, saw what was happening, and started yelling. The guards fled. Min-ho drove off at speed.

That night, seven or eight armed troops hammered on the door of the house. They searched, and found the two blue sacks but not the third, the small white one, which Min-ho had hidden outside the house. He and my mother were arrested and taken into custody at the Hyesan barracks of the Korean People's Army. Under interrogation, Min-ho insisted that everything was contained in the two blue sacks. He denied any knowledge of a third white sack, even though the army officer was certain he had seen three sacks. They locked him in a cell. Shortly afterwards, two uniformed interrogators entered and started beating him around his head with rubber blackjacks, and kicking him. Still he denied everything. He knew how much cash was in the white sack – I had told him. He said he'd rather die than let these bastards have it.

Oh, Min-ho.

I stood frozen listening to this, with my basket at my feet and mothers with children jostling past me.

From her cell, my mother could hear my brother's cries and howls as he was thrashed. She hoped he'd confess immediately but he didn't. Minute after minute it went on. She couldn't bear it. She banged on the iron door of her cell as hard as she could and yelled that she would tell them what they wanted to know. She confessed straight away to the small white sack and told them where it was hidden.

The amount of money took the soldiers by surprise. They called in a senior army commander. He said he had never seen so large a sum coming across the border. He thought it was a fund sent by South Korean spies, and that I might be an agent of the South Korean intelligence service, the *Angibu*. That was when they made Min-ho call me. When they heard my voice, they exchanged glances. The fact I no longer spoke with a North Korean accent was not a good sign. It increased their suspicion that I was a South Korean agent.

When the call came from the senior army commander, of course I had no idea what was happening. It was just as well, because my responses and my relaxed manner convinced him that I had acted privately and had just wanted to send some items and cash to my family. The army officers then presented my mother and Min-ho with a deal. Under normal circumstances, they said, the two of them should go to a prison camp. However, if they agreed to say nothing, they would be released. They agreed. The officers then gave the hairdryer and some of the vitamins to my mother, leaving her a few in each bottle, and stole everything else, including all the cash, my hard-earned savings.

Months had now gone by since Ok-hee and I had last heard from the broker who was meant to be preparing documentation for our supposedly 'lost' South Korean passports. With the alarming events in Hyesan, and the continuing delay, we became more and more nervous. What happened next convinced me that our fortunes were flowing in a very bad direction.

In a brief and urgent call my mother told me that she and Min-ho were departing Hyesan immediately to stay with Aunt Pretty in Hamhung. She would not be able to contact me again for some time.

Just days after she and Min-ho had been released by the army, Pyongyang had ordered one of its periodic crackdowns against corruption and capitalism. A team of *Bowibu* special investigators had arrived in the city. The neighbours knew that my mother had been in some kind of trouble. They had seen armed troops at her house. They denounced her and she was ordered to appear at the *Bowibu* headquarters in Hyesan, where she was told to wait, and waited for hours. She knew that people who entered that place sometimes did not come out. She asked to use the bathroom. Then she locked the door, climbed out through a tiny window, jumped over a wall, and ran down the street. The situation had become too serious even for my mother to solve with her usual bribes and persuasion. But she also knew how it went with these campaigns from Pyongyang – if you made yourself scarce while the investigation was on, you could usually return quietly when it had all blown over, without consequences. She closed up the house, and called to tell me she was leaving.

That settled it. Everything seemed dogged by such ill fortune that I became afraid. Using fake documents to obtain South Korean passports now seemed like the worst idea I'd ever had. It would most surely end in catastrophe, with Ok-hee and me being repatriated to North Korea. Ok-hee agreed.

We called the broker and cancelled the arrangement.

It was three months before my mother felt it safe to return to Hyesan. She took the precaution of presenting a new Chinese refrigerator and a large sum of cash to the head of the investigation team in order to have her name removed from the list of suspects, and went back to her house. The next-door neighbours who'd denounced her stared at her as if they'd seen a ghost. She had to greet these upstanding citizens and smile as if everything had been a harmless misunderstanding. 'The rumour was that you'd been deported to a prison camp,' they said. They had expected government officials to come any day to take possession of her house. Once she was inside and had closed the front door she sank to the floor. She realized she'd soon have to move again, to a new neighbourhood.

Chapter 35

The love shock

Another year passed in Shanghai. I found a well-paid new job, at a cosmetics company in the Mihang District. I was the interpreter for the owner, a Japanese gentleman who spoke neither Mandarin nor Korean very well.

I moved into a better apartment in Longbai. I liked my new street with its shady sycamore trees. Families lived at close quarters. It was an aspiring neighbourhood that retained a faint edge of slum, typical of Shanghai. Pensioners in Mao-era padded jackets would sit on doorsteps playing mah-jong, oblivious to the Prada-clad girls sweeping past on their way to work.

Most of the friends in my social circle, with the exception of Ok-hee, were now South Korean expatriates. We dined out often, and made excursions on weekends. I was twenty-five years old. I couldn't complain about my life. The emptiness in the core of me was something only Ok-hee understood.

One evening in early 2006, my friends thought it fun to go for upmarket drinks in the sky-bar of one of the luxury hotels on the Bund. Several of these bars had opened, competing to offer the most panoramic views of the Pudong skyline across the Huangpu River. In the group was a man I hadn't met before. We were introduced. I felt an instant and powerful connection with him, like an electric shock. He was the most flawless man I'd ever seen. Glossy black hair swept back, a beautifully proportioned face, a straight nose that ended in a fine point. Tailored suit and cufflinks. His name was Kim, he said. He was visiting on business from Seoul. We sat in the window and began talking. Almost at once the two of us were in a bubble, as if we were the only people in the bar. We forgot about the friends sitting next to us. The lights dimmed from pink to gold, and the view across the river began to sparkle, illuminating the clouds. He seemed reluctant to talk much about himself, and chose his words carefully, a reserve I found appealing. When one of our friends chimed in that he'd done some modelling, I wasn't surprised. I liked his manner. He wasn't trying to flirt, or impress me, but I could see in his eyes that he liked me very much. There was a trace of arrogance – of the confidence that comes with status and money. But that, too, I kind of liked. Something cut me loose from whatever kept me grounded. I was floating on air. After what seemed like minutes, someone said the bar was closing. We had been there more than four hours. I had never before experienced time contracting in such a way.

He called me next day and asked if I'd like to have dinner. He had one day left in Shanghai before returning to Seoul, he said. I already felt strongly enough about him to know that I would suffer once he'd gone, so I said no. I was afraid of being hurt.

I lay awake that night, regretting this. *You fool. Now you'll never see him again.*

In the morning I called him back. I asked if he had time for a coffee before his flight. When I saw him waiting for me in a café in Longbai, and he stood to greet me, I thought he had an aura of light. I asked if he could delay his return home. He made a call, and said he could stay a few more days.

I prayed again, something I only seemed to do in extreme situations. *I know this man is not a match for me. We come from different worlds. But please let me date him for a few days.*

The next week passed in a trance. Until now I had never been open to the possibility of romance. My emotional devotion to my mother and brother had always eclipsed all other feelings. The sexual instinct I knew existed inside me was one I'd always kept deeply hidden. In fact, I had hardly ever even kissed a man before.

Kim's few extra days in Shanghai turned into a month. That month would turn into two years. Soon he had rented an apartment just a few minutes' walk from mine in Longbai. We had entered into a serious relationship almost from the moment we'd met.

Kim had graduated from university in Seoul and was working for his parents, managing a small portfolio of property investments they had in Shanghai. He opened a door onto a world I had only ever glimpsed before. Money had never been a worry for him. His life seemed effortless, his problems all highly rarefied – to do with rental yields, occupancy, presentations to planning officials. He seemed unaware of the respect people showed him, because he'd never been treated differently. He had no difficulty getting tables at fashionable French restaurants on the Bund. When he flew in China on business, he'd take me with him. He had a dark side, I discovered, a reckless streak, which I suspected stemmed from the fact that he'd only ever done what his parents had expected of him and had never made his own choices in life. On one trip to Shenzen he took me to a private country club set in landscaped tropical grounds, with gleaming limousines and sports cars parked outside. The club had a late disco bar where breast-enhanced women got up to dance on tables. I was shocked, but Kim looked mildly bored. A bottle of complimentary champagne was presented to us. I don't drink alcohol, so Kim drank it all. I saw only flashes of this occasionally. Most of the time he was sensitive, loving and quiet. He was discreet to the point of secretive. He was someone I wanted to trust with my secret. I felt more and more certain he was the man I would marry. And that meant that South Korea was back on my agenda.

For the first time, I told my mother that I wanted to go to South Korea. She did not take the news well.

'Why do you want to go to the enemy country?' she said. 'This could cause us even bigger problems.'

But I could hear the resignation in her voice. Min-ho and I were the same, she said. Headstrong, disobedient, obstinate. Not even a beating in an army cell had budged Min-ho. She knew the Hyesan stubbornness in me would win out.

'I have no roots in China. It's not my home. South Korea is at least Korean.'

'But you'll have to marry soon . . .'

With each passing year she was becoming increasingly worried that I was unmarried. She'd been looking for a husband for me, she said – a man of good *songbun* who could earn money, and whose family she could trust with our secret. She talked of candidates in Hyesan she'd started vetting on my behalf. Again, she was adamant that she could bribe officials and fix documents so that I could return without punishment. I didn't have the heart to tell her that my reason for going to South Korea was to marry a South Korean man I loved.

About a year after meeting Kim I quit my job and lived for a while off my savings. With my free time, I started investigating in earnest how I might get to Seoul. Reading the posts on a South Korean website set up by defectors, I saw that dozens of people were asking the question I had: 'I am illegal in China. How do I get to Seoul?' Defectors who had made it offered their advice. I had thought there had simply been a rush of people trying to get to South Korea in 2004. Now it was 2007 and the flow of defectors was greater than ever.

I called the helpline of the website in Seoul. A sympathetic lady gave me a broker's number.

With great patience, the man talked me through my three options. Because I had a Chinese ID I could get a Chinese passport, he said. However, as I was single it would be hard to get a visa because I would not be able to convince the South Korean authorities that I would return to China. The easiest way, therefore, would be to marry a Chinese man with relatives in South Korea who could send us an invitation to visit. I dismissed that idea out of hand. But the second option was almost as bad.

This was to pay for a fake visa and fly directly. It would cost about $10,000. It was expensive and seemed extremely risky to me. If the visa were exposed as fake, I would be sent back to China and investigated by the Chinese police, who would discover that my whole identity was fake.

The third option was to travel to a third country, such as Mongolia, Thailand, Vietnam or Cambodia, which would give any North Korean who crossed its borders refugee status and allow them to travel to South Korea. That route would cost around $3,000. However, it could involve very lengthy periods of waiting while my status was assessed.

When the call ended I felt a wave of depression. None of these options appealed. I was no further forward. But I wasn't giving up now. After almost ten years living in China, I was no longer accepting of my indeterminate status. I wanted to resolve it. And I wanted to marry Kim.

A few nights later Kim and I were dining out with friends. I wasn't feeling hungry or very social. I was still mulling over what the broker had told me. Waiters served enormous steamed crabs. We messily picked the white flesh from coral-pink shells. When my bowl was cleared away, I saw that my paper placemat displayed a map of the world, with Shanghai at its centre. A red Chinese dragon undulated across the top and another along the bottom. I looked for the other countries the broker had mentioned, Thailand, Mongolia, Vietnam and Cambodia. I wasn't even sure where they were. It took me a minute to find them. Although all these countries were in Asia, China was so vast that none of them was near Shanghai.

Kim said: 'You all right?'

I told him I was just tired. I folded the placemat and put it into my handbag.

Next morning I awoke at first light.

Something was niggling me about that map. I retrieved it from my bag and spread it out on the table. I looked hard at each of the countries the broker had mentioned.

A tingling sensation spread across my scalp as the realization came to me.

I don't need a fake visa. I don't need to seek asylum in a faraway country. And I don't need to marry a Chinese man . . . all I need to do is get to Incheon International Airport in Seoul.

I called Ok-hee. Her voice was heavy with sleep.

'I think I've figured a way,' I said.

I knew that with a Chinese passport I could obtain a visa for Thailand. If I could book a flight to Bangkok, via Incheon International Airport in Seoul, then once I was in transit in Seoul I would declare that I was a North Korean and ask for asylum. Visas were for normal visitors. I wasn't a normal visitor. I was a defector. I would have to book a return ticket in order to allay any suspicions at the exit immigration in Shanghai.

Next time Kim and I ate out with our South Korean friends I asked one of them if such a route was feasible (without telling him why). He said: 'Are you nuts? Who flies a route like that?'

He had a point.

My ticket would have to be for Shanghai–Incheon–Bangkok–Incheon–Shanghai, a route that defied all logic. How would I explain to exit immigration in Shanghai that I was flying to Bangkok, which is south-west, on a 2,000-mile detour via Incheon, which is northeast, when I didn't have a visa for South Korea but was only transiting through the airport?

I would need a convincing story.

While I thought about this I applied for a Chinese passport. It was processed much quicker than I expected and arrived by mail.

I then applied for a Thai visa. The travel agent sent my passport to the Thai consulate in Beijing and it was returned a week later, visa included. I was almost ready to take the plunge – buying the round-trip plane ticket.

Ok-hee, meanwhile, couldn't apply for a Chinese passport using her fake ID. That would never work. So she paid a broker for a fake South Korean passport. That would at least get her to South Korean immigration control. She opted for a different route – taking the ferry from Qingdao to Incheon.

One thing remained. The matter I could put off no longer. I had to tell Kim the truth about myself.

Chapter 36

Destination Seoul

On a cold sunny weekend in December Kim was making lunch for us in his apartment. I broached the subject by saying I wanted to live in Seoul.

'Why?' He turned the gas up and was jiggling the pan, stirring chopped celery with a bamboo spatula. He was pulling a face. 'Korean-Chinese suffer from low status in South Korea,' he said over the hiss. 'You know that.'

'I know.'

One of my reasons, though I'd hoped I wouldn't have to spell it out, was so that we could marry.

I watched him add squid, and mushrooms, and salt and pepper.

'You have a good life here – better than you'd have in Seoul. You're Chinese. This is your country.'

This was not encouraging.

A dash of sake and soy sauce, and lunch was ready. It was delicious, but I ate in silence.

'Is this what's got into you lately?' He was speaking with a mouth full of steaming food. His reasoning was that I'd be half foreign in South Korea because I was Korean-Chinese. 'I tell you, people there don't make it easy for ethnic Koreans from elsewhere. They treat Korean-Americans as foreigners, and look down their noses at the Chinese.'

'I have a particular reason.'

'What's that?'

I took a deep breath. 'I'm not Chinese.'

'What do you mean?' He was lifting his bowl to scoop more food into his mouth.

'I'm not a Chinese citizen. My ID is a fake. I'm not even Korean-Chinese.'

He put his bowl down. 'I don't follow.'

'I am North Korean.'

He stared at me for a long moment as if I'd made a sick joke. 'What?'

'I'm from North Korea. That's why I want to go. I was born and brought up in Hyesan in Ryanggang Province, North Korea. I can't return home, so I want to go to the other part of Korea.'

He dropped his chopsticks on the table and slumped back in his chair. After a pause I thought would never end he said: 'I never expected this. I've heard you a hundred times on the phone with your family. They're in Shenyang.'

'No, they are in Hyesan, on the North Korean border with China.'

He gave a huff of incredulity.

'How could you keep this from me for two years?' His mouth was taut with hurt. 'How could you lie to my face all that time?' He was far more upset at my deceiving him than at learning that I came from the enemy country.

'Please try to understand,' I said, keeping my voice level. 'When I was in Shenyang, I had a serious problem and was almost sent back to North Korea because I had told people the truth about myself. I came to Shanghai because no one here knew me. Only one North Korean friend here knows the truth. Now, you do. That makes two people.'

Again he was silent for a long time, looking at me, seeing me anew. The winter sun slanted into the room, casting his face in sharp relief, and I thought I'd never seen him so beautiful. Gradually the hurt went out of his eyes, and was replaced by curiosity.

I told him the story of how I crossed the frozen Yalu River, and of my life in China. At the end of it he reached over and took my hands. Then he surprised me by laughing. A relaxed, gentle, would-you-believe-it kind of laugh. 'In that case you should definitely go to South Korea. Let's spend New Year here, then go.'

I think I loved him more at that moment than I ever did before or after.

I booked the ticket for January 2008.

***

My mother remained totally opposed, but relented when she understood there was no changing my mind. Kim was too important in my life now, but I still hadn't plucked up the courage to tell her about him. She still hoped I would one day return to Hyesan.

At this time, I entered my details into a defector site called 'people search' to see if I could find anyone from Hyesan. I put in the name of my last school and year of graduation and left my email address. Within a day, I had received a message from someone who said she was from Hyesan, though not from the same school. We talked by chat. When she said she was in Harbin, I mentioned that I was in Shanghai. I was reluctant to reveal more. I didn't say it, but I half expected her to be a man, and probably a *Bowibu* agent operating in China.

'Do you have a webcam?' she said. She must have sensed my suspicion. 'I'll turn on my video chat so you can decide if I am a woman, and not a spy. Okay?'

The picture came on. In the grey-pink half-light was a smiling woman of about my age, but to my surprise, her shoulders and chest were bare. Kim was sitting next to me and peered closer.

'Are you naked?' I said.

'Yes. Sorry, I'm at work.'

Kim and I looked at each other.

'If a customer calls, I'll need to switch the chat, so I don't have time to put clothes on.'

'Uh, what kind of job is that?'

'Video chatting,' she said brightly.

She said her name was Shin-suh. She had been trying to get to South Korea but had been caught in Kunming and deported back to North Korea. Kunming is the southwestern city that North Koreans head for en route to Southeast Asian countries that accept their asylum requests. A year later, she had escaped again and was doing this job to make money to pay a broker to get to South Korea.

'You chose that job?'

'No, of course not.' She gave a sad laugh. 'Most of the brokers who help defectors are human traffickers. They help women escape, not men. They're paid to bring us to China either as brides or prostitutes. What I'm doing is a kind of prostitution, I guess, but it's very new. I'd rather do this than be a real prostitute.'

By this time, all my suspicions had vanished. 'I'm going to Seoul soon. If I succeed, I'll help you get there,' I told her. I was determined to help this girl.

As the date of my flight approached I got more and more nervous about the check-in procedure at Shanghai Pudong International Airport. I was booked on a flight for Seoul with only a visa for Thailand.

Kim said: 'If you're worried, call the airport and ask.'

The official I spoke to at immigration was dubious. It would not be impossible for me to pass through, he said, but it would be difficult.

'First, look at the map. It's hard for anyone to figure why you would want to fly up to South Korea when you are going south to Thailand. Second, a lot of Korean-Chinese go to Seoul and don't come back. That's a problem for both countries. You will need to persuade us why you want to do it this way. If you succeed, we will stamp your passport and you can pass.'

I visualized the inspection process at the airport, trying to anticipate what might happen, and rehearse my answers. They might ask me anything, so I thought I should take all my documentation along with my passport – my driver's licence, my ID; all the detritus of a prosperous, settled life in Shanghai. I was ready.

Kim came to the airport and said goodbye. We had decided that travelling together risked complicating matters. 'I'll call you from Seoul,' I said. I didn't mention the alternative, not wanting to tempt ill fortune. In a few minutes, I was at the immigration counter.

'You're travelling to Thailand?' the man said, pursing his lips.

'Yes.'

'That's a weird way to go.'

'Excuse me?'

'Why are you travelling via South Korea? Your ticket is for Thailand and you're transiting at Incheon. It's a roundabout way to go.'

'My boyfriend is in Seoul. He's booked on the same flight as me from Incheon to Bangkok,' I said. 'We're doing the same on the way back.'

He held out his hand. 'Let me see your ID.'

Now he is suspicious. Perhaps he thinks the passport is a fake. I put all my documents on the counter. That seemed to help. By now, I had been there for ten minutes as he examined each, and I was holding up the line. I was afraid, but stuck. After what seemed like an age, he stamped my passport, looked up at me, and stamped it again. I took my documents and walked towards the gate.

I had a one-hour wait before boarding. Although it was mild in Shanghai, I was wearing a padded coat in readiness for sub-zero Korea. I was sweating with apprehension. Any moment now, I thought, that officer at the desk would realize this was a ruse. Police would appear to seize me and take me away. I kept glancing around nervously. As soon as boarding started, I rushed to the front. I took my seat on the plane and kept an eye on the door for the police. Finally, it was closed and the airplane taxied for takeoff. The stress flowed out of me like air from a tyre. My head sank back against the seat.

But within minutes I had started worrying about what would happen at Incheon. I did not have the documents to pass. For years I had been a fugitive in hiding. This would be the moment when I *gave myself up*. I felt a wave of terror.

After just an hour, the pilot announced the beginning of the descent. Minutes later we were flying over Seoul and Incheon. My heart was racing. I was excited, and very frightened.

Suddenly the clouds parted and I had a steep-angle view of a city that stretched to the horizon in every direction I could see. It looked like some endless geological formation, vast colonies of sand-coloured stalagmites with tiny cars moving between them.

The border between North and South Korea is narrow, and the distance from Pyongyang to Seoul is barely 120 miles. Yet the two countries are as far away from each other as any in the world. I thought of my mother and Min-ho. I had called them on New Year's Day. Min-ho gave me the upsetting news that our mother was in the hospital. She had severely scalded herself at home. This added to the confusion of guilt and loss I was feeling.

A hydraulic whine, and the wheels were being lowered for landing.

Would I ever see her again?

PART THREE

Journey into Darkness

Chapter 37

'Welcome to Korea'

I joined the crowd of disembarking passengers, not knowing where to go or what to do. It felt like a race. People wheeling carry-on luggage scurried away as fast as they could. A few peeled off into the restrooms, and I wondered if they, like me, were buying time before some encounter with destiny at the immigration barrier.

For so long I'd thought of my arrival in Seoul as the end of a long personal journey. I had not given much thought to what would happen once I'd got here. I found myself dashing along with everyone else, in small nervous steps. A sign coming up ahead directed any transit passengers away from immigration. My ticket would take me to Bangkok, if I wanted a way out. My stomach was filling with butterflies. I breathed in, slowed my pace a little, and committed myself to the confrontation ahead.

The crowd fanned out into lines behind the immigration counters. I joined one for foreigners. We moved steadily forward, one person every minute or so, until there were five people standing in line between me and the immigration officer. My mouth was dry but my palms were sweating. I had no idea what I would say to him. With a mounting anxiety I watched him look carefully at each person, scan their passport, check a screen. Four minutes and it would be my turn. I heard the commotion behind me and saw the line lengthening as passengers arrived from another flight. When I turned back, the line had moved forward again. Only three people in front of me. I was starting to feel stage fright, and embarrassment. *Two people in front of me.* There was no way of avoiding a public spectacle when I stepped across the yellow line and declared myself an asylum seeker. *One person in front of me.*

My courage failed.

I left the line, and went right to the back.

As I stood there I noticed a room over to the right. Through an open door I could see officers in navy uniforms working at computers, and three people sitting in front of them – two women who looked Southeast Asian, and a man who looked Chinese. I guessed there was something wrong with their documents.

This would be less embarrassing than the immigration counter. I walked into the office. No one looked at me.

My heart began beating so fast it made my voice sound strange, like a tape recording. 'I'm from North Korea,' I said. 'I would like asylum.'

The officers all looked up.

Then their eyes drifted back to their screens. The man who had looked up first gave me a tired smile.

'Welcome to Korea,' he said, and took a sip from a plastic coffee cup.

I felt deflated. I had thought my arrival would create a drama, but at the same time something primal in me reacted. He had just used the word *hanguk*.

North and South Korea refer to themselves by different names in Korean. The South's name, *hanguk*, means country of the Han, a reference to the Koreans' ancient ethnicity. Its official name, in English, is Republic of Korea. The North calls itself *chosun*, a name that derives from the time of Korea's Joseon Kingdom. Its official name is the Democratic People's Republic of Korea. Such is the hatred and ignorance created by a bloody history and by propaganda that we in the North grow up associating '*hanguk*' with *enemy*, and all things bad.

'Well done for getting here,' he said. 'Please wait a minute.'

He returned with two men in the same navy uniform, and a woman in a dark skirt suit. One of the men carried a small scanning device. They asked for my passport and scanned it. They shook their heads and tried again. Something wasn't right.

'Are you really North Korean?' the woman said. When she'd addressed her male colleagues she had not used honorific forms of address. This convinced me that she was the senior one, the intelligence agent.

'I am.'

'Your passport and visa are genuine,' she said. 'North Koreans don't come here with real passports. They have fakes.'

'It is a real passport, but that is not my real identity. I'm from North Korea.'

I realized with alarm that she thought I was a Korean-Chinese pretending to be North Korean so that I could get citizenship in the South.

Then my hand luggage caught her eye.

'This Samsonite is real, too,' she said curtly. 'It's not a fake.' I hadn't noticed the Western trademark so I didn't understand why she called my case 'Samsonite'. I had bought it because it looked sturdy. Later, I learned that South Koreans are very brand-conscious. Only foreigners and defectors carry fakes. She looked me in the eye, as if she'd caught me in a lie.

'Tell the truth now,' one of the officers said. 'It's not too late.' His tone was half threatening, half friendly.

'I am telling the truth.'

'Once you submit to an investigation by the NIS there's no turning back. If you're Chinese, you'll be jailed, then deported to China,' he said.

The National Intelligence Service was the agency that processed North Korean arrivals. I had heard that if they deported me there would be a huge fine to pay in China. There was also a risk that the Chinese authorities would discover my deception and return me to North Korea. I had made it to South Korea and now I was not being believed?

I've made a terrible mistake.

The man continued. 'Tell us the truth – right now. You won't get into trouble. We'll let you go back to Shanghai.' He paused to let this option sink in.

'I am telling the truth. My name's Park Min-young. I'm willing to be investigated.'

Even the truth sounded strange and dubious to me. I had not used that name in more than a decade.

'All right.' The woman shook her head. 'It's your decision.'

I spent two hours being questioned alone by her in a windowless room, and watching her taking notes. When I thought we'd finished, two other men in suits and open-necked shirts arrived. They were older, one in his forties; the other, with steel-grey hair, in his fifties. From the way she greeted them, I understood that they were her superiors. Then she left. The men started questioning me all over again, from the beginning. They also didn't believe I was North Korean. The older man had an aggressive edge to his voice.

By this time I was tiring and getting hungry, and starting to lose the thread of the questions.

The irony. In Shenyang, I'd had to convince suspicious police that I was Chinese, not North Korean. Here, I was trying to do the opposite.

After two more hours they told me we were going to the NIS processing centre in Seoul. They led me through a side exit to a waiting car and driver. By now it was early evening and dark. I had been at the airport for five hours. The vehicle was a gleaming civilian car that smelled new. I sat in the back with the younger man. We drove past the terminal building and looped around on a six-lane highway lit sodium amber by the streetlamps.

'This is the way into Seoul,' the younger man said. He was the nicer of the officers who had questioned me. His steel-haired colleague in the front said nothing.

I tried to assess my situation. *I'm not in jail. They haven't put me back on the plane.* That counted as progress. This thought was quickly superseded by a less comforting one. *What would my friends back home think if they knew who I was with right now?* To North Koreans, the *Angibu*, as they call the NIS, was the sinister agency behind all road and rail disasters, building collapses, faulty products, supply failures and unexplained fires. Many people executed in North Korea, especially high-ranking cadres, are accused of having aided the *Angibu*.

'We've been busy,' the man said. 'This is our second trip to the airport today. Just before you landed, 150 North Koreans arrived and are now being processed.'

'How many?'

'One hundred and fifty. Each week we're getting about seventy from Thailand and about the same number from Mongolia and Cambodia.'

They were experiencing the biggest-ever surge of defectors, he said, caused by a huge crackdown on illegals in China – part of a social clean-up before the 2008 Summer Olympics in Beijing.

He asked me what I felt about the country I was now in, and started giving me basic facts about life expectancy, healthcare, average income. It sounded like a spiel he'd given many times. His aim was to puncture the false beliefs learned from propaganda – that people here are impoverished and persecuted, that the American soldiers stationed in Seoul gleefully kick children and the handicapped. North Korean propaganda is so grotesquely over the top that, in debunking it, the South Koreans have no need to exaggerate. As long ago as the 1970s, when South Korea began rising towards the major league of world economies, all it took for North Korean defectors to unlearn decades of propaganda was a tour around a Hyundai automobile production line, or the Lotte Department Store in Seoul. This even worked with highly indoctrinated commandos captured after failed secret missions to the South.

We were driving in fast rush-hour traffic along the Han River near Yeoido, a high-rise business district; great work-hives coruscated with light. I looked up and saw a vision of plated gold glass, which I recognized from TV dramas.

'The Sixty-three Building,' the agent said. 'A landmark. Sixty-three floors. We don't build them too high, or they'd be targets for a North Korean attack.'

So much light. So much wealth.

All this had been going on while I was growing up, less than 300 miles away to the north. I shook my head as the full realization of where I was struck me. For a moment I felt so excited I could hardly breathe. I was on the other side of my divided country. I was in the parallel Korea. It was vital and real: compared with the sloth and gloom of the North, the energy and light everywhere was astounding me.

We arrived at the monolithic processing centre of the NIS. Armed sentries stood guard outside. The huge gate opened automatically without a sound, and I felt my excitement wane. My 'real investigation', as the agents put it, would soon begin.

Chapter 38

The women

I spent my first night in Seoul in a general detention room shared with about thirty North Korean women. The moment I entered, faces turned toward me, and I knew I would have trouble. Most of the women were older than me. Their eyes took in my fashionable Shanghai clothes, and I saw resentment. I had come straight from the airport. They looked as if they'd spent years behind bars. Straight away, one of them demanded that I give her my clothes.

About twenty of them, I learned, had indeed just come from prison. They had escaped on an epic journey across China to Thailand, where they had been jailed by Thai police before being released to the South Korean embassy. The experience had brutalized them. They lost no time in making sure I learned every detail. Some 300 women had been packed into a space built to hold 100. Often, there wasn't even room to sit. If they didn't have cash to pay for a good spot, newcomers had to sleep next to a stinking latrine. In these conditions, tempers were continually at boiling point, and fights broke out. The Thai authorities released only a few detainees each week, so the wait lasted months. Since pregnant girls were given priority, some of the nastier women accused them of being queue-jumping sluts who'd deliberately conceived en route to Thailand. These accounts shocked me. I had thought that once defectors had made it out of China to another country they could safely claim asylum. But in many of the women's stories, the real nightmare had begun only once they'd left China. The exceptions were the few women who had escaped via Mongolia, where the authorities had treated them well, housing them in decent facilities with their own kitchens.

Violence was so casual among the women that the NIS guards had warned them: physical fighting was a criminal offence and would hinder their progress toward South Korean citizenship. Despite this, heated rows erupted almost every day in our room.

Almost all of them considered me soft, and a fraud. 'You would never have survived Thailand,' was a common snipe. 'You're not North Korean, are you?' was another. 'You look and sound Chinese.' I let them believe whatever they wanted – I owed them no explanation – but their attitude saddened me deeply. They were on the cusp of freedom, yet their negativity was so caustic it could have dissolved the bars on the window. North Koreans have a gift for negativity toward others, the effect of a lifetime of compulsory criticism sessions.

Lesbians were a frequent topic of conversation. In the humid crush of bodies in the Thai women's prison, I learned, everything took place in public, including sex.

The dominant woman in our room was a large, imposing figure with hair cropped like a soldier's. The others referred to her as The Bully. She'd established her primacy in the Thai prison by physically assaulting any challengers. I was told she was a lesbian, and that her girlfriend was in a separate room. The woman herself was candid about it, and made her attraction to me plain.

This was the first time I had ever known that North Korea has gay people. I am embarrassed to admit that I had thought of homosexuality purely as a foreign phenomenon, or a plotline in TV dramas. One woman in the room told me that homosexuals in North Korea are sent to labour camps, that they suffer alone and cannot even confide in their families. I had not known this either. In fact, this was the first of many things I was to learn about my country. My political awakening was only just beginning.

To avoid being bothered I had adopted a brusque manner, and said little. Unfortunately, this afforded me no protection from The Bully. I can only imagine how difficult her life had been in North Korea, and what she must have suffered there; even so, she made my time in this room pure hell. I am 5 feet 2 inches tall and weigh just 100 pounds. She was so much larger than me she could have flattened me with one blow. Initially I tried to befriend her, for my own safety. But as the days passed, teasing turned to taunting, with an increasingly aggressive, sexual edge. 'I won't do anything bad to you until you're asleep.'

Twice, a guard came in and told her to cool it. She terrified me, but I knew the one thing I should not do was show fear. Soon, she was singling me out almost hourly. She couldn't leave me alone. I realized I was going to have to talk back to her, even though she was older than me and, according to Korean culture, should be respected. Each day her taunts made me more tense and nervous, but I kept it hidden behind a mask of indifference. No one stood up to her, not even the older women.

One of the younger of us was a subdued girl called Sun-mi. We struck up a friendship of sorts. She had been caught three times in China, she told me, and each time she was sent back to North Korea, where the *Bowibu* kicked her and beat her with batons. They asked over and over if she had met any South Koreans or Christians in China.

'What are Christians?' she said. 'I didn't know, so they kept hitting me.'

The slightest noise, I noticed, of a door closing or of a chair scraping, sent Sun-mi into a bunker in her mind.

On an afternoon toward the end of my first week in the women's room, Sun-mi was watching a television show I knew she'd been looking forward to. I was reading a book. The Bully entered, sat directly in front of Sun-mi so that she blocked her view of the screen, picked up the remote, and changed channel.

It's funny how the final straw is invariably a trivial incident.

I heard a voice yelling. It was mine. It was using foul language, which I had never used before in my life, and it was speaking disrespectfully to an older person – also a first. In a scene that still seems unreal, I was directing a torrent of invective at this woman – the worst I could think of, finding within myself a rage I never knew I possessed. The others gaped open-mouthed. The Bully looked diminished, suddenly. I didn't stop until I was out of breath. In the silence that followed there was just the sound of my panting.

One of the oldest women there turned to her. 'This is what your behaviour's earned you. The disrespect of a young person. You've been humiliated.'

After two weeks in the women's room, a guard came for me. It was time for my face-to-face interrogation with a special investigator. I was taken to a windowless cell, and kept in solitary. It was grim, but I was relieved to be by myself. The cell had a wooden desk, two chairs and a metal-frame bed, with a blue woollen blanket and a small white pillow. It was five steps long and four steps wide. A bare bulb cast an anaemic glow; a tiny surveillance camera watched me from one corner. The door was kept locked. Beside it was a telephone that connected me to a young guard who would unlock the door when I needed the bathroom.

On the second morning, a middle-aged man in a suit entered, looked at me, glanced at his file, and left. A minute later, he returned.

'You're twenty-eight?'

'Yes.'

'Your name's Park Min-young?'

'Yes.'

'And your *present* age is twenty-eight?'

'Yes, that's correct.'

This man was my interrogator. I wondered why he'd double-checked and looked confused. The information must have been there in his hand.

He asked me to write out my life story in as much detail as I could. Some people submit a thick wad of paper, like an autobiography, he said. This document would form the basis for his questions. He also asked me to draw a map of the part of Hyesan where I had lived. I spent a long time doing this and put in as much detail as I could remember.

Often during the questioning he went silent and stared deep into my eyes, tilting his head slightly as if searching for something. It was unnerving. It crossed my mind that this was some bizarre form of flirting. After what the women had told me about the Thai prison, nothing would have surprised me. I tried to keep a blank face. I didn't want to give him any ideas.

I remained in solitary for a week. At first, I'd felt intimidated by my interrogator, but after a few days I looked forward to seeing him every morning at nine. He was my only human company. During one of my long afternoons alone, for something to do I practised my Chinese calligraphy, writing down my thoughts and feelings on a couple of pages. I described the oppressive bleakness of the cell walls and stated my conviction that a room was incomplete without a window. Then I screwed the paper up and threw it in the trash can. The next morning, the young guard came into my cell.

'Did you write this?' he asked. He was holding my crumpled sheet of paper.

So they're checking my trash.

'What does it say?'

'Just my thoughts and feelings,' I said. 'Is that allowed?'

'Yes,' he said, surprised. 'I studied Chinese at university, that's all. So I tried to read it. I just wondered why you wrote it.'

'There's nothing to do.'

Early the next morning, he opened the door and put his head in.

'It's snowing. Would you like to see?'

He led me to the bathroom, opened the window, and left me there. It was just before dawn. A bar of gold along the horizon illuminated the underside of the clouds. Snowflakes were floating like goose down, such as I hadn't seen since I was a young girl. It was far below freezing. Lights burned in every building I could see, and dotted all across the city were glowing red crosses. *There are so many hospitals*, I thought. (Later I learned that the crosses marked churches, not hospitals. I'd never seen such signs in North Korea or China.) It was magical. I thought of that far-off thundery day in Anju when I'd waited for the lady in black to come down with the rain. 'If you grab her skirt, she'll take you back up there with her,' Uncle Opium had said. I'd been scared stiff she'd carry me away into another realm. In a way, she had. And I was looking at it.

The next day, the interrogator smiled for the first time. The questioning was over, he said. 'I believe you're North Korean.'

'How did you know?' An enormous grin spread across my face. By now I felt as if I'd known him for months. 'The women think I'm Chinese.'

He made a modest gesture with his palms. 'I've been vetting people for fourteen years,' he said. 'After a while you get a feel for the psychology. I can usually tell when people are lying.'

'How?'

'From their eyes.'

I felt my face redden. That explained the lingering eye contact. He hadn't been flirting at all.

'Still, you were a curious case,' he said. 'You're in the one per cent that I've seen in fourteen years.'

One per cent?

'First, you're the only person I've met who arrived here easily, by direct flight from where you were living. Second, it took you no time to get here – just a two-hour journey – and, third, you didn't have to pay any brokers. That's what I mean. You just jumped on a plane. Was it your idea?'

'Yes.'

'Then you're a genius.' He was quite different now, talkative and friendly. 'I knew things would go smoothly with you, because you didn't lie about your age. Most North Koreans do. The old ones claim to be older than they are in order to claim benefits. Young people make themselves younger so that they're eligible to study for free. But you said you were in your late twenties. When I came to question you, I expected to meet someone in her mid-thirties, but you looked about twenty-one. I thought I had come to the wrong cell so I went back to check. Why would a North Korean who looks twenty-one admit she's in her late twenties? Because she's honest, I thought.'

I smiled, but a part of me thought I'd missed a trick here.

The next morning I awoke refreshed. It was the first sleep I'd had without nightmares since I'd arrived at my uncle and aunt's in Shenyang more than eleven years before.

Chapter 39

House of Unity

With a large group of others I boarded a bus early in the morning for the two-hour drive to Anseong, in Gyeonggi Province. The morning was clear and mild. This was my first proper look at my new country by daylight. The trees were budding with bright green leaf. Within the city, and surrounding it, far into the distance, were many soft green hills, an iconic Korean landscape familiar to me. As the sun rose, one crest of low hills would materialize in the haze; then the row behind it, and then, faintly, the row behind that. Hanawon, which means 'House of Unity', was among these hills. It is a facility in the countryside south of Seoul that enrols defectors on a crash course, teaching about the society they'll soon join. Without the two-month stay there, most North Koreans would not be able to cope. As many discover, freedom – real freedom, in which your life is what you make of it and the choices are your own – can be terrifying.

I was high on optimism. I vowed to myself that I would succeed in this beautiful country, no matter what. I would make it proud of me. I thanked it with all my heart for accepting me.

The facility is nothing special to look at – a complex of classrooms, dorms, a clinic, dentist, and a cafeteria, all surrounded by a security fence – yet there is probably nowhere else like it in the world. It is a kind of halfway house between universes, between the parallel Koreas. People who've crossed the abyss begin to adjust at Hanawon. Few find the transition easy.

We were given an allowance to buy snacks and phone cards. I immediately called Kim. This was the first call I'd been allowed to make since arriving in the South. He shouted with joy when he heard me. As time had dragged on, he'd become seriously worried.

'I thought they'd sent you back to China,' he said.

We had a long talk, and when I heard that gentle, relaxed laugh of his my heart swelled. I could not wait to see him.

Next I called Ok-hee. She had arrived by ferry and had been processed much faster than I had. We talked excitedly. She already had an apartment in Seoul, she said, and was going to job interviews.

When I replaced the phone I wanted to jump in the air. My new life was just weeks away.

Later, at the time I had agreed with my mother, I called Hyesan. She gave me the news that Min-ho had a serious girlfriend. Her name was Yoon-ji. My mother said she was very beautiful and from a family of good *songbun*. Her parents adored Min-ho. This brought a lump to my throat. I was never going to meet this lucky girl.

This complex in Anseong was for women only, and I shared a room with four other girls. I was told that every week the aggressive women I'd been with in the NIS detention room had gone out to meet the bus to see if I was on it. They were so convinced I was Chinese that they'd been taking bets on whether I'd been caught. When I met them again, however, they had softened. I learned that some of them were plagued by guilt over family members they'd left behind, or by memories of terrifying treatment at the hands of the *Bowibu*. They carried that darkness in them, so strongly that it obscured their hopes for the future. Despite the tight security, some of them obtained alcohol from the outside and would get rolling drunk, for which they were severely reprimanded by the staff at our morning assemblies. In this more lax environment, fights often broke out, too. The Bully was there, but she avoided me.

My nightmares had stopped, but curiously, it was here, in this haven, that many defectors' ordeals caught up with them, and tormented them in dreams. Some suffered breakdowns, or panic attacks at the thought of the super-competitive job market they were about to enter. Psychologists were on hand to talk to them, and medics too, to tend to chronic, long-neglected ailments.

Many arrivals found it hard to shake off old mentalities. Paranoia, a vital survival tool when neighbours and co-workers were informing on them, prevented them from trusting anyone. Constructive criticism, which everyone needs when learning a new skill, was hard for them to take without feeling accused.

I attended classes on democracy, our rights, the law and the media. We were taught how to open bank accounts, and how to navigate the subway. We were warned to be careful of conmen. Guest lecturers visited. One was a North Korean woman who'd set up a successful bakery in the South. Her self-belief inspired me. Another was a priest who introduced us to the Catholic faith (many defectors embrace Christianity in the South), but his justification for the celibacy of priests and nuns caused much mirth among the women. Another speaker was a kindly policeman called Mr Park who told us what to do in case of emergencies, such as needing an ambulance or reporting a crime.

We also attended some extraordinary history classes – for many at Hanawon, their first dogma-free window onto the world. Most defectors' knowledge of history consisted of little more than shining legends from the lives of the Great Leader and the Dear Leader. This was when they were told that it was an unprovoked attack from the North, not from the South, that began the Korean War on 25 June 1950. Many rejected this loudly, and outright. They could not accept that our country's main article of faith – believed by most North Koreans – was a deliberate lie. Even those who knew that North Korea was rotten to the core found the truth about the war very hard to accept. It meant that everything else they had learned was a lie. It meant that the tears they'd cried every 25 June, their decade of military service, all the 'high-speed battles' for production they had fought, had no meaning. They had been made part of the lie. It was the undoing of their lives.

We ate three good meals a day, each one different, and everyone put on weight. Eat as much as you like, the staff said. Once you leave here, it may not be so easy to eat well. In fact the instructors warned us that life, generally, would be challenging. It might not be easy to find a job, they said. We'd have bills to pay, and if we didn't pay them we'd get into debt. This was a source of extreme anxiety for those who owed large sums to brokers, who waited daily for them outside the main gates. The staff gave us the impression that the path to a happy and successful future was winding and obscure. I had hoped to hear: 'Work hard, do your best, and you'll succeed.' They were trying to manage our expectations, but this vague uncertainty made me nervous. Soon I would no longer need to live by my wits. I would have the freedom to shape my own life. But whenever I tried to picture what lay ahead, I saw not clarity but a swirling fog, and hidden in it were unresolved questions to do with my mother, with Min-ho, and with Kim.

To prevent the creation of a North Korean ghetto, the South Korean government disperses defectors to towns and cities all over the country. We can't choose where we are sent. Ninety-nine per cent would prefer Seoul but, given the shortage of housing, only a few were selected. Each of us was given a grant of 19 million won (about $18,500) for housing expenses.

I desperately hoped to live in Seoul. I thought my best chance of finding a job was there, and it was where Kim lived. I thought of him every day at Hanawon. I daydreamed about him in classes. I tried to picture his apartment in Gangnam, what it would be like to meet his family, his stylish friends, how he spent his Sunday mornings – with espressos, and jazz music, and stock-market news.

My mood plunged, however, when I realized that only ten people out of hundreds would be chosen for an apartment in Seoul. *Ten people.* So to avoid any accusations of unfairness, Hanawon selected the people destined for Seoul by a transparent lottery of numbers placed in a box. In a packed auditorium, a staff member shook the box, as if it were a game show, and picked out ten numbers. One by one, he called them out: *126, 191, 78, 2, 45* . . . Each winner threw up her arms, cried with happiness, and was embraced by her friends.

I was only half-listening. The whole spectacle depressed me. I was trying to imagine where else I might get sent in the country.

201, 176, 11 . . .

The man was looking around the auditorium. 'Eleven? Who has it?'

The west coast wouldn't be so bad.

'Eleven? Come on.'

A memory came to me of a summer on the beach near Anju, and my father telling me how the moon made the tide go out.

I felt a sharp pain in my arm. The woman next to me had poked me. She was pointing at the number in my hand. 'Eleven – that's you.'

Chapter 40

The learning race

I was met off the bus by Mr Park, the smiling policeman who'd taught us about personal security at Hanawon. 'You've moved to my neighbourhood,' he said. 'I'm here to help.' He was in his early forties and was from the Security Division of the National Police Agency. His calm authority reminded me a little of my father. He helped me find my feet, and to do the paperwork to apply for my South Korean ID and passport. Mr Park remains one of the most warm-hearted people I have ever met in South Korea.

My new home was a small, unfurnished, two-room apartment in the Geumcheon district of southwest Seoul, near Doksan Subway Station. I was on the thirteenth floor of a twenty-five-storey block. It had a view of similar blocks and the street. There was a large hill behind it. This was not an affluent neighbourhood.

Red Cross volunteers had shown me to my apartment. When they said goodbye, and my metal door closed, echoing down the corridor with a clang, I was alone. Not in hiding, but free. I stood at the window for a long time, watching life go by below, and the shadows of the buildings lengthen as the sun moved into the west. I didn't know what to do, I realized. I could go out and buy a mattress and a television and watch soaps all day; I could let laundry and unwashed dishes pile up; I could stand here and wait for summer to turn to autumn, and autumn to winter. The world would not interfere. Freedom was no longer just a concept. Suddenly, I felt panicked. It was so frightening and unsettling that I called Ok-hee and asked if I could stay at her apartment that night.

Ok-hee was very relieved to see me. After we'd embraced and congratulated ourselves on achieving our dream, we sat on the floor and ate instant noodles. Her own experiences since arriving in Seoul made a sobering story. Despite living for years in Shanghai, as I had, Ok-hee was not finding life here easy. She told me of an experience she'd just had after a job interview. The interviewer told her that he would call her to let her know the company's decision. After days without hearing, she phoned the company and was told that they hadn't called because it was impolite to reject someone directly.

North Koreans pride themselves on their directness of speech, an attitude that had been encouraged by Kim Jong-il himself. Foreigners are often taken aback by the bluntness of North Korean diplomats. Ok-hee's experience was the first hint I got that the two Koreas had diverged into quite separate cultures. Worse was to come. After more than sixty years of division, and near-zero exchange, I would find that the language and values I thought North and South shared had evolved in very different directions. We were no longer the same people.

The next day Kim flew home from Shanghai and came straight to my apartment. I melted when I saw him. It had been three months. We spent a long time simply hugging, pressing our faces together, whispering how much we'd missed each other. I'd missed his touch, his fragrance, his calming voice. He'd grown his hair longer. If it were possible, he was more handsome than he was before.

Later he took me to a big cinema complex in Yongsan. He suggested buying snacks to take into the theatre, and asked me what I wanted. I read the illuminated menu above the counter. It was in Korean. I couldn't understand a word. What were *na chos*, *pop corn*, and *co la*? Of course I knew these snacks, from China. But English transliterated into Korean words baffled me. And, as I soon found, there were many more. When people mentioned that they were in the *elebaytoh*, leaving their *apateu* to catch a *tekshi* to a *meeting*, I felt embarrassed. I had no idea what they were talking about. I needed to learn. In fact, I needed a new education.

I had grown up in a communist state where the Fatherly Leader provided for all. The most important quality for all citizens was loyalty, not education, nor even the capacity for hard work. Social status was fixed by the *songbun* of one's family. In South Korea, too, social status matters a lot, but here it is not hereditary. It is determined through education. And although education is a great leveller in South Korea – even the children of the wealthy get nowhere if they do poorly at school – it brings with it oppressions of its own. It is partly the reason why South Koreans are, according to surveys, the unhappiest people in the developed world.

Everyone I seemed to meet was desperate for a good education in order to avoid sinking to the bottom of the pile. In the stampede to avoid this fate, 80 per cent of school students go on to university. Even K-pop stars and athletes take degrees to avoid being perceived as the other 20 per cent. Mothers enrol their children in extra tuition from kindergarten to give them a competitive edge. The pressure mounts so much that school years can be torture. Because so many are awarded degrees, extra credentials are needed if a job candidate is to shine – proficiency in English, and so on. If, after all this struggle, a student gains a position in one of South Korea's star conglomerates, such as Hyundai, Samsung or LG, then they have made it.

North Korean defectors flounder because the education they received back home is worthless in a developed country. If they are too old to return to school, they have to opt for menial work. If they are young enough, they find themselves lagging far behind, and lacking confidence. I had been vaguely aware of this while living in Shanghai, but the reality began to bite during those first weeks in Seoul. I knew then what they meant at Hanawon when they said life would be 'challenging'. Without a university degree, I would be no one.

Because North Korean defectors are usually in low-paid, low-status jobs, they are looked down upon in South Korea. The discrimination and condescension is seldom overt, but it is felt. For this reason many defectors try to change their accents and hide their identity when looking for work. I was deeply hurt when I learned this. I had kept my identity secret for years in China. Would I have to hide it here, too?

With Kim's help, my adjustment was going more smoothly than it was for the other defectors I'd known at Hanawon, some of whom were looking for service industry or blue-collar-type jobs where they'd be fed at work. I didn't want to do that. I was done with waitressing. I wanted a life that wasn't day-to-day and hand-to-mouth. This took a little time to figure out. After a few weeks, I made the decision to enrol in a six-month course to become a certified tax accountant. I was good with figures, and thought this would position me well for a job. My fellow students were all women. I would soon learn from them how hard it was for South Koreans themselves to be happy in their own society.

Many of them had failed to find jobs with prestigious companies and had become depressingly resigned, believing that fate was against them. Minor flaws – being too plump, or too short – and misfortunes in love became exaggerated and were perceived as causes of failure. Still, I couldn't help feeling sympathy for them. Every country has worries of its own. Sometimes their complaints sounded like plotlines from TV melodramas.

Within only weeks of being reunited with Kim, I began experiencing a romantic melodrama of my own. When Kim and I had lived in Shanghai, our feelings for each other were so strong I was convinced we would marry. I'd waited for him to propose. But after two and a half years, he had not proposed. Now, I understood what had been stopping him.

Kim had grown up in Gangnam, the affluent, fashionable district on the south side of the Han River. His family had profited greatly from the boom years, becoming millionaires from soaring property values. He was highly educated and his parents were also graduates of prestigious universities. As crucial as education is in South Korea, it is not an end in itself. It is the means toward status, and social status is the insurance against the fear that everything may one day turn upside down. In a country that went from being third-world to the world's fourteenth-biggest economy in the space of one lifetime, hunger and instability are still lingering memories. If all else fails, a person with status will have family and connections to fall back upon. Kim's friends came from similar backgrounds. Some were well-known actors and models – part of Seoul's beautiful set. When we'd go for a night out, some of the girls my age would arrive in luxury Western sports cars. Their parents had impressive job titles in the Korean conglomerates. Yet I had nothing

– no family, no job, no degree, no money. I had no *back*, as the South Koreans say, from the English word 'background', meaning that I had no connections, no support.

I didn't feel sorry for myself. I'd shared a similar belief system in North Korea. Uncle Poor had grown up in a high-*songbun* family, but he'd ignored family advice, married the girl from the collective farm, and had sunk in the social scale. Kim could rebel against his parents, run away with me, and marry me. We might even be happy for a year or two. But the romance would fade. The disappointment he had caused his family would gnaw at his conscience. Life with me would wear him down until, as I imagined had been so with Uncle Poor, he'd conclude that his marriage had been a big mistake.

Kim had realized this before I had – probably when we were living in Shanghai – and had been trying to think of a way forward.

'I want you to go to university,' he said, driving me home after one of these nights out with the beautiful set. 'If you could pass the exams to be a doctor or a pharmacist, it would really please my parents.'

I stared ahead and said nothing. I had not even been introduced to his parents.

The next day, however, I investigated. The medical courses were expensive, and only the very brightest students passed the exams. Worse, the NIS had told me that because I'd left North Korea without graduating from secondary school, I would have to take a two-year course to become sufficiently qualified merely to apply for college. This titanic effort to please Kim's parents would take a decade.

In that summer of 2008, I watched the Beijing Summer Olympic Games on television with Kim and a large group of his friends at an apartment in Gangnam. When the South Korean athletes were winning, they cheered tumultuously, as did everyone watching in nearby apartments. I heard the roars rising across the whole neighbourhood. They chanted '*uri nara!*' (Our country!) and '*daehan minguk!*' (Republic of Korea!) I was cheering, too, but I couldn't shout *uri nara*. I tried to, because I wanted to fit in, but my heart went quiet, and the words wouldn't come out.

My heart was rooting for North Korea. I was proud to see my country winning gold medals. But I couldn't cheer. North Korea was the enemy.

Later, I turned down Kim's offer of dinner and went home to my little apartment, where I could still hear distant cheering and celebrations from the other blocks. The experience had depressed me. That night I lay awake on my mattress, watching the reflected glow of the city on the clouds. The sky over Seoul was a thick amber broth that obscured the stars. In Hyesan, I could see the Milky Way from my bedroom window.

The Olympics sparked a full-blown identity crisis in me. It had probably been building for a while, fuelled by the insecurity I was feeling over Kim, and by my lack of education.

Am I North Korean? That's where I was born and raised. Or am I Chinese? I became an adult there, didn't I? Or am I South Korean? I have the same blood as people here, the same ethnicity. But how does my South Korean ID make me South Korean? People here treat North Koreans as servants, as inferiors.

I wanted to belong, like everyone else around me did, but there was no country I could say was mine. I had no one to tell me that many other people in the world have a fragmented identity; that it doesn't matter. That who we are as a person is what's important.

As if reaching for a well-thumbed book, my mind turned again to thoughts of going home to North Korea. But now that I was a South Korean citizen it was illegal for me to go to the North. If I did go, at best the North would parade me for propaganda purposes as someone who'd rejected the South (this happened with some people who decided to go home); at worst I'd be imprisoned or shot.

My mother could tell I was lonely and unhappy. I spoke to her every Sunday. But I did not want to burden her. She had worries of her own. Ever since armed troops had searched her house after I'd sent the money over with the three sacks, she'd been living under a cloud. The incident had drawn the attention of the *Bowibu*, and whenever a crackdown was ordered from Pyongyang she'd find herself on a list of people to be banished to internal exile in some remote mountain village. Each time she'd have to pay an enormous bribe to the investigators to have her name removed, but feared she could not go on doing this for much longer.

Had they known the truth – that her daughter had defected to the South – they would have had no hesitation in arresting her and Min-ho.

Life in Hyesan was getting worse, she said. And hunger had returned.

I began to feel desperate for her. Surely it was time for her to come to South Korea?

Gently, each Sunday, I began to raise the possibility of her coming to Seoul.

'I will never, ever leave,' she would say.

Slowly, I pulled myself out of my despondency. I had taken such risks to get to here. I couldn't give up now. I had made a promise to myself, on that bright morning on the way to Hanawon, that I would succeed in this country and make it proud of me. I would steel myself to succeed – no matter what. There would be no failure.

After working very hard, I obtained my accounting qualification at the end of 2008. A law firm offered me a job with a monthly salary of 1.3 million won (about $1,200), a respectable sum. But after some thought I turned it down. I figured that without a degree I would never be able to move on to anything greater.

I started to contemplate the gruelling university entrance exam.

By the time I qualified for university I would be thirty years old. I would be thirty-four when I graduated. Could I do it? I posted the question in an online question forum. It provoked a lot of comments. 'It will be tough working alongside people ten years younger than you,' one said. 'Give it up and get a job,' was another. Another common response was: 'Your best bet is to get married.' They might have added *before it's too late*.

The one person who encouraged me was Mr Park. He really wanted me to succeed, and encouraged me to go for it. Before applying, however, there was something I thought I should do – get a new name.

In Hanawon I had heard about defectors whose family back home . had been punished when the *Bowibu* learned they were in the South. There were almost certainly spies among the defectors, who reported back to Pyongyang. For these reasons, many changed their names. This wasn't the only motive. Others did it because fortune-tellers told them a name change would bring better luck.

When I told Mr Park I wanted to have a new name with a special meaning, he introduced a *jakmyeongso*, a professional name-giver. I paid the lady 50,000 won ($45) and gave her my date of birth and the two parts of my given name.

'One of these names has brought you ill fortune,' she said softly.

I couldn't help smiling. I was thinking of my mother taking me to Daeoh-cheon all those years ago for a dawn reading with that grizzle-headed mystic. This one was more presentable, a middle-aged lady with a bubble perm. I immediately found myself in a familiar frame of mind when I watched her close her eyes. I thought the whole thing was ridiculous, yet I wanted to believe every word.

I decided to help her.

'I'm always feeling cold.'

'Yes,' she said, taking the hint. 'Yes, you have a yin not a yang consti-tution, so you need to warm yourself with a warm name.' She presented me with five choices of name. I chose Hyeon-seo.

'With this name, the strength of the sun will shine on you.' But she warned me: 'This name is so strong it could bring you great fortune, or it could overpower you and bring great misfortune. Therefore, I suggest you also take a nickname, to balance out the overwhelmingly positive force of "Hyeonseo".'

No, I thought. *No more names. Hyeonseo it is.*

In the summer of 2009, I applied to several universities under my new name. To gain an added credential I started studying English from a textbook, but found it extremely difficult. If any universities were going to invite me for interview or to sit the entrance exam, they would do so in September and October. I would have to wait a few weeks. If they accepted me, my next few years would be divided predictably into semesters and vacations.

But just as life was starting to feel settled and structured, I was pitched straight back into the abyss.

Chapter 41

Waiting for 2012

'People may be hungry now,' my mother said. Her voice trailed off uncertainly. 'But things will get better. We're all waiting for 2012.'

I groaned. This date was the centenary of the birth of Kim Il-sung, now less than three years away. For years, Party propaganda had been trumpeting it as the moment when North Korea would achieve its goal of becoming a 'strong and prosperous nation'.

I knew nothing would change, but how could she? She might grumble about life, but she had no perspective and still shared the regime's values. It is hard for outsiders to grasp how difficult it is for North Koreans to arrive at a point where they accept that the Kim regime is not only very bad, but also very wrong. In many ways our lives in North Korea are normal – we have money worries, find joy in our children, drink too much, and fret about our careers. What we don't do is question the word of the Party, which could bring very serious trouble. North Koreans who have never left don't think critically because they have no point of comparison – with previous governments, different policies, or with other societies in the outside world. So my mother, along with everyone else, was waiting for the mythical dawn of 2012.

'Omma, you said life there is getting worse. It will never happen,' I said. 'Listen. I've met so many North Korean families here. Usually one person comes first, then from here they arrange to bring the rest of the family out.'

'I've seen too many executions of people who've tried to get out,' she snapped. 'I don't want Min-ho jailed because of us. I don't want to be shot at Hyesan Airport with your aunts and uncles sitting in the front row.'

'But Omma, life's so much better here. You can have whatever you like. The government gives us plenty of money to settle.'

'You said you weren't happy.'

'I was just moaning.' My theme was starting to break her resistance. 'I haven't seen you in nearly twelve years. My twenties have come and gone and I never saw you once. I want to marry and have children, but what's the point if you'll never see us? If we don't do something now, we'll never meet again in our lives.'

There was a long pause and I realized she was crying quietly. The thought of being separated for ever was unbearable, she said.

I kept the pressure up over three or four weeks. 'Come for eighteen months,' I said. 'If you don't like it, you can always go home. It'll be easy.'

I was lying, of course, but I had to convince her and I believed the lie was justified. We'd be reunited, and she would be able to live free from danger. I pushed this theme because she had already begun researching the process of getting the records changed to make it appear as if she'd never left.

Still, she wavered.

Then, a sensational event in Hyesan changed her mind. Wanted posters went up all over the city with the face of a well-known Party cadre, Seol Jung-sik, the provincial secretary for the Socialist Youth League. Soon the gossip was that he'd defected. Locals in Hyesan were astonished. My mother thought, *If a big shot like Seol can leave, why can't I?* The timing could not have been better.

On the Sunday after it happened she came out with it. 'I've made up my mind. I'll go.' She kept her language vague in case the *Bowibu* was listening. She was nervous. 'Will it be safe?'

I almost yelled, I was so happy. 'I will make it one hundred per cent safe,' I said, knowing this was a promise only the president of China could make.

'Your brother won't go.'

This brought me down to earth. 'But he must. You must both come together. It'll be too dangerous for him to stay.'

'He'll be all right. He's got his own business, and he's going to marry Yoon-ji.'

'Marry?'

This was news to me. I knew about Min-ho's business. He was smuggling in motorbikes – the Chinese models Haojue and Shuangshi, but sometimes also high-end Japanese brands. In summer he would take the bikes apart and float them across the river on a raft. In the winter, he would ride them over the ice. He paid the border guards 10 per cent of whatever he made, and gave them cigarettes, Chinese beer or tropical fruits. Min-ho was resourceful and street-smart – his earliest memory of Hyesan was the famine, and it had toughened him – but, like me, he was stubborn. Once he set his mind on a course of action, it was difficult to change.

I should have felt happy for him. Yoon-ji, my mother had told me, was incredibly beautiful. When she had turned eighteen, special scouts that selected musicians and beautiful girls to attend upon Kim Jong-il came to her school and singled her out to join the Dear Leader's Joy Division. But to prevent her being taken away, Yoon-ji's mother had pretended that her daughter had health problems.

Min-ho said he'd help Omma get into China, but that he was staying behind. Yoon-ji's mother worked for the *Bowibu*, he said. He believed this would protect him. The family could be trusted with our secret.

There was nothing more I could say. It was clear that Min-ho felt strongly about this girl.

I started to plan. My first step was to contact the Reverend Kim, a middle-aged Protestant pastor whose organization demonstrated in Insadong, a popular market area of Seoul, every Saturday for North Korean human rights. Rowdy demonstrations are part of everyday life in Seoul. Any time I'd go downtown I'd see a lone protester outside a government building with a placard advertising his grievance, or workers with slogans on their headbands singing songs and punching the air. The first time I saw them I was amazed – citizens here could shout out their complaints without being arrested and publicly executed.

Using his contacts in China, Reverend Kim had helped hundreds of people escape. His specialty was shepherding defectors through the south-western Chinese city of Kunming and over the border into Vietnam, from where they could make their way to the South Korean embassy.

The journey across China is more than 2,000 miles and takes a week. It is dangerous, so much so that some escapers carry poison with them to kill themselves if they're caught, rather than face the consequences of being returned to the North. As South Korea does not wish to antagonize China by accepting North Korean asylum seekers at its embassy in Beijing and its consulates throughout China, it colludes with the Chinese authorities in keeping them away. Even if a defector makes it through an embassy gate, that person may have a very long wait. Some have waited seven years before China has granted permission for them to leave.

I found Reverend Kim on the sidewalk at one of his Saturday protests. Over the noisy chanting of a sit-down demonstration he told me that my mother would have to cross the Yalu River by herself, but that he could guide her from that point onward. It would cost $4,000. Alternatively, she could make her own way across China to Kunming and be guided from there to the South Korean embassy in Vietnam. That would cost $2,000. She would be in the hands of a Chinese broker arranged by him. I thanked him, and took his phone number, but I had a sinking feeling.

Brokers.

That evening I mulled this over in my apartment. Kim called and asked what I'd done with my day. I opened my mouth to tell him, and changed my mind. He would not understand. He would tell me it was insanely dangerous, and wonder why I wasn't content to let things be. He understood little about North Korea. It was the same with his friends – most of them did not want to think about the North, let alone talk about it. I would see a shutter come down behind their eyes if I mentioned it. The North was their mad uncle in the attic. A subject best avoided.

I had hoped Reverend Kim could somehow avoid using brokers, but I knew that even humanitarian organizations had to rely on some unsavoury characters at local level. As these brokers were breaking the law and their motivation was money, they were seldom trustworthy or pleasant. If a situation turned dangerous, they'd vanish like morning mist and leave their clients in the hands of the police, or worse. I would never forgive myself if that happened to my mother; if she were returned to the North. After talking it over with Ok-hee, I decided to use the broker only for the very final part of the journey – getting out of China.

I would go to Changbai, and meet my mother on the riverbank. I would guide her across China to Kunming myself.

Chapter 42

A place of ghosts and wild dogs

I pressed the bell feeling that familiar flutter of nerves. Suddenly I was seventeen again, standing outside this very door, at the start of my adventure. I shivered. It was much colder in northern China than it was in Seoul. I was wearing a thick, hooded sweatshirt, jeans, sneakers, and carried all my stuff in a backpack. I heard someone coming, and a latch jangling.

'My goodness,' my aunt said, looking me up and down. 'You've changed. You were only a girl when I saw you last.'

The difference in her appearance surprised me, too. She had become an old lady, thin and stooped, with swollen, rheumatic fingers. It immediately made me think how much older my mother must have become.

My aunt invited me in. She had redecorated the apartment, and showed me around. The guitar was still in my old room. My uncle was away on business, she said.

I had long repaid the debt I owed him, and had stayed in touch. I hoped time had healed the hurt I'd caused all those years ago when I'd fled this place to avoid marrying Geun-soo. I'd heard that he'd married, and was glad for him. It had released me from my penance never to marry. I wondered whether he had provided his fearsome mother with the grandchildren she'd wanted. I didn't dare ask.

My aunt was warm and welcoming. It was clear that all was forgiven, if not forgotten. I was relieved, because I needed her help again. And it was a big favour to ask.

'My ID card?' She was taken aback.

I lowered my eyes. 'I'll mail it back to you in two weeks' time.'

For my plan to work, I needed to borrow a genuine Chinese ID that my mother could use. When I explained this, my aunt laughed. I was grateful for that laugh.

'Well . . . I suppose so.'

I had timed everything finely, and couldn't stay long at my aunt's. Having taken her ID, I told her apologetically that I had to leave immediately. She shook her head, gave me 500 yuan (about $75), and wished me all the luck in the world. Within an hour I was on an overnight coach to Changbai.

I stowed my aunt's ID carefully in my wallet. I had enough cash with me for the broker's fee, for food, accommodation and travel. The money was the last of my savings from Shanghai. I'd been living off that and my small monthly stipend of 350,000 won ($320) from the South Korean government.

It was now the end of September 2009. All going well, in two weeks' time I would be back in Seoul, and my mother – a shudder of apprehension and excitement ran through me – my dear omma would be safe in the South Korean embassy in Ho Chi Minh City, claiming asylum. This meant I would still have enough time to take the entrance exams and attend interviews at any universities that had accepted my application for the 2010 academic year beginning the following spring.

Mr Park the policeman had warned me to be extremely wary. 'Tell nobody you're a defector.' There had been cases of Chinese police handing defectors over to the *Bowibu* even though they were travelling on valid South Korean passports. So as soon as I'd passed through immigration at Shenyang, I hid my South Korean passport and took out my old Chinese ID. This made me feel safer.

It was 3 a.m. by the time I arrived in Changbai. I checked into a two-star hotel to make preparations. Once Min-ho had brought my mother across, my plan was to have a few days' vacation with them both before Min-ho returned to Hyesan. To help them blend in as Chinese I bought some trousers for him, and some colourful, good-quality clothes for my mother, who would have to throw away any North Korean-made items.

I went to several hotels in the town to see which would be safest, and decided on the Changbai Binguan, the hotel with the largest lobby, and where we wouldn't have to walk past the reception desk every time we came and went. It was also the most expensive hotel in town, and the last place Chinese police or *Bowibu* agents would expect to find an escaped North Korean. I checked in the next day and took a room with two double beds.

Min-ho had confirmed the plan – he would bring our mother over the next evening between 7 and 8 p.m. He told me where on the river they would cross. I knew the spot: there was a derelict house on the Chinese side.

My mother had prepared her departure ingeniously. If she had done what most escaping families did – leave everything and disappear – the authorities would come after Min-ho. But she also knew that if she sold the house, the authorities would still want to know where she'd gone. Either way, Min-ho would be questioned. To pre-empt this, she sold her house and told the city authorities that she was moving to Hamhung. However, instead of registering her residency in Hamhung, she bribed a hospital doctor there to file her death certificate and funeral documents. If the *Bowibu* investigated, it would appear as if she had died en route to Hamhung.

At 6.15 p.m. next evening, I began to get ready. I was frightened yet strangely exhilarated, my senses sharpened, my body tense with nervous energy. I set my phone to silent, dressed myself entirely in black, picked up the bag in which I'd put the new clothes for my mother and Min-ho, and walked calmly and purposefully through the hotel lobby. Outside I hailed a cab and directed the driver to take me to the point where the town ended, about 200 yards from the river. There, at the end of a row of low buildings, was the derelict house among the trees. I crouched down behind an old garden wall, and waited. The place was cold and damp and smelled of mouldering leaves and animal droppings. I peeped over the wall and saw North Korean border patrols passing on the opposite bank. In the half-tones beneath the trees, I felt camouflaged.

The sunset looked ominous, a palette of murky reds and yellows. On the other side of the water Hyesan seemed lifeless, a city dug from rock, or an intricate cemetery. A place of ghosts and wild dogs. I felt no nostalgia for it. Only defiance. *I dare you not to give me my mother.*

An icy breeze lifted swirls of leaves, and sent wavelets lapping across the surface of the river. If I hadn't felt so alive with nerves and excitement

I would have found somewhere warmer to wait. It was too cold to stand still.

Not long now. *I'm about to meet my omma again.* I could hardly believe this was happening.

Min-ho had told me he would lead her waist-high through the water, and help her up one of the ladders on the Chinese bank. *The water must be freezing.*

I checked the time on my phone every minute for an hour.

At 8 p.m. there was still no sign of them. A keening cry from a night bird made me jump.

A quarter of an hour later, night had fallen like a cloud of ash. I could see nothing on the other side of the river. The power was out in Hyesan.

The blood was no longer circulating in my hands and feet. The temperature was dropping by the minute. I didn't know whether my teeth were chattering from cold or panic. *Where are they?*

Another hour went by.

Then out of the darkness someone called: '*Ya!*'

My heart went into overdrive. Along the North Korean bank a beam of light was bouncing on the dirt track. Border guards, patrolling in pairs, greeting another patrol. They were passing every two minutes. I didn't remember there being so many guards. They were just fifty yards away from me. I could hear their conversation.

One patrol had a dog, which turned its head toward me and barked, setting off a dozen other dogs. A memory came to me, long suppressed, of seeing blood on the ice one morning. A failed escape. I put my hands to my ears. If the dogs would stop barking—

My phone was buzzing.

Min-ho's voice was fast and tense.

'We've had a problem.'

Chapter 43

An impossible dilemma

Quickly, Min-ho explained that just as he and my mother had been about to cross, they had walked straight into a border guard. Luckily he was someone Min-ho did business with. The guard told him there was a general alert out for a high-ranking family from Pyongyang who were attempting to escape this very night. There were extra guards all along the river, he said, as well as *Bowibu* agents. The whole area was in lockdown. The guard then asked Min-ho to stay a while and keep him company while he kept a lookout. At that moment, my mother had said good night, and had walked away.

Min-ho said he and my mother would try again to cross just before dawn.

I returned to Changbai. It was now midnight. The town was deserted and, alone in the dark, I felt exposed. I was too nervous to sleep, so I found an all-night diner. I ordered a bowl of bean-paste stew and went over what Min-ho had said. I couldn't believe this. I had picked the worst possible night of the year to bring my mother across, and it was already going horribly wrong. I willed myself to stay calm, and to think clearly. *In a few hours everything will be all right.* I couldn't finish the stew. I went back to the hotel and tried to doze for a while in my clothes.

I must have drifted off, because the next thing I knew the phone was buzzing next to my face.

'We'll be there at six,' Min-ho said. I jumped off the bed. Minutes later, as I was in the taxi, he called again. 'We're across. We're hiding in the derelict house.'

I was elated. I had not seen my dear mother in eleven years, nine months, and nine days. Now I was minutes away from her. I asked the driver to wait, and walked across the rough ground toward the riverbank.

The sky to the east was turning a faint duck-egg blue. Then, there, about fifty yards ahead, next to the derelict house, I made out the silhouettes of two figures. They were walking at a crouch, coming toward me.

My omma. In the half-light I saw a strained, old face, and a body moving very stiffly. Min-ho was behind her, protective and guiding with his arm around her.

I ran to meet them, but there was no time for a reunion. 'We have to go,' I said.

We were exposed, between the river and the town. At daybreak the Chinese border guards would start patrolling. The taxi driver, who I hoped was waiting out of sight on the road, might have got out and been watching. He could report us.

I pulled out the clothes I had brought for them. 'Put these on. Over what you're wearing. Quick.' Once they were dressed I led them towards the taxi. 'Act normal, but don't speak. He'll think you're locals.'

We got into the taxi. In case the driver reported us, I asked him to take us to a different hotel. We sat in silence for the ten-minute ride. I paid the fare. It wasn't customary to tip but I didn't ask for the change. We got out and, once he'd driven away, walked to the Changbai Binguan. It was so early that no one was around. The lobby was empty and the sole receptionist was engrossed in her cellphone. Once I had put my mother and brother in the elevator and told them to go to the room, I went over to the desk.

'Hey there,' I said, sounding casual. 'The lady's with me. I'll bring her ID when we come down for breakfast. The man's not staying. He'll go soon.'

'Fine,' she said, stifling a yawn.

I closed the hotel room door behind me. For a moment we looked at each other. Half a lifetime had passed since the three of us had been together. No one could speak. Then my mother broke down, and all her tension released. I held her. A lump rose to my throat. I had never felt such extremes of joy and sadness at the same time. She was weeping uncontrollably. Over her shoulder, Min-ho's face looked immensely sad.

He'd shared her pain all these years. And soon he would say goodbye to her and probably never see her again. We stepped back to stare at each other, taking in the changes in our faces, the ravages of time. My mother looked helpless and frail. My mind still held the image of her face the night I'd last seen her. She was forty-two then, and a woman of so much energy she could hardly sit still. Now she was fifty-four, but she looked much older. She was far thinner than I remembered, and her mouth was drawn and lined.

They were both different. Min-ho was a grown man. I could see the strength in his shoulders and arms. Eight years had passed since that brief reunion with him at Mr Ahn's house, cut short by the gang. He kept his feelings bottled up, as our father had, but his eyes brimmed with tears at the sight of our mother's distress. Her hands were shaking, touching my face, then touching her own face, then mine again.

'Omma,' I said. She saw the concern in my eyes.

'I've aged twelve years in the last twelve hours,' she said.

I laughed and hugged her again. She'd always made fun of her own appearance. As I held her I suddenly remembered the clothes she had on underneath were icy and soaking wet.

They were both visibly more relaxed after a hot shower, but I was back in worry mode. We were not safe. I had to stay in control, and be vigilant. By far the most dangerous part of the plan lay ahead.

'Why are you so spotty?' my mother said, as if no time had passed. It was exactly the comment she would have made when I was seventeen. The stress of the preparations had wreaked havoc with my complexion. 'If I'd known I'd have brought *bingdu* for you.' Crystal meth.

'I don't think so, Omma.'

'It's great for your skin. Mix it with water, wash your face with it, and it'll clear up in no time.'

'I use it for night driving,' Min-ho said.

There was no point debating this with them now. Two separate worlds were colliding in this room. Min-ho had put on the new jeans and top I'd bought for him. He looked handsome. *My brother.* I did not want to think about our imminent goodbye.

None of us had been to bed, but no one felt like sleeping. I wanted to know what had happened last night. After they'd run into the border guard on the riverbank, my mother had gone to wait at a friend's house nearby. Min-ho had kept the guard company for a few hours, then gone back to Yoon-ji's house, where he'd been living with her and her parents prior to the marriage. The wedding plans were under way, but a date had not yet been set.

'You should have stayed together,' I said, looking at both of them.

'I couldn't let Yoon-ji know I was helping Omma escape,' Min-ho said. If their relationship ever went sour, this fact could be fatal for him. 'If we'd come over last night, I was just going to call her and say I was here on business and would be back in a day or two. She was still asleep when I left this morning. I wrote her a note.'

Two guards had been patrolling when Min-ho had returned to the riverbank with my mother just before dawn. They asked him who the woman was. He told them she was a client meeting someone in China, and would be coming back.

'I told them she was paying me big money, so I'll have to give them something when I go back.' Min-ho hesitated, and I saw worry in his eyes. 'The funny thing was, while we were talking, more guards appeared. They were relieving the guards on duty further up the path. Suddenly, there were nine of them who'd stopped to talk. Some of them tried to persuade me not to cross with this woman. They trusted me, but they didn't know who she was. Leave her behind, they said. So we got delayed a bit while I argued with them.'

I told him he should have waited until they'd gone.

'It was getting light and I didn't want to run into a Chinese patrol on the other side. Anyway, the guys all know me. It's not a problem. I just said goodbye and crossed.'

The group of nine guards watched as he took my mother's hand and waded waist-deep with her through the water.

The irony was all too much. I started giggling and couldn't stop. The border crossing is the most dangerous moment for anyone attempting to escape. But my brother and mother had been waved off by every armed border guard along that stretch of the river.

Next thing I knew all three of us were weeping with laughter.

As we went down in the elevator the next morning I told my mother and Min-ho not to speak too loudly at breakfast. I would say something to them in Mandarin from time to time. Otherwise, we'd keep quiet, and not draw attention by speaking Korean. I was worried that Min-ho stood out. He was the youngest person in the hotel. The other guests were middle-aged or elderly.

After breakfast, we ventured out, disciplining ourselves to say as little as possible. Even though many people in Changbai spoke Korean as a first language, strong North Korean accents would be conspicuous. We went shopping at a market so that I could show them the wealth of goods on display. Then I took them to lunch at an upmarket Korean restaurant. I'd figured, again, that this was the last place anyone would expect to spot escaped North Koreans. But I also wanted to treat them. Soon Min-ho would be leaving us, and I wanted us all to have a wonderful memory of our last time together.

Back in the hotel room, Min-ho turned his cellphone on. It rang straight away. It was Yoon-ji.

She was shouting the moment he answered. My mother and I could hear every word. 'Where are you? Who's the bitch you were with?'

'Why?'

'Don't you know what's happening?'

'Calm down. What's the matter?'

'Everyone is going crazy here. The senior guard who let you across is here at the house. He's in a panic.'

'Why?'

'Someone informed his commander that you'd gone across with a woman. The commander says if you come back with her right now, you'll be all right. But if you come back alone, you'll be in deep trouble. And so will the guard, for letting you cross. They'll accuse you of human trafficking.' Min-ho's eyes bulged in disbelief. 'The guard is here. He's begging me to make you come. Right now,' she said. 'And who's this bloody woman you crossed with?'

'She's visiting relatives,' Min-ho sounded evasive, sheepish.

'Well why didn't you just take her across and come back?'

'She's paying me a big fee.'

'We've got money. Why take such a risk for this bitch?'

'Don't say that.'

'Bring her back,' she shouted.

'I'll call you later.'

He hung up and collapsed onto the bed with his hands over his face. My mother and I had heard everything.

Min-ho was in an impossible dilemma, the worst of his life. He had to go back but couldn't return with my mother – or they'd ask what she was doing in China. The answer could only be to meet me. If he went back alone, he'd be accused of human trafficking and interrogated. The *Bowibu* would break him and quickly get to the truth – that he was helping his mother to defect. He'd face political prison, a zone of no return. His life would be over.

I went to the window and my forehead hit the glass with a thump. Not in any of the disaster scenarios I'd envisaged had I imagined a complication such as this. For several minutes we said nothing, sunk in our own thoughts.

I broke the silence.

'Min-ho, if you go back, you'll be in terrible trouble,' I said, speaking slowly and evenly.

Min-ho looked as if he'd been cast in wax. My mother said nothing.

'If you both go back, it'll be worse. Omma can't go back with you. That leaves us two choices. We can hope that your connections with the guards will get you out of this . . .' I was talking to him but he made no sign that he was hearing me. 'The other choice . . . is don't go back.'

My words filled the room.

'Your friend the guard will be finished. I'm very sorry about him. But we're your family. Min-ho, you can't go back. You just can't. It'll be so dangerous. You have to come with us. I hadn't planned for this, but we'll figure it out, somehow.'

I knew there was no choice, but I had to let him decide. Both options were extremely risky. Min-ho would have to travel across China as an illegal. Also, I had budgeted for my mother and for the broker's fee, but didn't think I had enough money for him, too. I had no confidence we could all make it. But if he really thought he could go back, brazen it out, and bribe his way out of the problem, it had to be his own decision.

Min-ho was in shock.

'I can't go back.' His voice was a whisper. 'We all know that.'

I took his hand and my mother's hand, and held them. 'We'll leave together. We'll do the best we can.'

His phone rang. Yoon-ji again.

'Are you on your way?' she asked.

'It's going to take me one more day,' he said quietly.

He was buying time to figure out how he was going to tell her. Her parents liked him and had connections that could help him. But if they thought he was running out on her, they also had the power to stop him getting far. The *Bowibu* were permitted to operate in China to track down escapers.

'You've got to come back,' she cried. We could hear her weeping. She'd sensed he wasn't going to come.

In the morning, we decided to leave Changbai as fast as possible. Min-ho was dreading turning on his phone. It rang within seconds. Yoon-ji was calling again. She was calmer now. She said she had a feeling that he wasn't coming back. Her parents were in the room with her.

'Tell me . . . the woman you're with. Is she really a stranger? Or is she your mother? Just say the truth.'

'She's my mother,' he said. 'My sister came for her. That's why I crossed.'

Her parents had figured it out. She started crying again.

'Min-ho, please come back.' She was begging him. 'You left me a note but all the time you knew you were going for good. How could you leave me sleeping without saying goodbye?'

My mother clasped her hand to her mouth. This was breaking her heart.

Min-ho's lip trembled. 'Please believe me. I wanted to go back. I still do. But I can't take Omma back. So how can I go back alone now? Check the money in the drawer. It's all there. If I were going for good, would I leave it all there?'

'I believe you,' she said. 'Just come back.'

'Min-ho.' A man's voice, now. Stern. Yoon-ji's father. 'Please return right away. I'm begging you, for Yoon-ji.'

Min-ho didn't answer. He was breathing deeply. The look on his face was one I remembered from when he was a little boy and wished something wasn't happening to him. I took the phone from his hand.

'This is Min-ho's sister,' I said, hearing the coolness in my voice. 'We want him to go back; he wants to go back. Whatever he does now is dangerous. But please understand that returning now is the more dangerous option.'

'I know it's a serious problem,' he said, 'but we will do whatever we can, whatever the cost, to take care of this.'

'Good. Thank you. We will also try to think of a way,' I said. 'Let's speak again tomorrow.'

I could hear Yoon-ji in the background crying almost hysterically. I ended the call. The scale of this disaster was clear. These two were in love.

I turned off the phone, and without expecting to, burst into tears. I was exhausted. I looked over at my mother, who had remained silent this whole time. I could only imagine the guilt she was feeling. She had been the rock of our lives, always able to solve any problem, fix any situation. Now, she could only watch as her children struggled with a calamity that had struck just a day after our reunion.

'I'm going to take a shower,' Min-ho said.

My mother shot me a puzzled look. He closed the bathroom door. We heard him turn on the taps and flush the toilet. Then the shower came on with a hiss. My mother and I glanced at one another and then we looked down. We could hear him sobbing. It was agonizing to hear. He had nothing left but his body and the clothes on his back. His mother and his sister could do nothing. No words would be enough.

A few minutes later, he came out, dressed and towelling his hair dry. We pretended we hadn't heard. He had regained some composure.

'So, Nuna, what's the plan?' He'd called me older sister on the phone, but it was gratifying to hear it from him in person.

'We're leaving this town in under an hour.'

Chapter 44

Journey into night

I left Min-ho with my mother in the hotel room while I went to the coach station to buy tickets. Outside in the bustle of the town I seethed with nerves, as if everyone I passed was reaching for their phones to call the *Bowibu*. At the station, I realized what was unsettling me. There were police everywhere – Security Police in navy uniforms, People's Armed Police in olive-green uniforms. What was going on?

When I asked for the tickets, the woman at the counter held out her hand. 'Your ID and those of the other travellers.'

This was a surprise. 'IDs?'

'It's National Day,' she said flatly, 'in case you hadn't noticed.'

That explained the police. It was 1 October. Nor was it any ordinary National Day. This was 2009, the sixtieth anniversary of the founding of the People's Republic of China. There was always heightened vigilance on this date to prevent anything marring the celebrations. But the sixtieth was considered so propitious an anniversary that security was at maximum.

I gazed about in disbelief. Not only had I picked the worst possible night for my mother to cross the river, I'd picked the worst day in a decade to travel.

'Min-ho, could you borrow an ID from someone in Changbai? Anyone.'

Min-ho said he could try a few business contacts.

The first man ran a used motorcycle shop. He came out as he saw us approach, wiping his hands on an oily, stained T-shirt.

'What're you doing here? Who's she?' was his greeting. He wasn't fat, but his posture was so slouched that his gut hung over his belt.

Min-ho said that he was buying family gifts for *Chuseok*, the Korean harvest festival that was two days away. He introduced me as a cousin from Shenyang, and said he wanted to go to Shenyang, but needed to borrow an ID for a few days.

'If I lend it to you and you get into trouble, what am I supposed to do?'

Min-ho had told me this man was honest, but a born coward when it came to bending the rules.

'Report it stolen,' I said.

He puffed out his cheeks and shook his head slowly.

Min-ho's second contact was a motorcycle parts trader, a friendly man with a patchy beard. We took him for lunch, and gave him the same pretext. I also offered to pay him 1,000 yuan ($150), and to return the card to him in a week's time.

'What if you get caught?' he said, lighting a cigarette.

'Say you lost the card, and get a new one.'

He blew out a mixture of laughter, nerves and smoke. 'There are an awful lot of cops around. They're checking everyone.' I could see that he wanted to say no. Instead he said: 'Give me a day. I'll think about it.'

We had no choice but to wait. I went to Mrs Ahn's house to see if she could help. The house was boarded up. A neighbour said that she had moved away.

We were out of options. It would have to be the second trader or nothing. In the meantime I had to book another expensive night at the hotel.

I was back in one of those tight corners where I found myself closing my eyes and muttering to my ancestors, beseeching, desperate, asking for their help. But I expected no miracles. Our predicament seemed hopeless.

The trader called the next morning as we were eating breakfast.

'I'm scared shitless about this, but Min-ho has helped me make a lot of money. I owe him.'

When we had the ID in our hands I noticed that the man's age was thirty-eight. Min-ho was twenty-two, and looked nothing like him. Still, it was the gender that counted. I figured that's all the police would look at. The card was also in a different format from mine – it was in both Chinese and Korean scripts, which I'd never seen before.

The parts trader told us the police had launched a massive nationwide social clean-up campaign prior to the sixtieth anniversary celebrations. Travellers were facing checks and roadblocks everywhere. The sensible thing would have been to wait two weeks until things had calmed down, but I didn't have enough money. We had to move. I did not want to panic my mother and Min-ho. I reassured them that I had faith in our good luck. If fortune was with us, we'd be protected no matter what. If it wasn't, there was nothing we could do.

At the coach station I bought three 160-yuan ($25) tickets for the coach leaving at 2 p.m. the next day. It had sleeper bunks on two levels and in three rows, split by two aisles. I asked for the three bunks at the back of the bus on the second level. My hope was that if the coach was stopped, the police would come through and collect all the IDs. At the back they would neither see us nor check closely that the IDs were ours.

The coach left on time. Our epic journey had begun. My stomach tightened with trepidation. But I was also hopeful. Getting that ID for Min-ho made me think fortune had turned our way. We travelled southwest out of the town, along the Yalu River. The first leg of the journey, to Shenyang, was about 250 miles. It wound through hilly countryside and would take twelve hours.

I held my camera up to the window. I had taken a few shots of Hyesan the previous day. This fleeting view would probably be the last time I'd ever see the place. It made me reflective and sad, glimpsing the high white wall of our old home on the riverbank. I thought of far-off days in spring, before the famine, when my father skimmed stones with us across the water, when the world beyond the river had seemed vast and mysterious.

The coach passed the customs post at the end of the Friendship Bridge. I took a few last pictures. Then, less than five minutes into our journey, the coach slowed, and pulled over.

We leaned into the aisle to see what was happening. The hydraulic door opened with a hiss. A soldier in green uniform and cap climbed in, carrying an automatic rifle.

I felt my guts coil.

I looked out of the window on Min-ho's side. A group of People's

Armed Police was manning what looked like a temporary checkpoint. Jeeps were parked along both sides of the road ahead.

The soldier moved down the aisle. He was not demanding IDs, he was checking people's eyes, looking each passenger in the face. Why? For signs of nervousness? For anyone who doesn't belong? It was only at that moment that I realized Min-ho was the only man on the coach. Every other passenger was a woman. Min-ho did not even look Chinese. He was weathered and had darker skin than Chinese men his age. Sunblock is unheard of in North Korea. In the street earlier, I'd given him my baseball cap to keep the sun off his face. Now he had pulled it over his eyes and pretended to be asleep.

The soldier moved slowly, taking in each face. I could hear my heart pounding in my ears. He had now checked more than half of the passengers.

I glanced at the bridge with its flags flying. I could see North Korean guards on the far side.

The soldier was just feet away. He met my eye. Then he spotted Min-ho.

It seemed to happen in slow motion. I swung my legs off the berth and blocked the aisle. I felt something metal and hard in my hand. It was my camera. Without thinking, I pointed it at the soldier's face and took a picture. Somehow, the flash was on.

'Hey, hey, hey,' he said.

Then I swung around and pointed it through the window and started snapping pictures of the armed police at the checkpoint.

He grabbed my arm. 'No photos.'

'Oh.' I smiled stupidly with my hand over my mouth. 'Sorry. You look awesome in your uniforms.'

Behind him I noticed that every passenger on the coach had craned their heads into the aisle to watch.

'It's illegal. Delete them now.'

'Aw,' I said, sounding put out. 'Can't I keep this one?'

'No. Now. Quickly.'

The passengers all looked like locals from Changbai. I looked like a girl from somewhere foreign and fashionable. With luck, they all thought I was some clueless tourist. The soldier was embarrassed and annoyed. He knew the whole coach was watching.

'Here's the one of you,' I said. His face looked blanched and stunned. 'Look, I'm deleting it.'

Then he turned and stomped down the aisle to escape the stares. The automatic door closed behind him.

I slumped back into my berth. *What just happened?* I had a sensation of coming back to reality, as if I'd just come off stage and the performance had left me exhausted. We had more than 2,000 miles ahead of us. How often would this happen?

For the rest of the journey to Shenyang we lay in our berths without speaking. When the sun set the other passengers also settled into sleep beneath rough blankets.

I lay awake listening to the hum of the engine, as the road unrolled endlessly from the darkness. I was too unnerved to sleep. My mind was running far ahead of the coach, probing for danger.

Chapter 45

Under a vast Asian sky

My aunt had wanted me to bring my mother to her apartment for a day or two to acclimatize, but we hadn't time to waste in Shenyang. I had thought carefully about the next section of the journey. A flight to Kunming would have been fastest, taking just six hours, but it was out of the question. The airport authorities would certainly scrutinize our IDs. The train would take two full days, but ID checks on trains were even more worrying because they would be face to face. The least perilous option was going by road. It would be gruelling. With all the transfers and waiting times, I figured the journey would take a week. And although there would be more police checks, the driver usually handed all the IDs to the policeman who'd check each with a handheld machine, but wouldn't match them against the owners.

We braced ourselves again. We were going to cross eight vast provinces of China by coach.

If we encountered any more problems like the one on leaving Changbai, we would pretend that my mother and Min-ho were deaf mutes and that I was their guide. It was a desperate, crazy, ridiculous idea, but it was the only one I had.

The next leg of the journey was to Zhengzhou, the capital of Henan Province, on the Yellow River, almost 900 miles southwest of Shenyang. It would be an eighteen-hour ride. We reached the first police checkpoint one hour into the journey. As I had hoped, the conductor collected all IDs and handed them to the policeman, who took them away for inspection. In our ordeal on the coach at Changbai I thought I'd seen the soldier glance down to the back as he'd entered. He had probably spotted Min-ho straight away. This time, I had opted to sit up front in the most conspicuous place. We'd look as if we had nothing to hide. Again, we took seats on the second level, with Min-ho at a window, me in the middle and, as the seat beside me was taken, my mother behind me, also in the middle section. Ten minutes later, the policeman returned and handed the cards back to the driver.

The moment the automatic door closed, we breathed again. We were in the clear.

The three of us began talking freely. We felt rested. We'd had a good night's sleep at a hotel in Shenyang. So we chatted, and ate snacks. The coach was full. By this time, if they didn't think we were Korean-Chinese, every passenger would have guessed we either came from a minority ethnic group, or we were foreigners. The coach stopped twice at restaurants on the expressway and the passengers filed off to stretch their legs, use the washrooms, and eat.

Seven or eight hours later, the coach stopped again. It was in the early hours of the morning and we were somewhere near Beijing. Up ahead, blue lights revolved and flashed on the top of a police jeep. Again, the conductor collected our passes, handed them to a policeman. Ten minutes later, the policeman climbed in. He had the IDs in his hand. He told the driver to pull off the road, and turn the interior lights on.

I caught a draught from the air con overhead and felt beads of cold sweat on my brow.

The policeman looked at the top card, called out a name, and a passenger lumbered down the aisle to claim it.

'Name?' he said. 'Your residence? Where're you going? What's the purpose of your visit?' After the passenger had answered the last question, the policeman handed over the ID.

The full horror of what was happening sank in.

He's looking for illegals who can't speak Mandarin.

I felt exposed and helpless. Our high-spirited conversations in Korean had given us away. A muscle began to spasm just beneath my eye. I had to grimace to make it stop.

This is it. We're finished.

I looked over to see if my mother and Min-ho had caught what was happening. Min-ho was surreptitiously sipping from a cheap bottle of Maotai, the Chinese liquor. The rank, sickly smell of it had already reached my bunk. He'd said his strategy, if questioned, was to be drunk. He quietly screwed the cap back on and closed his eyes. His lips were pressed tightly together. I felt immensely sorry for him, and for my mother. This was all my doing. They could be safe at home now. *They will pay the price for my selfishness.*

Min-ho's distraction strategy was not going to work.

'Chang-soo.' The policeman was calling the name on Min-ho's ID. The name was Korean but he was pronouncing it in Mandarin. Min-ho's eyes were still shut. There was nothing I could do.

He called the name out again. No response. Then he called it a third time, irritated now. I pushed Min-ho, pretending to wake him. The other passengers watched as he climbed down from the bunk. I could see his legs wobbling. He was moving slowly as if stepping forward to be shot. My heart was bleeding for him.

But I could not do as a broker would have done – shrink back into my bunk, look out of the window, and abandon him to his fate.

I'll take the bullet for him.

'What is your name?' the policeman asked in Mandarin. Min-ho stood helplessly in front of him with his head lowered. He said nothing. The policeman looked at the card and looked up at him.

'He's deaf and dumb,' I said in Mandarin, climbing down from my bunk.

'Who are you?'

'We're together,' I said. He found my card.

'Really? He's deaf and dumb?' The policeman was holding my ID and Min-ho's out in front of him. 'Yours is in Chinese. But his is foreign.'

'That's Korean script,' I said. 'For Korean-Chinese from the north-east the ID is in both languages.'

'Never seen that before.'

'She's right,' the conductor chipped in. I turned my head and saw the driver tap the watch on his wrist in a show of irritation. 'The cards are all like that in the Korean autonomous provinces.'

The novelty of the Korean script had distracted the policeman from the ID's photo and date of birth. He still looked suspiciously at Min-ho. Then he handed back the card.

Suddenly, a loud, ape-like grunting noise behind me distracted everyone. My mother had clambered down from her berth. She was gibbering as if unaware she was making any sounds, and waving her arms about in a show of extreme annoyance, or as if she'd skipped her medication. The performance was so startling the policeman took a step backward.

He swore. 'Another one?'

'She's with me, too,' I said, sounding apologetic. 'I am guiding them both.'

Reluctantly, the policeman gave back our cards without further questions. The entire coach was watching this bizarre piece of theatre. They'd heard us chatting for hours. They might have been too surprised to speak, but not one of them gave us away. I had fifty-two accomplices to a crime, and they were all total strangers.

A minute later the coach was back on the expressway. Min-ho and my mother looked like people just spared the firing squad. Behind me I could feel the heat of the other passengers' stares. I wanted to turn and say something by way of an excuse, or to thank them, but I was too embarrassed and scared. The rest of the journey lasted eight hours. My mother and Min-ho did not utter another word.

We arrived in Zhengzhou in the late afternoon and from there travelled to Guilin, the capital of Guangxi Province, unnoticed among a group of tourists on their way to see the famous karst hills along the Li River. We dozed for much of the twenty-four-hour journey. Occasionally I'd pull back the curtain and see a vast Asian sky over endless low hills. The chill northeast was far behind us. We emerged in subtropical China. Another overnight ride westward, and on the morning of the seventh day we reached Kunming, in Yunnan Province.

I was feeling a mounting sense of purpose and excitement. We were so close to the edge of China. The border to freedom. We were going to make it. We were going to pull this off.

Reverend Kim's broker was waiting for us in the ticket hall of Kunming coach station. He was a tanned, middle-aged Chinese man dressed in black jeans, a cheap leather jacket and tinted glasses. He introduced himself as Mr Fang. I had an instant bad feeling about him.

I was his client, and was paying for his services, but from the moment he greeted us he behaved as if we'd been sent to irritate him, and he was doing us a favour. I watched him glance at my mother and shake his head. She had once ranked highly in her society and was the wife of a senior military officer, but in this fellow's eyes she was an empty-handed old woman on the run. His body language showed contempt; his manner of speaking even more so.

I'll admit that, as a Korean, I'm sensitive to how I'm treated. In our hierarchical culture, everyone is either above or below you. Honorific language is used with anyone further up the hierarchy. The safe bet when meeting strangers is to use polite forms, until you can place their age, or status. But this man began speaking to us in language reserved for kids. He was especially dismissive of Min-ho.

'That fool's taking his time,' he said when Min-ho was in the station bathroom.

If we'd been in Seoul, I'd have told him plainly to his face to watch his manners, but I kept my anger banked down. I could not allow my feelings to interfere with our goal. I forced myself to treat the situation as another type of checkpoint, to be passed with calm nerves and composure. My family's safety came first.

Mr Fang's Korean was so thickly clouded with Mandarin that I had to keep asking him to repeat himself. I'd never heard Korean so mangled. In the end I had to ask him to speak in Mandarin, which further annoyed him.

My mother and Min-ho, meanwhile, were not reacting well to the fug of humidity we'd stepped into off the coach, or the pervasive reek of gasoline fumes. To make matters worse, the oily fried food we'd been eating at expressway restaurants all the way from Shenyang was taking its toll. Their bodies weren't used to it. They now had stomach cramps. Min-ho, who possessed such sinewy strength, had become listless and wan at the very stage of the journey he needed to be taut and alert.

Mr Fang led us to a guesthouse for the night. It was the cheapest kind of lodging, in a rough neighbourhood of old, single-storey houses separated by narrow, litter-strewn dirt alleyways. When I turned on the bathroom light, tiny lizards darted across the walls; the shower head was a spigot with a sock tied over it.

Mr Fang sat down on a bed. Payment was the first thing he mentioned. Without asking if we minded whether he smoked in our room, he lit a cigarette.

I took out my cash. From my experience of gangs and brokers I knew that the worst thing I could do was betray any sign of desperation, or appeal to his pity. I spoke as if this was a controlled, manageable situation.

'When I arranged this with Reverend Kim, we only planned for my mother. But there was a problem and my brother had to come with us. Right now I only have the money for one person.'

'We had an agreement.'

'We still do,' I said. 'As soon as I return to Seoul, I'll pay the extra to Reverend Kim. He can transfer it to you.'

The man swore under his breath. 'That's not going to work, little Miss.'

'It will, because I'm giving you my South Korean ID card.' I took it from my wallet and handed it to him. 'You keep it. You and Reverend Kim now know exactly who I am, and where I live, and can come after me if I don't pay. And I will pay.'

The ID was the only thing I had that might persuade him to trust me.

He seemed to weigh the card in his hand for a moment, gauging its value, then slipped it into his jacket pocket.

'They leave tomorrow,' he said, nodding to my mother and Min-ho. 'They will be guided early in the morning over the border. Into Laos.'

Where? 'No, we're going to Vietnam.'

'That was the plan, but two days ago a group of North Koreans was caught in Vietnam and sent back to China.'

I glanced at my mother. She wasn't following the Mandarin, but she could see the alarm in my eyes.

'The Vietnamese used to allow you people to go to South Korea,' he said. 'We don't know why this has changed, but it means that route is not safe now. We can't risk it. We're switching to Laos.'

My head was spinning. 'Where's Laos?'

'Next to Vietnam. Same distance from here. Seven hours away.'

'Is it safe?'

'Safe?' He gave a snort. 'Nothing is guaranteed. But we've been doing this a long time. We can get you across the border and to the South Korean embassy in Vientiane.' He saw another blank look on my face. 'That's the capital. I'll get your mother and brother there.' He took a final drag on his cigarette and flicked it through the open window, trailing orange sparks.

'Well, I'm going too,' I said.

'No, you're not.' He shot me a look of glinting suspicion, as if I were trying to steal his trade secrets. 'You're going back to Seoul.'

'I'm not leaving them. They need me.'

'They'll be in safe hands.'

'They don't speak Mandarin and they don't know about anything outside of North Korea. I'm staying with them.'

'Too dangerous. You'll be a liability, little Miss.'

My fists clenched. *If he calls me that one more time . . .*

'Everything we're doing is illegal,' he said. 'With a South Korean passport you can enter Laos for fifteen days without a visa. They don't even have passports.' He gestured casually at my mother and Min-ho. 'If you're caught with them you'll be arrested for helping illegals. They'll think you're a broker and put you in jail. You'll be no help to anyone there. They need you to arrange things for them in South Korea.'

'I could travel on my Chinese ID,' I said.

The moment the words were out, I knew this was a bad idea.

He seemed to read my mind. 'And if something goes wrong, do you want to get sent back to South Korea, or to China? If the Chinese figure out you're a defector, too . . .'

The thought was left hanging in the air.

He had me. There was nothing I could say.

Every hour of the day for the past week, I had been my family's sole lifeline. But now control was being taken from me. I would have to leave them in the hands of a man I absolutely did not trust.

At dawn the air was already humid and noisy with the cries of unfamiliar birds. The alley smelled of rotting garbage. It took us just minutes to prepare ourselves. My mother would take only a small bag, and gave me her winter clothes. I went out to buy toiletries for her and Min-ho. I checked the remaining cash in my wallet. I did not have much left, and still had to buy my plane ticket to Seoul.

I went with them to the coach station. I gave Min-ho 1,000 yuan ($150). I wrote my South Korean cellphone number down for him and my mother and told them to memorize it.

We said our goodbyes. I did not want to let go of their hands, but Min-ho gave me his grin and said: 'Nuna, we'll be all right.'

I watched the coach until it had turned the corner and disappeared from view. *Please be safe.* The dice were rolling again. Now it was all in Fortune's hands.

I stayed behind in Kunming until I'd heard from Min-ho, who called that evening. They had arrived at the border without incident. They would cross at dawn, when Mr Fang would bribe the guards. At 5 a.m. he called again.

'We're in Laos.'

Relief washed over me like warm spring water. The end of the journey was in sight. For days my nerves had been wound to breaking point. Now, as the tension drained from my body, I was so tired I could barely move.

I found a post office and mailed back the two borrowed IDs. Then, with some hesitation, I called my boyfriend Kim in Seoul. I hadn't spoken to him for more than a week, and had told him nothing about what I was going to do. I had not answered his worried text messages. When I told him where I was, however, his shock was greater than his hurt.

'*Where?*'

In the background I heard the business meeting he was in go quiet.

I briefly told him what I'd done, and that my family was now in Laos, heading for the South Korean embassy.

There was a stunned pause on the end of the line. Finally he said: 'I don't know what to say.' Then I heard that gentle laugh. 'Come back quickly.' He thought I was insane, he said, but I heard the note of admiration in his voice. 'I've got to hear all about this.'

I sat in the back of the taxi satisfied that I'd accomplished a difficult mission. And I couldn't wait to get out of the grime and humidity of Kunming. We were approaching the departures terminal when my phone rang.

It was Mr Fang. I didn't hear him at first because a plane roared so low overhead I could see the streaks of rust on its fuselage. All I got was the word *problem*. My stomach turned to stone.

'Problem?'

I was staring at the back of the taxi driver's head, with the phone at my ear.

'The police picked them up.'

Chapter 46

Lost in Laos

I screwed my eyes shut. *This can't be happening to me.*

'Which police? Chinese?'

'Laotian.'

'Where? When?'

'I don't know.'

'You don't know?' My voice rose to a shout. 'Where are they and what are you going to do?'

'There's nothing I can do, little Miss,' he hissed. 'They were stopped at a checkpoint by police. We could have rescued them. You didn't give me enough money.'

'I gave you 50 per cent – as agreed.'

'We were working with police and one of the guards at the checkpoint. If you'd given me a hundred per cent of the money, I could have paid to have them let go. But you didn't.'

With a tremendous effort I kept my anger under control. Anger would only cloud my thinking, and I had to think.

'All right. OK. Where do you think they are?'

'Probably Luang Namtha.'

'Luang Namtha?' *Where the hell is that?*

'The first town, about twenty-five miles from the border.'

I ended the call, and covered my face with my hands.

Until two days ago, I hadn't known Laos existed. I had never even heard the name. Or maybe I had forgotten it. Laos was one of North Korea's few remaining allies in the world, and still communist. The Lao People's Democratic Republic, to give it its official name, would have congratulated the Dear Leader on his birthday each year, and this would have been reported in the media. Pyongyang makes headline news of diplomatic pleasantries – the regime's attempts to suggest that the ruling Kim is loved and admired the world over.

Laos. I couldn't even picture it. Just a dark place on the far edge of China that had swallowed my mother and my brother.

The taxi pulled over. There were people everywhere wheeling luggage.

All the strength had gone out of me. My voice sounded wan. 'Please take me to the coach station.'

'You said the airport,' the driver exclaimed.

'I know. But now I'm going to Laos.'

He turned and peered at me as if I needed a psychiatric ward, not a coach station.

'All right,' he said slowly, starting the car again.

I called Min-ho but his battery had died or the phone had been taken from him. *How can I contact them now?* Somehow, I would have to find him and my mother by myself.

I felt so weak when I reached the coach station I could barely lift my backpack. I removed all the cold-weather clothing and gave it to the taxi driver. He was grateful, and again looked at me oddly.

My journey ended at noon the next day, at the last station in China. My mother and brother had been here twenty-four hours earlier. During the long ride, and with some dinner, my energy had started to revive. I asked for directions, hoisted my backpack, and walked toward Laos.

The Chinese passport control was in a modern building surrounded by low hills dotted with tropical trees. The sky was a beautiful, washed blue, I noticed, clearer than anything I'd seen in Shanghai or Seoul. Vast white clouds sailed over the hills.

About twenty people were waiting in line to have their passports stamped. A few were backpacking white Westerners in high spirits. I looked at them with envy. They were inhabitants of that other universe, governed by laws, human rights and welcoming tourist boards. It was oblivious to the one I inhabited, of secret police, assumed IDs and low-life brokers.

Standing apart from them was one white man no one could miss.

He was in his early fifties, strongly built, and extremely tall, looming head and shoulders above everyone else. He had that pinkish skin and sandy-coloured hair that North Korean kids would gawp at on the rare occasions they saw a Westerner. He and I seemed to be the only lone travellers.

We crossed the border. The contrast with modern China was stark. The Laotian passport office was a squat, mud-colour building. It was clear at once that this was a poor country. We filed on board a sputtering twenty-seater bus. The tall white man got on also, folding his legs awkwardly between the wooden seats.

Bouncing through the hilly countryside on this boneshaker, I stared again at the clean turquoise sky. It made the vegetation seem extravagantly lush – hardwood trees and rubber trees, by the look of them, and fields of sugar cane, and wild flowers everywhere, enormous purple hibiscus and golden jasmine hanging down from the canopies of the trees. In a more relaxed frame of mind I probably wouldn't have noticed such things so keenly, but in my anguish I was seeing all this as beauty denied to me. I would not have any chance to enjoy it.

Laos is one of those big, small countries, like Korea. It's a little larger than both Koreas combined, and much longer than it is wide, about 650 miles from north to south. It is landlocked and poor and surrounded by better-known countries – China, Vietnam, Thailand, Burma and Cambodia. I had entered the country at its northernmost tip and was heading south.

The journey to Luang Namtha took an hour. When I got off, the tall white man and three or four others got off too.

Luang Namtha is the capital of the province of the same name. There were many Westerners about, wandering the markets, and lounging on hostel verandas. Apart from the police station and one or two guesthouses the town was made up of single-storey houses, with telegraph wires crisscrossing every street. I had to find a local who could help me, so I asked directions for the local Chinese restaurant. The owner was a tubby, friendly family man, who reminded me a little of Mr Ahn.

'I'm looking for two North Koreans who were arrested yesterday,' I said in Mandarin. I gave him a big smile. 'If you can help, I'll eat my meals here every evening.'

He laughed. 'Well, start at the immigration office,' he said. 'There's a holding cell there.' Straight away he offered to take me there on the back of his scooter. His name was Yin, he said.

The immigration office was closed and looked deserted. I stood outside, tilted my head back, and shouted: '*Omma-ya! Min-ho-ya! Na-ya!* (Mother! Min-ho! It's me!)' Nothing.

'Let's try the police station,' the man said.

The police shook their heads when we asked them. No North Koreans here, they said. Our last stop was the prison, some distance away. The police told us this place was for real criminals. I didn't expect my family to be here. It was a compound of single-storey buildings surrounded by a high mud wall. Again, I yelled as loudly as I could: '*Omma-ya! Min-ho-ya! Na-ya!*'

Outside the main gate, off-duty guards were sitting around with some local girls. They had taken their uniform jackets off and were drinking beer from bottles and laughing. 'No North Koreans here,' they said, 'just drug dealers and murderers.' They added that this was not the sort of place someone like me should be visiting.

Darkness falls fast in the subtropics. Yin offered to take me to my guesthouse, saying it was dangerous for me to walk alone in the street. I thanked him and told him I'd be fine. I was clinging to any hope now. I thought there might be a chance that my mother and Min-ho had escaped and were wandering around. As I approached the lights of the town, the traffic increased – tuk-tuks slowed down beside me; the drivers shouted and whistled at me in Lao and stirred up clouds of dust and exhaust fumes. I walked around for hours, looking at every face I saw.

It was a Friday night. My search could not resume until after the weekend. I had no choice but to stay in town.

On Monday morning I went straight to the immigration office. A group of men in dark green uniforms were sitting about on the benches outside. The place seemed sunk in torpor. I sensed straight away that nothing here happened quickly. They eyed me with suspicion. I introduced myself as a volunteer from South Korea who'd come to Laos to help two North Koreans. I showed them my passport and the visa.

None of them stirred. I thought no one had understood me.

Then one said: 'Yes,' in Mandarin, and swatted a fly from his face. 'Two North Koreans were caught at the border and brought here.'

Chapter 47

Whatever it takes

At last I was getting somewhere. 'Can I see them?'

'You'll have to make an official request. At the police station,' the man said. 'There's no point doing that until we've completed the paperwork.'

Nothing about the attitude of these men suggested that paperwork was given any priority. But I was finally on familiar ground.

I spent the next seven days going back and forth between the police station and the immigration office, establishing relations with the officials, working on them to build a rapport. I knew I would have to bribe. I tried to think how my mother would have dealt with this – with a combination of charm, persuasion and cash. I was friendly. I flattered them. I learned their names and their foibles. I went to the immigration office early each morning, before anyone else, and waited on the bench outside, so that mine was the first face they saw. I took packets of cigarettes for everyone. If I didn't do that, if I just sat and waited until I was called, I knew I could be here for weeks, or months. Here, an administrative matter that could have been dealt with in minutes would stretch to hours, or days. The humidity of the afternoons sapped the life out of everyone. But each day, I felt I was inching closer towards my goal.

The officials in immigration wanted Marlboro Reds, they had told me, the most expensive cigarettes. Once it was plain to them that I was agreeable, and opening a channel to them, their corruption became naked. At every one of my visits they'd ask how much money I had withdrawn from the ATM.

'A hundred dollars,' I'd say. Or: 'Just fifty.'

With a flick of the hand they'd ask to see it. Then I'd hand over the wad of kip, the local currency, to show them; they'd take about half the notes, sometimes more, and give the rest back to me.

After a few days of this extortion, and the cost of my meals and my lodging, my money was almost gone. I had no choice but to make the call I was loath to make – to Kim in Seoul, who immediately transferred funds. I was immensely grateful, and told him this was strictly a loan. I would repay him, just as I had repaid my uncle in Shenyang.

After my morning visit to immigration, I had little to do in the afternoons, so I would sit and read in a place called the Coffee House, a Western-style café that served Thai and Western food. I could remember a little English but could not read the menu, so I asked a waiter what another customer near me was eating.

'Noodles,' he said, using the English word.

I ate noodles every day. After a week, I wanted a change and rang Kim to ask him the English word for *bab*.

'Rice,' he said.

'Lice,' I repeated.

'Not lice, rice. They're two different things. You must ask for rice.'

'Got it. Lice.'

I had my lunch every day at the Coffee House and dinner at Yin's Chinese restaurant. To cut down on spending, I started skipping breakfast. I didn't care. It made me feel solidarity with my mother and brother. I didn't dare imagine what they were eating, or how little. One afternoon at the Coffee House I saw the tall sandy-haired man again, who had gone very pink from the sun. His eyes met mine in greeting as he lumbered by, like a giant. I smiled.

After seven days, the immigration office chief, a big lazy man whose gut strained against his green uniform shirt, said that he would take me to where the two North Koreans were being held. I felt an enormous relief.

We got into his car. He said: 'How much money are you bringing?'

I showed him what was in my wallet. Without counting, he helped himself to half. There was no pretence about a fee or expenses. This casual, shameless robbery by one of the town's senior officials angers me now, but at the time it didn't. I had a single-minded strategy to reach my family. *Whatever it takes*, I thought. *I'll do whatever it takes. Humans are selfish and care only for themselves and their families. Am I any different?*

To my surprise, we arrived at the main prison I had visited the first day, where the people drinking outside had told me indifferently that there were no North Koreans here. If I'd known that my omma and Min-ho were indeed in this place I would have visited every day, even if all I could do was send them good thoughts. I would have yelled over the wall: '*Omma-ya! Min-ho-ya!* Don't worry. I'm here.' I would have come from the immigration office every afternoon and sat here until dusk had fallen and the cicada sounds filled the night.

The prison wardens told me I could meet my mother in the women's section of the prison, but would not be allowed into the men's section to see Min-ho. They led me through a courtyard of mud walls to a large black gate. With a clanking of locks and a ferrous groan it opened sideways. Standing behind it, alone, was my mother.

She glared at me for a moment with an odd, distant expression. Her appearance devastated me. She was much thinner. Her hair was greasy and plastered to her head. For some reason she had one hand on her hip and was tilting oddly to one side.

Suddenly she ran toward me, threw her arms around me and began to sob. She had on the same clothes and rubber flip-flops as when I'd last seen her in Kunming.

'I thought you'd gone,' she wailed. 'I thought I'd never see you again. A second ago I thought I was dreaming, so I pinched my side until it hurt.'

No wonder she'd looked at me strangely.

She ran her hands over my face, just as she had after she'd crossed the Yalu, making sure I was real.

Holding her in my arms, I too had begun to cry, but I forced myself to stop. I wiped my eyes with the palm of my hand and composed myself. I didn't want to complicate matters by letting the guards know I was her daughter.

I sat with her in the prison courtyard. She was being held in a cell for foreign women. One Chinese woman had been there for ten years, she said. Pictures of her family hung on the walls. They had no clean water. They had to drink and wash from the same ration of dirty water each day. A couple of days earlier, they'd heard the guards beat a Thai male prisoner to death. His wife was in the same cell as my mother, and she wailed without cease.

'It's pure hell,' she said. 'We should never have left home.'

Images I'd blotted out until now – of fouled latrines, female violence, public sex and a murderous lack of hygiene – came flooding into my mind.

There was nothing I could say, but there was no going back now. The police had taken all the money I'd given her in Kunming. I slipped her some local currency when the guards weren't looking so she could buy some food.

After I'd seen her I returned to town and at once called the South Korean embassy in Vientiane.

'It's dangerous for you to stay there by yourself,' the consul said. 'Leave Laos now, and let the embassy take care of matters.'

This sounded encouraging. 'How long will it take to get them out?'

'We have to go by the book, unfortunately. There are no shortcuts. We'll submit a request for information and ask permission to visit, but of course that all takes time—'

'How long?'

'Five to six months.'

My head slumped into my hand. But I was not surprised. I'd seen for myself the sluggish apathy of this country's bureaucracy.

I simply could not leave my mother and Min-ho in that place.

The prison interpreter turned to me. 'Five thousand dollars,' he said simply.

My mouth fell open. I looked from him back to the superintendent. His elbows were on his desk, his fingers tapping together. He did not blink. A slow-turning electric fan ruffled his hair, which he periodically smoothed back into place.

'Impossible,' I said.

The superintendent shrugged. 'In US dollars,' he said, and made an *up to you* gesture with his hands.

Over the following days, I went early to the prison, with gifts and bribes for the superintendent. Again I was creating a rapport. The interpreter told me that I was very lucky – until two years earlier, Laos had sent all defectors back. The policy had only changed after an international outcry.

'Now, we just fine them,' he said.

Slowly, I managed to bring the amount down. Negotiations finally stalled at $700 apiece. Every time I was allowed into the courtyard to see my mother, the superintendent took half of my cash, however little it was. I would sit with her in a shaded spot and update her on my progress. When I told her I was struggling to raise the funds, she handed me a small dirty plastic cylinder. Inside was the cash I'd given her earlier. She'd only used a little to buy drinking water.

I figured that $700 was probably close to the official fine, but it was still far out of my reach. By this time almost all the money Kim had sent had been used up. To add to my worries, during my next visit to my mother she had brought along three bedraggled people to meet me – North Korean defectors who had been caught a month earlier. They were an old woman, and an unrelated middle-aged mother and her daughter. My mother was overwhelmed with compassion for them. She wanted me to help them, too. I looked at them in dismay, yet I knew I would try to help. They handed me all the money they had hidden in their private parts. It came to $1,500 – far short of the total we'd need.

By now my fifteen-day visa was about to expire. The two female officials who ran the visa office in Luang Namtha told me they could go to the capital, Vientiane, with my passport to renew my visa, but as it was expiring in just one day, they would have to fly. I'd have to pay their airfare and expenses. It would come to several hundred dollars.

I walked back to the Coffee House in a trance. I felt as if I was being fleeced of everything I had, and my family held to ransom. I slumped into a chair in the window and tried to think, but every thought came to a dead end. There were no options. I had no idea what to do.

I closed my eyes. I was about to start beseeching aloud the spirits of my ancestors, not caring who heard me, when a very tall figure blocked my light and spoke to me in English. I looked up. Sunlight glinted through sandy hair.

'Are you a traveller?' he said.

Chapter 48

The kindness of strangers

The tall white man had said the word 'traveller'. I vaguely knew it but I hadn't understood his question. By now I had got to know the waiters at the Coffee House, and called over the one who could speak English and some Mandarin. He translated for us.

'Most people only stay here a day or two,' the tall man was saying. 'You've been here weeks, like me. Are you on business? I'm just curious.'

This was the first time a white person had ever spoken to me. His eyes were a pale blue and he had a trim, sandy beard that was turning grey. He seemed more shy of me than I was of him. The English threw me. I couldn't find the words. I gestured for him to join me, and opened an English–Korean translation function on my cellphone.

Slowly, and with many embarrassed laughs and pauses, we communicated. I told him that I was a South Korean volunteer trying to help five North Korean defectors who were now in prison for illegal entry into Laos. The man looked very surprised, and I saw pain in his eyes. I searched for more words and told him that the Laotian government was demanding a huge fine.

'How much?' he asked.

'Each person, $700. American money.'

He scratched his beard and stared into the road for a while. Then he made a gesture that said, *Wait here a moment*. And another to indicate that he had to make a phone call. He walked to the other end of the café, made a call, and returned after a few minutes. I would never in my life have imagined what happened next. He tapped the words into my cellphone.

In Korean it said, *I just made a phone call to a friend in Australia. After talking it over, I've decided to help you.*

My defences shot up. *Why?* Why would a white, fifty-something male all of a sudden care about the problems of some Koreans he'd never met?

I searched his face for a clue. I dismissed the thought that his motives were sexual – I think I would have detected that in his eyes. I decided that he was probably making some feel-good gesture that he would end up not honouring. I told myself not to get any hopes up.

'Thank you,' I said, in English. He seemed to sense my doubt.

He again tapped into my phone. It said *I met two North Korean women while I was travelling in Thailand. Their story moved me very much.*

He again made the *Wait here* gesture.

I watched him walk across the street to the ATM. He returned holding a thick wad of green bills.

To my astonishment he was putting hundreds of US dollars into my hand. 'This is some of the money for the fines. I'll withdraw the rest tomorrow.'

Was I dreaming? I was struggling to comprehend what had just happened and express gratitude at the same time.

With the help of the cellphone dictionary and our translator waiter, the tall man explained that he was on a two-year journey around Southeast Asia. He'd intended to leave for Thailand tomorrow, but was willing to stay and help if I wanted him to, and visit the prison with me.

'Of course,' I said, when I finally understood.

This kindness and willingness to become involved completely floored me. My next thought was that if this impressive man came to the prison with me, I would not have to face that superintendent alone.

'Great,' he said. 'Why don't you move to my guesthouse? It's easier to talk there. We'll go to the prison together in the morning.' He said this very carefully, and in a way so that I would not misunderstand his good intentions.

I nodded dumbly.

'We'll have dinner later if you like,' he said. 'Bring your bag.'

'Sure,' I said blankly.

He held out his hand. 'My name's Dick Stolp. From Perth, in Australia.'

I shook his hand. I had not even asked his name. He turned to walk away but I held on to him. In halting English I said: 'Why are you helping me?'

'I'm not helping you.' He gave an embarrassed smile. 'I'm helping the North Korean people.'

I watched him go.

Something marvellous happened as I walked outside. All that locked-up beauty I'd seen in this country, and felt I was being denied, suddenly opened. I could smell the scent of jasmine in the trees; the sun and the stately white clouds were celebrating my mood. The whole world had just changed.

Dick's guesthouse was far nicer than mine. I had not expected him to pay for my room, on top of what he'd already done, but he did. When you've lived your whole adult life as I had, calculating the cost of even the smallest decision, such generosity wasn't easy to accept. It involved a loss of control. All I could do was say thank you. Not once did he ask for anything in return. I had never before experienced such detached generosity without some connection or debt attached. If we had been two lone Koreans from Hyesan meeting in Laos, or two young people in a crowd of old people, I might have understood the impulse. But Dick's simple kindness took no notice of age, race or language. It crossed my mind that perhaps he was so rich that money meant little to him, but I learned later that he was not a rich man.

At dinner I joined Dick at a table with five others: a German couple in their fifties, a middle-aged Chinese woman who made documentary films, and a young Thai woman with her German boyfriend. Everyone spoke in English. I had a very hard time following, but I didn't care. I was so relieved not be alone. I realized I would have to learn English. It was the world's common language. It was a relaxed and enjoyable evening. I laughed and smiled for the first time since leaving Seoul.

Dick and I rented a scooter to go to the prison. We took fruit, food and blankets.

He didn't know the lady in prison was my mother, and that her son was my brother, and that I was North Korean myself. But if he had, it wouldn't have changed anything. I wanted to tell Dick the truth about my identity. He deserved to know. But North Koreans wear masks from such long habit that it's difficult to cast them off.

I held on to him as he drove the scooter. On the way he stopped at the ATM to withdraw the rest of the money for the fines.

My most basic assumptions about human nature were being overturned. In North Korea I'd learned from my mother that to trust anyone outside the family was risky and dangerous. In China I'd lived by cunning since I was a teenager, lying to hide the truth of my identity in order to survive. On the only occasion I'd trusted people I'd got into a world of trouble with the Shenyang police. Not only did I believe that humans were selfish and base, I also knew that plenty of them were actually bad – content to destroy lives for their own gain. I'd seen Korean-Chinese expose North Korean escapees to the police in return for money. I'd known people who'd been trafficked by other humans as if they were livestock. That world was familiar to me. All my life, random acts of kindness had been so rare that they'd stick in my memory, and I'd think: *how strange*. What Dick had done changed my life. He showed me that there was another world where strangers helped strangers for no other reason than that it is good to do so, and where callousness was unusual, not the norm. Dick had treated me as if I were his family, or an old friend. Even now, I do not fully grasp his motivation. But from the day I met him the world was a less cynical place. I started feeling warmth for other people. This seemed so natural, and yet I'd never felt it before.

Reverend Kim had warned me of many checkpoints along the road to Vientiane. The journey by road would take eighteen hours and pass through three provinces, each governed independently enough for us to risk being jailed and fined another three times. His advice was to hire a police van for the whole journey. This sounded like a good idea. If the uniformed immigration police took us, we would have protection.

The immigration police chief told me it was possible, but the sum he asked for was exorbitant. I pleaded poverty and bargained him down to $150 a head for the six of us: my family plus the three other North Koreans. But I still did not have enough.

Once again, Dick stepped in and paid.

***

The police told Dick he could not go with us to Vientiane. He insisted, thinking his presence would help protect us, but they were adamant. They didn't want him there. In the morning he rented a scooter and followed the van to the prison. The van, a new Toyota, was at least comfortable.

The five prisoners were led out and I saw Min-ho for the first time in weeks. He was very pale and his face was covered in terrible acne. But he grinned at me, as if there'd been nothing to complain about. *My tough brother,* I thought. I felt proud to be the sister of such a man.

By this time, they all knew who Dick was and what he had done. One by one they shook his hand and bowed with gratitude and disbelief. The old lady managed to say in English: 'Thank you very much.'

The van's engine was running; we were ready to go.

Dick said he was leaving for Thailand. He gave me his phone number and email address, and then one final, overwhelming gift: the money for my flight home. 'You need this more than me.' He was saying goodbye to me before I could thank him properly. He swung his leg over the scooter and rode away, shouting: 'Get in touch if you need me.'

My angel vanished as suddenly as he'd appeared.

We set off for Vientiane, six of us accompanied by a senior policeman, the prison translator and a police driver. As part of the deal, I had to pay for the meals of all three of them along the way, and they ate gluttonously when we stopped for lunch and dinner.

As Reverend Kim had warned, there were regular checkpoints along the road, but the van was waved through each time. This gave us a tremendous feeling. We passed through hilly countryside dotted with mahogany trees, and small picturesque villages. The windows were open to let in the breeze, and everyone seemed to breathe deeply, scenting freedom.

Min-ho told me what had happened after I'd last seen him and my mother in Kunming. Near the border Mr Fang had guided them to the foot of a hill. 'This is as far as I take you,' he had said. 'The border's over that hill.' Min-ho listened carefully to his directions. 'Keep going straight and you'll come to a small, empty house. Go inside. A man will come. Follow him.'

He and my mother were shocked to find themselves suddenly alone, and in complete darkness. They started to climb. The terrain soon became thick jungle, and a light rain was falling. It was extremely slippery and there was no path to follow. They had to pull themselves up by grabbing at branches and vines until their hands and faces were scratched and bleeding. In pitch dark they had no sense of where they were; they tried to keep moving in a straight line, up what now seemed like a mountain, not a hill. It was almost too much for my mother. She said that if Min-ho hadn't been with her, she would have lost her way and died.

After a couple of hours, when they were almost down the other side of the mountain, a figure sprang up in the darkness in front of them. A man had been crouching in the undergrowth and stood to block their way. Min-ho could make out the glint of a badge on a uniform. The man held up the fingers of one hand and rubbed them together to mean *money*. Then he made another gesture to indicate two cuffed hands.

Money, or I arrest you.

Min-ho had separated the money I'd given him and put it in different pockets. He took out 300 yuan ($45). 'No,' the man said in English. Min-ho gave him another 500 ($75). The man smiled and let them on their way.

Shortly after, and by some miracle, they found the empty house the broker had described. It was hidden in thick forest. Another man was indeed waiting there. He gestured for them to sleep, spread out some flattened cardboard boxes, and lay down. They watched as he fell asleep. He looked poor, my mother thought.

When it was light, he loaded them into a tuk-tuk and drove them to a bus station. He pointed at a particular bus and told them to get on. Min-ho assumed the man would board it with them, but he disappeared. Again they were on their own with no idea where they were heading.

'One of the broker's men is sure to be on the bus,' Min-ho said, trying to reassure my mother. 'He'll make himself known at the right moment.'

In fact, the broker's man, a policeman, was supposed to be at the next checkpoint, but due to a mix-up was not manning his post when the bus arrived. My mother and Min-ho were handcuffed and put into a police car. I was glad I only learned this now. The thought of my omma in handcuffs would have tormented me. At the prison, Min-ho's remaining cash was taken off him by the gangster inmates who helped the guards maintain control.

We arrived in Vientiane in the early morning. It was not like any capital city I'd imagined. There were no tower blocks. It was almost entirely low-rise, with buildings separated by lush tropical greenery. There seemed more gardens than buildings.

We turned onto a leafy street of large, official-looking buildings topped by flagpoles. I assumed this was the embassy quarter. My eyes were scanning the road ahead, searching for the South Korean flag.

We stopped outside one of these buildings, which had a plaque written in Lao. There was no South Korean flag.

'What's this place?' I said to the translator.

'The Vientiane immigration office,' he said. 'Let's get out.'

I was immediately on my guard. 'Why?'

'Just procedure. Someone from the South Korean embassy will come this afternoon.' In my dealings with the prison superintendent, I had built up a rapport with the translator and had slowly won his sympathy. He seemed decent and more honest than the others. I watched as he got into a long conversation with the senior police officer. The translator had told me we would go directly to the South Korean embassy. He did not seem pleased with what the senior police officer was telling him.

'What's happening?' I said.

'Don't worry. Please get off.'

We took our bags from the van and were taken to the second floor of the immigration office. We left our bags in a corner and sat down to wait in silence. I had an uneasy feeling about this. Then an immigration official entered and called my name. 'Please follow me.'

I told my mother and Min-ho I'd be back in a few minutes. One of the North Korean women asked me to buy toiletries.

'We just have a few questions,' the official said as we walked along a corridor.

'I don't want to be separated from the group.'

'It's all right, I'll take you back.'

He led me to an air-conditioned conference room where four officials in green uniforms were waiting. One was a lipsticked woman in her mid-forties who was introduced as the chief of the immigration office. Her epaulettes had gold stars. She spoke in Lao. One of the officials in uniform translated into Mandarin.

'Do you know why we're questioning you?' she said coolly.

'I have no idea.'

'Because you're a criminal.'

Chapter 49

Shuttle diplomacy

I opened my mouth but words failed me. My first thought was that this was some absurd misunderstanding, or that I'd been brought into the wrong room.

I looked around at each of the officials. They were all watching me. 'Why am I a criminal?'

'The North Koreans entered our country illegally,' she said. 'They are criminals. You helped them.'

I'd been feeling a simmering anger ever since we'd stopped outside this building, guessing that there'd be one more attempt to fleece us before we gained asylum. But when I heard my family labelled 'criminals' my temper exploded.

I was shouting. 'Criminals? They are not criminals! Have they killed anyone? Robbed anyone? I've met plenty of robbers in this country and they're all police! These people are refugees seeking asylum.'

I should not have lost my calm, because I was no longer thinking clearly.

The woman chief remained unruffled.

'They're here illegally. We can't overlook that. And you helped them.'

I tried to regain my composure, but I was still enraged. 'This is my first time in Laos. I'm only trying to help them reach asylum. It is not my job. I am NOT a broker.'

I felt a stab of fear in my stomach. In my outburst just now had I said the word 'family'? I wasn't sure. Only now was I recalling the warning from Mr Park the policeman to tell no one that my mother and Min-ho were related to me. If this woman realized that I too was

North Korean, I would lose the protection of my South Korean passport.

'We know it's your first time here,' she said. 'But you're still a criminal.'

If my mind had been clear, I'd have guessed, from what I knew by now of Lao bureaucracy, that she probably wanted me to admit to a charge so that I would pay a fine. But as I refused to accept that I was a criminal helping criminals, she couldn't proceed to the matter of payment. It didn't help that I was now clearly starting to rile her.

'You could go to prison.'

'I'm just a volunteer,' I said, taking out my phone. 'I'm calling the South Korean embassy.'

'You're not calling anyone.'

She gestured with her finger to one of the officials. He stepped towards me and took the phone from my hand.

'This is Laos,' she said. 'Your embassy has no power here.'

The official who'd taken my phone was now demanding my passport also. I had no choice but to give it to him.

The woman spoke to the others in Lao for a minute, then said: 'For now, you may go. Come here tomorrow morning. We need to talk again.'

I returned to the room where the others had been waiting. They'd vanished. All the bags were gone except my lone backpack, left behind like some menacing clue. I ran straight back to the interrogation room.

Again I was shouting. 'Where've you taken them?'

'To a hotel,' the Mandarin-speaking official said. The woman chief had turned her back on me. 'There's nothing you can do for now.'

Downstairs, the lobby of the building was deserted. It was lunchtime. Two long corridors led away from either side of the empty reception desk. I made sure no one was around and slipped along one corridor, looking into each of its rooms, then the next. At the end of the second corridor was a row of iron cell doors. All but one were shut. I peered inside. It was chilly and smelled of damp concrete. The walls were black with mould, and the ceiling so low it would have been impossible to stand upright. They were like livestock pens. *Surely they're not here?* There was no sound from behind the locked doors.

I didn't dare shout *Omma-ya! Min-ho-ya!* in case they heard upstairs.

Outside, it was so hot that the streets were deserted. I spotted a motorcycle taxi rank waiting for fares, and in a mixture of English and sign language asked a driver to take me to the South Korean embassy. Minutes later I saw the South Korean flag, and the embassy itself, but the guard at the gate told me to come back after lunch.

I wandered further along the street, looking for somewhere to sit. It was cooler here, beneath a canopy of plane trees. Then just to my left, on the other side of the street, I saw a flag that made me do a double take. The embassies of both Koreas were just yards from each other. For the second time that day I felt caught in an absurd situation. East and West Germany had long since reunified. So had North and South Vietnam. Why were we the only nation on earth still suffering from a bizarre division that should have vanished into history? Why was my family paying the price of that division in this faraway and unwelcoming country? I stood still in the empty street, thinking that my whole life lay in the distance between these two flags.

'Welcome,' the consul said. 'We don't get many Korean travellers here.' He invited me into a meeting room.

I explained to him that I'd come from Luang Namtha, bringing five people who were now being held by immigration in Vientiane. 'We expected to come directly here.'

'Yes.' He rubbed the bridge of his nose beneath his glasses. 'We received a message from immigration in Luang Namtha that five North Koreans were on their way. But what's your connection to them?'

'I called you a month ago. Do you remember? To tell you that my family was imprisoned in Luang Namtha. You said that you'd take care of things, and that I should leave.'

'Ah. Yes.' He gave a look of mild surprise. 'You didn't leave? I'd never have thought you would manage this much. And you've done it alone? In a month? Amazing. Really.'

He sounded like a bored uncle trying to show an interest in a child's drawing.

'We were told you'd go to the immigration office this afternoon,' I said. 'What's the next step?'

He gave a small apologetic laugh. 'I can't just go there when I like. I have to wait until they call.'

'But they're holding five North Koreans. They took my passport and my phone. Can they do that?'

'We have no authority here. We can't tell them what to do. But we'll see if we can find out what's going on.'

On each step of this journey, every time I thought I'd spied hope, disappointment would plant itself firmly in the way. As I got up to leave, I told him something my mother had mentioned – that a group of twelve North Koreans had been caught a few days previously and thrown into Luang Namtha Prison just before she and Min-ho left yesterday. 'But I'm sure you knew that.'

'No, I didn't,' he said, as if I'd told him a crazy-but-true fact. 'I'll look into it.'

I wondered how many North Korean refugees were sitting in prison cells around the country, waiting for this man to do something.

The next morning a junior diplomat accompanied me to the Vientiane immigration office. In hindsight, this was not a good idea. The meeting took on the feel of a summit between two nations. It was held in a large conference room lined by national flags. Across a long, polished table we faced five uniformed immigration officials, including the woman chief.

She insisted on conducting the meeting in Lao, and refused to budge from her position that I had committed a criminal offence by aiding illegal aliens. I would go to prison if I did not pay a statutory fine of $1,300.

'She's really furious with you,' the diplomat whispered when we'd stepped outside the room for a moment. 'She said you were extremely rude.'

I saw that I'd made a tactical mistake. Had I returned alone and contrite, and apologized to her, I might have been let off, but matters had gone beyond that. By bringing a diplomat I had escalated the whole issue up a level.

I showed my wallet to the immigration officials and explained my predicament. I had $800 that Dick had given me on the last day when he realized I didn't have enough for my fare home to Seoul. It was sufficient for a one-way ticket. The woman took all the cash and handed back my passport and phone.

'Don't ever come back to my country in this way,' she said. 'If you do, you'll be imprisoned as a broker. However . . .' She gave me the most insincere smile I'd ever seen on another woman. 'You may return as a tourist.'

I wanted to slap her face.

'We've granted a twenty-four-hour extension to your visa,' she said. 'If you're still here this time tomorrow we'll arrest you. Understand?'

'I'd like to leave your country right now,' I said. 'But I have no money left for a ticket.'

She pressed her lips together. *Not my problem.*

On the way out of the building, the Korean diplomat reassured me that my mother, Min-ho and the other three North Koreans would be taken to the embassy the next day. All would be able to leave for Seoul after that. A few days, he said.

They say people tend to believe what they want to believe, and I really wanted to believe this news. It was so wonderful to hear. I thanked him profusely. I should, of course, have tested the truth of what he was saying by asking further questions, but I was distracted by another immediate concern.

'I've got nothing left for a ticket out of here. Could the embassy lend me the money?'

Regrettably, he said, getting into his car, it was not embassy policy to lend money.

Stupidly, I thanked him again. I was so grateful that my family's ordeal was almost over that it was a few minutes before it occurred to me, as I stood alone again in the street, that he'd driven away knowing that I was penniless and had nowhere to go. When I later learned that embassies have an obligation under international law to protect and support their citizens, I found the attitude of the South Korean embassy in Vientiane very hard to understand.

I had no idea what to do. I thought I would have to sleep in the street. Within moments of me turning on my phone it rang. It was Dick. I was beginning to think he was some divine being. When I explained the situation – in broken English – he offered to send more money, but I said no. He had given so much. I would figure something out for myself.

I dawdled in the street for a while, but I knew I had only one option

– to ask Kim. This was hard to do, harder than asking Dick. My pride did not want him to see me needy and desperate. It simply confirmed the gulf of status between us. I was afraid of repulsing him. He transferred the money, and again I insisted this was a loan, of which every penny would be paid back.

I left Laos the next morning.

It was the first week of December. I'd come from the subtropics to a bright, freezing day in Seoul, with high blue skies and air so cold there were ice crystals patterned like feathers on the inside of my apartment windows. I immediately had to shop for clothes. I'd given all my winter wear to that puzzled taxi driver in Kunming.

That evening I was curled up in Kim's apartment in Gangnam, cradling a coffee, wearing his knitted sweater, listening to jazz and describing my adventure. It seemed surreal, somehow, to be so suddenly back in the comfort and safety of the other universe, watching Kim, who'd never left it, stare at me as he tried to comprehend what I'd been through. He was silent for a long time, and kept shaking his head in bemusement at the sequence of disasters and the twists of good fortune we'd had in overcoming them. He was also deeply impressed by Dick Stolp.

'To meet someone like that,' he said, 'at that moment, and in that place? It's incredible. You've been very lucky.'

'I've been lucky to have you, too,' I said.

The jazz track we were listening to had ended. Silence filled the room.

I had been away so much longer than I'd expected – two months – that I'd missed the university entrance tests and interviews. It would be another year before I could apply. I didn't really mind. I figured I'd be so busy helping my mother and Min-ho cope with life in Seoul.

The day after I returned I called the South Korean embassy in Vientiane. I was in a positive mood, and expecting good news. I got through to an answering machine telling me in English to press various buttons for different services. I tried them all day but could never get through to anyone. It was the same the next day and the day after. I was not too concerned, however. I expected that my mother and Min-ho would arrive any day, and knew that once they were being processed by the NIS, they would disappear off the radar for a while. Even so, I would have liked some confirmation from the diplomats in Vientiane.

After three weeks without news I was anxious. Kim tried to reassure me, telling me that nothing would happen quickly in Laos. Finally, in the fourth week, my phone rang with a number I did not recognize. It had an 856 prefix, the code for Laos. The voice was very faint.

'Nuna?'

'Min-ho?'

'Yes, it's me.'

'You're still in the embassy?'

'I've borrowed this phone. Will you call back?'

Why is he whispering? I called him straight back. He answered before the phone had rung once.

'I'm in Phonthong Prison.'

Chapter 50

Long wait for freedom

My apartment seemed to go into a spin around me. I was clutching the phone so tight my nails dug into my palm.

'What?'

'It's where they put foreigners,' Min-ho said. 'It's much bigger than the prison in Luang Namtha . . .'

I was in that nightmare again, pitched straight back into the darkness. My lip began to wobble. But my kid brother was sounding imperturbable. It was as if he were describing a new school he'd started.

'There are white people here, and black people, everyone except locals . . .'

'Whose phone is this?'

'My Chinese friend here in the cell,' he whispered. 'It's against the rules to have them.'

My head fell into my hand. 'Why, why, why aren't you in the South Korean embassy? They told me they'd get you the next day.'

'The embassy? I've seen no one from there . . .'

Min-ho explained that after I left the immigration office, the officials took him, my mother and the others to the cells on the ground floor. *So they were in those mouldy concrete cells at the end of that corridor.* A few days later they were taken to Phonthong Prison. My mother was there too, in the women's section. Min-ho hadn't seen the sun for weeks, he said, and his skin had gone very white. Yet he sounded cheerful. I marvelled at his ability to endure any physical discomfort or hardship. I realized then that it would be the pressures of the rich world he'd have trouble coping with.

'There are two South Koreans here. One's doing five years for selling amphetamines. The other had some sort of business disagreement in Laos. When they found out we were from the North they bought food from outside with their own money and gave it to me and sent some over to the women's prison for Omma and the others. They've been here for a long time, but they encourage me. They're telling me not to worry. They say a lot of North Koreans pass through and then get sent to the South Korean embassy. It's the normal process, Nuna. Don't worry. We'll be all right.'

Min-ho and his Chinese friend were sharing a cell with two others, he said, from Britain and from Ghana. The British man was serving a long sentence for possessing marijuana. His name was John and he was very kind.

'Guess what, Nuna? I'm learning English!'

At that the floodgates opened. I cried until my eyes and nose were streaming. Through the tears I managed to say: 'We can speak English together when you get here.'

Min-ho, in his characteristic way, was enjoying discovering the world, albeit from the inside of a prison cell. Starting from the very bottom. I admired him so much. He was not letting the prospect of months or even years in prison cast him down. He was facing the future, preparing for the next phase of his life.

At least now I understood why that junior diplomat had been in such haste to drive off. He'd deliberately been untruthful about my family getting out in a day or two. He knew the process, but didn't want me hanging around and getting into more trouble. Still, there was reason to hope the ordeal would end soon, and happily. Now that I thought about it, there had never been any suggestion, even from the Laotian immigration chief when she was furious with me, that my mother and Min-ho might be handed over to the North Korean embassy, or sent back to China.

My mother and Min-ho spent another two months in Phonthong Prison in Vientiane before being handed over, as Min-ho's friends had predicted, to the South Korean embassy. They then spent another three months there, in an embassy shelter where they joined the queue of North Koreans being slowly processed for exit by the Lao government.

Finally, more than six months after I'd returned from Laos, in the late spring of 2010, I received a call from the National Intelligence Service in Seoul. Among the North Korean arrivals being processed, the agent told me, was a woman claiming to be my mother, and a man claiming to be my brother.

The release of tension in hearing those words, and the deadpan, bureaucratic way the agent had said them, set off a fit of giggling in me, and I couldn't stop. I tried to apologize to him. To his credit, he said: 'Take your time. You must be relieved.'

They had arrived.

It was over.

Chapter 51

A series of small miracles

Under new rules introduced after spies were discovered among the North Koreans seeking asylum, my family's period of processing by the NIS was longer than mine. They were questioned for three months before being moved to Hanawon, where they stayed another three months. The women who had been held in Laos with my mother and Min-ho arrived at the same time. Sadly, after making it all the way here, the older lady died of cancer.

In these weeks while I was waiting, I was contacted out of the blue by Shin-suh, the friendly video-chat girl who'd appeared naked on my laptop screen in Shanghai. She'd been trying to reach me, she said, but my change of name had made me hard to track down. I was thrilled that she'd made it to Seoul not long after me. I invited her over. But when I opened the door, the girl on my doorstep was a stranger, not the person I'd seen on the video-chat. It flashed across my mind that this was a trap. There were rumours throughout the defector community of *Bowibu* spies and assassins in our midst.

My confusion amused her. 'It's me, Shin-suh.' She clapped her hands together and laughed.

I recognized her voice. She explained that she'd spent $20,000 on a total plastic surgery overhaul – eyes, forehead, nose, lips, breasts, everything. Her South Korean boyfriend had been so turned off by the transformation that he'd broken off their relationship.

When I told her that I had got my family out of the North, the light went out of her eyes. She became quiet and pensive. Like me, she missed her family with an almost physical pain. She wanted to get hers out too, she said, but she was terrified of the risks. She had suffered far worse than I had. Like many North Korean women, Shin-suh had been trafficked, tricked by men who had posed as brokers helping her to escape. She considered herself fortunate that she'd been sold to an adult video-chat business, and not as a bride to an impoverished Chinese farmer. It made me blush to recall how, as an eighteen-year-old, I'd thought the worst thing in my life would be to go through with a marriage to the affluent, harmless Geun-soo in Shenyang.

A week before my mother and Min-ho emerged from Hanawon I decided to have the long-overdue talk with Kim. I did not want to postpone it any longer. My family was about to join me. A new chapter was beginning, and I knew Kim would not be a part of it. My experiences had made me a realist. I was not going to be a romantic fool hoping that he'd defy his parents and marry me, nor did I expect him to. He'd never done anything to displease his family. Pining over lost love was for TV dramas, not for me. My priority now was to help my mother and Min-ho adjust to a new life. I had to move on.

'I don't think we have a future,' I said to him. I think he'd guessed from my tone why I'd come to his apartment this evening.

After a long, heavy pause he said: 'I know. You're right. It would be hard to deal with my family.'

We sat for a while just looking at each other across the sofa in his apartment, listening to the sounds of the city. I hadn't expected to feel as sad as I did. It was such a shame. We liked and respected each other very much. He'd come home from the gym and was wearing a sweatshirt that showed off his body. He was a beautiful man, and kind. But his future was as closely connected to his past, and to his family, as mine was to mine. And that meant separate destinies.

'There's not much left to say then.' If I wasn't going to cry, I needed to get this over with quickly.

'I guess not,' he said.

I smiled at him warmly. 'Let's part as friends.'

We embraced, and I left before he saw me break down.

Two days later I was waiting anxiously at the top of the subway stairs for my mother and Min-ho. It was now August 2010, almost a full year since our drama in Changbai, and nine months since I had last seen them in Laos. When I caught sight of them I bounded down the stairs and into their arms. At last they were free, South Korean citizens. My worry was how well they'd cope with the 'free'.

'You told me it would all take two weeks,' was the first thing Mother said. 'If I had known how long and awful the journey was going to be, I doubt I would have agreed.'

'Well, we're all here now,' I said. 'That's what matters. Min-ho, look at you. You were too thin last time I saw you. Now you're too fat.' Actually, he looked much healthier.

'No way,' he said. He grinned at me, and I saw my father in him. 'I'm hungry. Let's eat.'

Their eyes were everywhere. The subway had disgorged my family into the bustling area near City Hall. Their senses were being assaulted by the sights and sounds of the most modern city in the world. Seoul is bright with signage that competes to grab attention, and illuminated advertising designed to entice and allure. Streets are solid with more traffic than a North Korean could ever imagine. Crowds moved in every direction. These were the modern Koreans, whose language was recognizable to my mother but whose fashions, attitudes and indifference toward the thousands of foreigners of all races living unmolested in their midst were so at odds with what she had known. Everywhere she looked was a vast hive of activity, and prosperity.

I had invited Ok-hee along, to join us for *seolleongtang*, ox-bone soup.

'Eat a lot, Omma,' I said. I was concerned that she looked frail. I'd hoped she would look relaxed and healthy after Hanawon.

'I was too stressed to eat most of the time,' she said.

We chatted freely until the restaurant closed. I was so happy, and kept holding their hands. I had been fantasizing about a scene like this for more than a decade.

My mother's first few days of freedom in the developed world were overtaken by a series of small miracles. She struggled to keep up. At Dongdaemun, a popular night market of street-food vendors, she was transfixed by the ATM where I'd withdrawn cash. 'I can't figure it out,' she said. She thought an extremely small teller was crouched inside a tiny room in the wall, counting out notes at high speed. 'The poor thing, stuck in there without a window.'

'Omma.' I started laughing. 'It's a machine.'

The travel card I gave her also flummoxed her. When we got on a bus, she swiped it over the reader, as I had shown her, and a mechanized woman's voice said '*hwanseung imnida*' (transfer), meaning that the fare had been paid.

'Do I need to reply?' my mother asked loudly.

Later, in the street, she asked me if the kids she kept seeing were from South Korea's equivalent of some sort of Socialist Youth League.

'No, why do you say that?'

'They salute each other, like this.' She held up her palm.

'Omma, that's called a "high five".'

One evening, as we were strolling after dinner she said: 'It wasn't all bull.'

'What wasn't, Omma?'

'All these cars. All these lights. I'd seen them in the illegal South Korean TV dramas, but I'd always thought it was propaganda, that they'd brought all the cars in the city to the same street where they were filming.' She shook her head. 'It's astonishing.'

Chapter 52

'I am prepared to die'

That September 2010, I was accepted by the Hankuk University of Foreign Studies for an undergraduate course in Chinese and English that would start in spring the following year. Min-ho had an apartment of his own. My mother looked for work so that she could help support me. Her previously privileged position of authority in North Korea – at the government bureau in Hyesan – counted for nothing in Seoul, so she took a job as a cleaner in a small motel where rooms were charged by the hour. She received board and lodging at the motel, with one day off per month. She was getting old, and wasn't used to the hard physical labour. Within a few weeks in the job, she was changing sheets on a bed when she slipped a disc in her spine, collapsed in agony, and soon after had to have surgery.

My mother's brave attempt at a new life in the South began to falter. It didn't help that she saw Min-ho struggling, too.

Among the 27,000 North Koreans in the South, two kinds of life have been left behind: the wretched life of persecution and hunger, and the manageable life that was not so bad. People in the first group adjust rapidly. Their new life, however challenging, could only be better. For the people in the second group, life in the South is far more daunting. It often makes them yearn for the simpler, more ordered existence they left behind, where big decisions are taken for them by the state, and where life is not a fierce competition.

My mother, who had arranged the paperwork for her own death before leaving Hyesan, had also left money behind with Aunt Tall, on the understanding that she might return. She began to miss her brothers and sisters so much that she would weep for them every night after work. She started endlessly recalling tales of the long-ago antics of Uncle Opium, or the hardships of Uncle Poor, or the business tricks of Aunt Pretty. Then, finally, one night, she came out with it.

'I want to go home.'

'Omma.' It was what I'd dreaded to hear. 'You can't. You know what they'll do.'

'I am prepared to die,' she said, stoically gazing into space. 'I want to die at home.'

'Don't say that.'

'I never see the sun,' she said. It was winter, and dark when she got up for work, and dark when she finished. 'Did I come here for this? There's no meaning here, no future.'

We had this conversation in one form or another for the next few months. She never once accused me of doing the wrong thing by persuading her to defect, but I started to feel that I had made a terrible mistake. I had taken an enormous risk with our lives, and at a great cost in effort and money, so that we could be together. But despite my best intentions, my mother was now miserable. She was caught in a dreadful dilemma: she longed to go home, but then she would be separated from me once more.

At first I encouraged her to be patient. It wasn't easy to adjust to life here, I said, but she would succeed. It would just take a little time. But when she started saying that she wanted to die in the North, I knew I could not ignore her.

With a heavy heart I told her I would help her get back there safely, if that's what she truly wanted. Over several weeks, I weighed the risks. It was unbelievable that after all we'd been through I was now trying to figure a way of guiding my mother all the way back to North Korea. But if her mind was made up, what choice did I have?

The return trip to the North would not be nearly as arduous as our long journey to Seoul. We could get back to the border at Changbai easily, as South Korean tourists, and I could hire a broker to take her over the river. But she had to be sure – really, absolutely sure – that she could cover her tracks when she was back there.

I lay on my bed, unable to sleep, staring at the beige blanket of the sky over Seoul. *Am I really going to do this?*

'Omma,' I said the next day. 'If they find out you've been in China, they'll arrest you and beat you. If they find out you've been here . . .' I didn't need to say anything. We both knew what her fate would be. I looked her in the eye. 'I need to know your plan will work.'

'It will work,' she said. 'I know exactly who to bribe at the records office and he's all right. Then your Aunt Pretty will help me move to a new city. No one will ever know I've been away.'

That seemed to decide it. Min-ho was very unhappy about this. He missed home as much as our omma did. He was having adjustment problems of his own, and didn't want to lose his mother, too.

Over the next week I began to plan her journey. But when I tried discussing dates and practicalities with her she became reticent, distracted, as if she were preoccupied with some inner turmoil.

At the same time, I was trying to convince Min-ho to try for university. He was restless and disaffected. My greatest fear was that he'd turn to crime. Smuggling in North Korea may have been illegal, but the police gave it a nod and a wink, and, informally, it was a socially accepted form of business. But in South Korea, society would not tolerate it. The idea of college terrified Min-ho. He looked brought down whenever I mentioned it. His worthless North Korean education had put him years behind other students his age. I told him to take a year to think about it.

He had already found a job on a construction site, which he tackled with his usual doggedness, working so hard that he was promoted to team leader within weeks. After six months, however, he quit, telling me that if he didn't do something now, he'd spend the rest of his life on building sites. He would try for university. I was enormously relieved and pleased by this, and it was quickly followed by more good news.

'I won't go back,' my mother said abruptly one morning.

I'd guessed she'd been having doubts, and had stayed quiet hoping they'd take root.

'I'd miss you and your brother too much,' she said. 'I'd be able to see your aunts and uncles and your cousins, but I'd miss you so much that I'd be in double agony.' She'd been staying at my apartment that night. Later, when she had gone to work, I cried miserably. My relief was marred by the fact that I'd condemned her to experience loss and regret for the rest of her life. I was acutely aware that I had done this to her.

By the spring of 2011, it had been nine months since my mother and Min-ho had been living freely in Seoul. Just when I thought both of them were beginning to settle down and adjust to the reality of their new lives, another drama occurred that almost tore us apart all over again.

Min-ho had re-established contact with Yoon-ji, his fiancée, and called her regularly. He wasn't giving up on her, and over many conversations had convinced her to join him in the South, making all the complex preparations with brokers to get her across China. I did not deter him. He knew the dangers. But he had his heart set.

He applied for his passport, got a Chinese visa, and went to get her, but by the time he reached Changbai, she had changed her mind. She didn't want to create problems for her parents, she said.

A few days later, on my first day at university, he called me. It was a beautiful spring day. I was crossing the campus, looking at a map to locate my faculty building.

'I'm in Changbai.' His voice rang strange, as if we were in a dream. 'I'm looking across at Hyesan right now.'

'You shouldn't go that close. Someone might recognize you.'

'Nuna, I'm very sorry to tell you this. I'm going back.'

'That's not funny.'

'I cut my hair today, dumped my jeans, and bought trousers that look North Korean.'

My blood froze. 'What? When?'

'Now. I'm crossing back now.'

I screamed. 'Min-ho, you can't.'

'Yoon-ji's mother will take care of everything. It'll be like I never left.'

I tried to focus. I had to stop him. I felt a horrible tension building in my head.

'Min-ho, listen to me. Once you go over, you can never come back. Think about this.'

'I have no future in Seoul,' he said. 'I don't know if I can handle college. In Hyesan, I can marry Yoon-ji. I know what to do to make money.'

'You're not sure, because you've just arrived and it's still scary. But after a year or two, you'll be fine.'

He fell silent and I could hear him breathing deeply, that trick he had when he wished something wasn't happening.

'Min-ho. You're my brother. I can't lose you again now. You're the man in our family. Think of Omma. What will this do to her? We've had a hell of a journey, and we're still not finished. It's hard, but we can overcome this. You and me, we're young. We can do anything. Remember how hard it was to get here? But we did it. You want to throw that away?'

'What about Yoon-ji?' His voice was faint and so sad.

It was the dilemma all three of us had. Every choice we made cut us off permanently from someone we loved.

'She'll be all right.' I came in hard, addressing what I guessed lay behind this – his underlying fear that he would never find a woman in South Korea interested in him. 'There are many girls here. I have friends. I'll start introducing you. They know you're my hero.'

'Maybe.'

'Or we can go to America together. We can get our degrees and go to America. There's uncertainty in Korea, but America's the country of freedom.'

'America? Why the hell would I go there?'

'We can do anything, Min-ho. We can go anywhere. We are free people. We only have to set our heart on it, and we can do it.'

We talked like this for over an hour. Slowly he came back to reality. The whole time I was walking in circles in the middle of a quadrangle, with students flowing around me, chatting, pushing bicycles.

'I think of the path along the river all the time,' he said. 'I miss knowing what I'm doing.'

'I know.'

'But you're right. I'll come back. I'll try again.'

He hung up. I found a bench and sat down. My whole body was shaking. I felt like a pilot who'd narrowly averted a plane crash.

Chapter 53

The beauty of a free mind

Not long after my family had arrived, Ok-hee introduced me to an organization called PSCORE (an acronym for 'People for Successful Corean Reunification'), which helps improve the lives of North Korean defectors. One Saturday evening she and I joined a group of PSCORE volunteers for a night out in Hongdae, a district of crowded bars thumping with music and clubs popular with Seoul's students. The others in our group were South Koreans and, curiously, three young male Westerners. At dinner I found myself sitting next to one of them. Ever since meeting Dick Stolp in Laos, I was much more curious about Westerners. If even just a few of them were as wonderful as Dick, I was interested to meet more. And I confess that I was also struck by how fine-looking this one was, next to me. He was fair-haired, with chestnut-brown eyes and a friendly, unassuming manner. He was in his mid-twenties, I guessed.

His name was Brian, he said. He was a graduate student at Yonsei University in Seoul. He asked where I was from.

'A city called Hyesan,' I said matter-of-factly, as if everyone knew where that was, and watched with amusement as he scratched his chin.

'Hyesan, Hyesan,' he muttered. He was trying to think where it was on the map. 'That's weird. I know this country pretty well.'

'It's in the North,' I said. 'Near China.'

He turned to me with a look of wonder. 'You're kidding me.' I was the first North Korean he'd ever met.

He told me he was from Wisconsin. He saw the blank look on my face. 'In the USA.'

We spent the rest of the evening deep in conversation. I was struck by how open and honest he was about everything. He spoke without guile or evasiveness. He wasn't defensive, or status-conscious. I felt completely at ease with this stranger. I was honest with him, too, until the very end of the evening. Foolishly, I'd brought up the subject of age.

'Well, how old are you?' he laughed.

'Twenty-five.' It was an instant, reflexive lie. I'd snapped straight back into that cynical mode of calculating every benefit. It also came from years of lying about my identity. I'd shaved a few years off so that I'd seem more attractive to him. I didn't feel too guilty, and didn't imagine we would meet again.

What I did not expect was that Brian would call me, that we would start dating, and that a few months after meeting, we would start a serious relationship. That small lie did matter now. I kept putting off telling him the truth until it became unbearable. I had to get it over with.

'Brian, I've got to apologize,' I said, while we were walking in the street. 'I lied to you. I'm not twenty-five. I'm twenty-nine.'

'Oh.' He gave me a puzzled look. 'I don't care about that. But I want you to know that you can always be honest with me. I'm not going to judge you.'

Brian was the first to show me a free intelligence, with a humorous, sceptical mind that took nothing as given. It made me open unexamined thoughts of my own. He made me realize that the wider world cares about the suffering in North Korea, and is well informed about it, too. His attitude emboldened me to confront the stultifying prejudice in South Korea against defectors – something they would never experience in the United States. Most defectors I knew in the South hid their identities out of fear of being seen as low-status. I was damned if I was going to hide mine. Now that my family was safely with me, I had nothing to hide.

But Brian also presented me with a problem I had not foreseen. It wasn't just South Korean prejudices I was confronting. I had to change some defectors' attitudes, too, and some of them were very close to home.

My mother and Min-ho knew that I'd got romantically involved with someone. They wanted to meet him, and wondered why I kept making excuses, not even telling them his name. As my relationship with Brian deepened, I realized they would have to know. In the end, I decided shock would be the best therapy.

And so it was that Brian was introduced to my mother and to Min-ho in a restaurant, and they found themselves face to face with one of the reviled Yankee jackals of North Korean propaganda. We sat down in silence. My mother, normally the epitome of good manners, gaped at him with her mouth open. She and my brother looked stunned and offended. I knew what they were thinking. A well-known saying in North Korea goes: 'Just as a jackal cannot become a lamb, so American imperialists cannot change their rapacious nature.' I acted as interpreter. After a brief and excruciating dinner, Brian left as soon as he politely could. Min-ho remained silent and stared at the table. My mother said only one thing, muttering to herself: 'I've lived too long. I'm too old for this shit.'

Later Min-ho admitted to me that he'd hated Brian on sight. He was a *miguk nom*, he said. An American bastard.

I did not feel bad for offending them. I felt bad for Brian, who was decent and kind and had done nothing to deserve their contempt. But I knew I would achieve nothing by having a row with my mother and Min-ho. They had only been out of North Korea a few months. Some convictions would not change overnight.

Slowly, I started speaking out in defence of defectors, and about the human rights abuses in North Korea – first, in defector group meetings, then in small public speeches, then on a new television show called *Now on My Way to Meet You*, in which all the guests were female defectors, given new clothes in vibrant colours to dispel public perceptions of North Koreans as shabby and pitiful. The show had a big impact in transforming attitudes in South Korea toward defectors.

I started thinking deeply about human rights. One of the main reasons that distinctions between oppressor and victim are blurred in North Korea is that no one there has any concept of rights. To know that your rights are being abused, or that you are abusing someone else's, you first have to know that you have them, and what they are. But with no comparative information about societies elsewhere in the world, such awareness in North Korea cannot exist. This is also why most people escape because they're hungry or in trouble – not because they're craving liberty. Many defectors hiding in China even baulk at the idea of going to South Korea – they'd see it as a betrayal of their country and the legacy of the Great Leader. If the North Korean people acquired an awareness of their rights, of individual freedoms and democracy, the game would be up for the regime in Pyongyang. The people would realize that full human rights are exercised and enjoyed by one person only – the ruling Kim. He is the only figure in North Korea who exercises freedom of thought, freedom of speech, freedom of movement, his right not to be tortured, imprisoned, or executed without trial, and his right to proper healthcare and food.

By coincidence, it was at the time I was having these thoughts that something happened that no defector expected.

My mother and I were watching television on the evening of 17 December 2011 when news came through that Kim Jong-il, the Dear Leader, was dead. He had died on his private train, the distraught North Korean news anchor said, from the 'excessive mental and physical strain' of his lifelong dedication to the people's cause.

I turned in shock to my mother. We were yelling. Her palm was raised. She was giving me a high five. Ok-hee was on the phone straight away. We wanted to celebrate. Naively, we thought major changes were about to happen in the North.

We couldn't believe it. He was seventy. We'd all thought he had at least ten more years in him. An entire scientific institute in Pyongyang was dedicated to his longevity. He had access to the best healthcare in the world, and the best food. Every single grain of rice he ate was inspected for imperfections.

Our mood soured a few days later, however, when we saw footage of the forced public outpouring of crying and wailing for this callous tyrant. Kim Jong-il had been a disastrously bad ruler, doing almost nothing to alleviate one of the worst events in Korean history, the Great Famine. Yet from his point of view, he'd been highly successful – his power had remained absolute, he'd died peacefully, and he'd passed the reins to his youngest son, Kim Jong-un.

Brian brought stability to my life. I felt settled and less distracted; I attacked my studies and began to gain confidence at school, especially in English. I continued speaking out on behalf of defectors, and then something else occurred that I could never have anticipated. I was chosen through a worldwide talent search to give a talk at a TED conference. (TED stands for technology, education and design, and holds annual conferences to present interesting ideas to a broad audience.) In February 2013, I was flown to California to tell my story before a large audience.

To my astonishment the talk received an overwhelmingly positive response from people all over the world. Some of the most inspiring messages came from China, a country I love but which caused me so much hardship. Many expressed their shame at the complicity of their government in hounding escaped North Koreans. I also received hate messages, calling me a traitor, and worse. Brian laughed those off and suggested I did the same.

Later that year, I was invited to New York to testify before the United Nations Commission of Enquiry on Human Rights in North Korea, alongside some defectors who had survived the North Korean gulag. The international outcry that followed the Commission's verdict on North Korea's crimes against humanity finally brought me to the attention of the regime in Pyongyang. Its Central News Agency, in its inimitable style, proclaimed this: 'One day, the world will learn the truth about these [. . .] criminals. The West will be so embarrassed when they realize they invited these terrorists [to testify].'

Behind the bluster, I sensed fear. Dictatorships may seem strong and unified, but they are always weaker than they appear. They are governed by the whim of one man, who can't draw upon a wealth of discussion and debate, as democracies can, because he rules through terror and the only truth permitted is his own. Even so, I don't think Kim Jong-un's dictatorship is so weak that it will collapse any time soon. Sadly, as the historian Andrei Lankov put it, a regime that's willing to kill as many people as it takes to stay in power tends to stay in power for a very long time.

So when might this suffering end? Some Koreans will say with reunification. That should be our dream on both sides of the border, although, after more than sixty years of separation, and a radical divergence in living standards, many in the South face the prospect with trepidation. But we can't sit on our hands while we wait for the miracle of a new, unified Korea. If we do, the descendants of divided families will reconnect as strangers. Reunification, when it happens, and it will happen, may be less turbulent if the ordinary people of North and South can at least have some contact, be permitted to have family vacations together, or attend the weddings of nephews and nieces. The least that could be done for defectors is to ensure that they know, when they risk everything to escape, that they will not be lost for ever to the people they left behind, that they have supporters and well-wishers the world over, that they are not crossing the border alone.

With the wide publicity I received after these events, my mother could no longer ignore the fact of my relationship with Brian. He had been so supportive of me. What's more, the attention I was receiving for my work was causing a change of attitude in her and Min-ho. Through me, circumstance was forcing them to take a more international view of their lives. Slowly, they were starting to see themselves as citizens of a larger world, rather than displaced people from a tiny area of Ryanggang Province, North Korea.

Nevertheless, the next step was a major one for my mother to accept. She became quiet and forbearing when I told her the news.

'Omma, Brian has asked me to marry him. It means so much to me that I receive your blessing.'

Epilogue

Incredible as it may seem in our connected world, I lost touch with Dick Stolp shortly after leaving Laos. The email server I was with went out of business, and with it, all my addresses. I wrote letters to the editors of several Australian newspapers hoping that they'd be published and that Dick would see one of them and get in touch. I wanted him to know what his kindness and his heroism had achieved. None of my letters was published. It was only after the attention generated by the TED talk that an email eventually appeared in my inbox. 'Hyeonseo, is that you?' Dick wasn't sure that it was me he was writing to, since he'd had no idea I was North Korean. An Australian news programme, *SBS Insight*, got wind of the story and flew me to Australia to thank Dick in person. TV cameras were there to film the reunion. Normally, such public pressure would have kept my North Korean mask firmly on my face, but the moment I saw Dick's towering figure and the same gentle, kind smile I'd seen that day outside the Coffee House in Luang Namtha, I threw my arms around him and wept.

I know that the mask may never fully come off. The smallest thing occasionally sends me back into a steel-plated survival mode, or I may ice over when people expect me to be open. In one edition of the popular South Korean defectors' show, each woman's story was spoken through floods of tears. But not mine.

I still go through bouts of self-loathing. Somewhere, years ago in China, I stopped liking myself. After leaving my family behind, I felt I didn't deserve to celebrate my birthday, so I never did. I am perpetually dissatisfied. No sooner do I achieve something than I become unhappy with myself for not doing better, and achieving the next thing.

I try to appreciate what I have and keep a smile on my face. I have recently graduated from university, thanks to that friendly encouragement from Mr Park the policeman. Min-ho is at university, speaks English, and these days is best of friends with Brian. Both of them laugh, now, at that dinner when they first met. In many ways it symbolized the ludicrous misconceptions created by politics.

And my mother, my wonderful omma, cries far less. She even manages to smile from time to time, especially when Brian mangles something in Korean. Those she left behind – my uncles and aunts – still appear to her in dreams. She tries to be strong for me, but some nights I hear her weeping quietly.

Perhaps the most remarkable step in my mother's own journey came when we asked her to Brian's hometown in the Midwest to attend our wedding. She surprised me by neither objecting nor complaining.

And so, my mother accompanied us on a journey into the belly of the Yankee imperialist beast, the United States of America. Had her mother, my grandmother, who'd hidden her Workers' Party card in a chimney from American soldiers sixty years before, and worn it for the rest of her life on a string around her neck, been able to see my mother marvel at the view from the hundredth floor of the John Hancock Center in Chicago, or watch her, as I did, sitting in an American diner, sampling American food, she would not have believed her eyes. She would surely also have been astounded, as Brian and I were, to see her asking a waitress, in English, for another cup of coffee, and humming to herself, gazing across the sunlit canyon of skyscrapers, completely at her ease.

List of Illustrations

Hyeonseo with her mother, or 'Omma', 1984, at a photography studio © Hyeonseo Lee.

Hyeonseo's mother with Aunt Pretty, her younger sister © Hyeonseo Lee.

The Mansudae complex of skyscrapers in Pyongyang. Courtesy of breathoflifestar

A housing estate on Kwangbok Street in Pyongyang. Courtesy of breathoflifestar

Placards from the vast, extravagant performance of the Mass Games that captivate foreign audiences. Courtesy of breathoflifestar

Visitors bow to the bronze statues of Kim Il-sung and Kim Jong-il on Mansu Hill. Courtesy of breathoflifestar

A procession float featuring a painting of Kim Jong-il. Courtesy of breathoflifestar

Factory workers going to work together in the city of Hyesan, on the border of China's Changbai County. © REUTERS/Reinhard Krause

A building in Hyesan pronounces slogans as Kim Il-sung looks over women working in front, 2009. © REUTERS/Reinhard Krause

Hyesan, from the Chinese border. Photograph by Hyeonseo Lee

An infamous picture, seen around the world in May 2002, taken at the Japanese consulate in Shenyang, China. Kim Han-mi, aged two, watches her mother being dragged by Chinese policemen as her family attempt to enter the Japanese consulate in order to seek asylum. The Han-mi family, including her uncle and grandmother, had dashed into the Japanese consulate gate in Shenyang, China in May 2002. Two male relatives had slipped through successfully, but the two women and the girl were forcibly apprehended, sparking a diplomatic incident between Japan and China. This image of Han-mi looking on as her mother was being wrestled to the ground was broadcast worldwide. © REUTERS/Kyodo

Hyeonseo and her family at Navy Pier in Chicago © Hyeonseo Lee.

Hyeonseo's mother and brother in their first water fight. Photograph by Hyeonseo Lee

Hyeonseo (misspelled on her identification panel) testifying at the United Nations Security Council in April 2014 © Hyeonseo Lee.

Hyeonseo with the US ambassador to the United Nations, Samantha Power.

Acknowledgements

This book would not have been possible without the support of many people around me.

Primarily, I want to thank my family for always being by my side. The separation from my mom and brother was heartbreaking, so I'm eternally grateful that they had the courage to risk their lives and leave their homeland in order for us to reunite. My husband, Brian, has also been a constant source of love and encouragement.

The dedicated team of professionals around me have been essential in the production of this memoir. I've been fortunate to have had the guidance of my literary agent, Kelly Falconer, my speaking agent, Oliver Stoldt, and all the wonderful people at HarperCollins who have always believed in me and the importance of sharing my story.

Additionally, I must thank my co-writer, David John, for his effort and dedication, as well as my good friend, Mike Breen, who enhanced the book by sharing his invaluable insights on the Korean Peninsula.

Finally, I want to thank the people at TED for caring about my story and making me the first North Korean to speak on the TED stage. I also owe a debt of gratitude to all the people around the world who have enthusiastically encouraged me and continue to help me raise awareness about North Korean human rights.

Index